Thai

PHRASEBOOK & DICTIONARY

lonely planet

Acknowledgments

Editors Samantha Forge, Jodie Martire, Branislava Vladisavljevic, Tracy Whitmey

Production Support Chris Love

Language Writer Bruce Evans

Cover Researcher Naomi Parker

Thanks
James Hardy, Angela Tinson

Published by Lonely Planet Publications Pty Ltd
ABN 36 005 607 983

8th Edition – September 2015
ISBN 978 1 74321 452 7
Text © Lonely Planet 2015
Cover Image Girls in traditional dancing costumes, Bangkok – Travel Pix Collection / AWL
Printed in China 10 9 8 7 6 5 4 3 2 1

Contact lonelyplanet.com/contact

acknowledgments

This 8th edition of Lonely Planet's *Thai phrasebook* is based on previous editions by Lonely Planet's Language Products team and translator Bruce Evans, who provided the Thai translations and pronunciation guides as well as many cultural insights. Bruce lived in Thailand for more than 20 years and has translated a number of books from Thai to English. Bruce would like to thank Annie Main for help with some of the more obscure terms, his wife Lek for help with Thai idioms, and Thai proofers Benjawan and Mike Golding for valuable suggestions. The Phrasebuilder chapter was based on some of the grammar material Joe Cummings wrote for earlier editions of this language guide.

make the most of this phrasebook ...

Anyone can speak another language! It's all about confidence. Don't worry if you can't remember your school language lessons or if you've never learnt a language before. Even if you learn the very basics (on the inside covers of this book), your travel experience will be the better for it. You have nothing to lose and everything to gain when the locals hear you making an effort.

finding things in this book

For easy navigation, this book is in sections. The Basics chapters are the ones you'll thumb through time and again. The Practical section covers basic travel situations like catching transport and finding a bed. The Social section gives you conversational phrases, pick-up lines, the ability to express opinions – so you can get to know people. Food has a section all of its own: gourmets and vegetarians are covered and local dishes feature. Safe Travel equips you with health and police phrases, just in case. Sustainable Travel, finally, completes this book. Remember the colours of each section and you'll find everything easily; or use the comprehensive Index. Otherwise, check the two-way traveller's Dictionary for the word you need.

being understood

Throughout this book you'll see coloured phrases on each page. They're phonetic guides to help you pronounce the language. Start with them to get a feel for how the language sounds. The pronunciation chapter in Basics will explain more, but you can be confident that if you read the coloured phrase, you'll be understood. As you become familiar with the spoken language, move on to using the actual text in the language, which will help you perfect your pronunciation.

communication tips

Body language, ways of doing things, sense of humour – all have a role to play in every culture. 'Local talk' boxes show you common ways of saying things, or everyday language to drop into conversation. 'Listen for ...' boxes supply the phrases you may hear. They start with the phonetic guide (because you'll hear it before you know what's being said) and then lead in to the language and the English translation.

food 153

safe travel 185

sustainable travel 201

dictionaries 205

index 255

thai

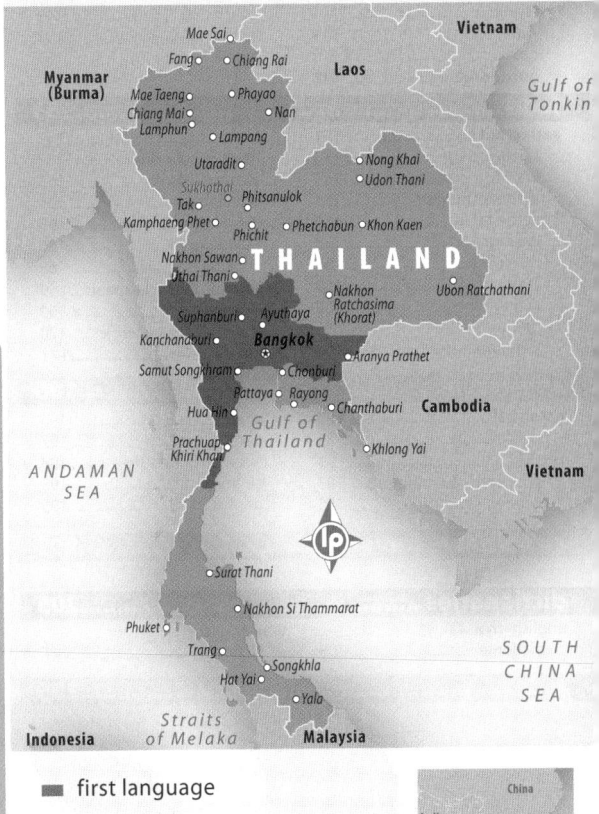

- first language
- second language

For more details, see the **introduction**.

8

Cradled between Cambodia, Laos, Malaysia, and Myanmar, the Kingdom of Thailand is something of a Tower of Babel, with numerous dialects spoken from north to south. What has come to be known as Standard Thai is actually a dialect spoken in Bangkok and the surrounding provinces. Standard Thai is the official language of administration, education and the media, and most Thais understand it even if they speak another dialect. For this reason all the words and phrases in this book are translated into Standard Thai.

Thai belongs to the Tai language group, meaning that it is closely related to a number of languages spoken outside the borders of present-day Thailand. Some of these are Lao (Laos), Khampti (India) and Lue (China). The Isaan dialect, spoken in the northeast of Thailand, is linguistically identical to Lao. Thai has borrowed a number of words from languages such as Mon (Myanmar) and Khmer (Cambodia). Ancient languages also continue to influence Thai. Just as English relies on Latin and ancient Greek for coining new words or formalising rules of grammar, Thai has adopted Sanskrit and Pali as linguistic models. More recently, English has become a major influence on Thai, particularly in words related to technology or business.

The elegant characters of the Thai script are a source of fascination for those experiencing the language for the first time. The curved symbols seem

at a glance ...

language name:
Thai, Siamese
name in language:
ภาษาไทย pah-săh tai
language family:
Tai
approximate number of speakers:
25–37 million
close relatives:
Khampti, Khmer, Lao, Lue, Mon, Nhang, Shan, Zhuang

introduction

to run together but they are all divisible into distinct alphabetical units. There are 44 consonants which are classified into three categories depending on the kinds of vowels they are associated with. Vowels are indicated by symbols, or combinations of symbols, that may appear before, after, above, below or even around the consonant. The Thai government has instituted the Royal Thai General System of Transcription (or RTGS) as a standard method of writing Thai using a Roman 26-letter alphabet. You'll notice its use in official documents, road signs and on maps. The system is convenient for writing but not comprehensive enough to account for all the sounds in Thai. In this book we have devised a phonetic system based on how the language sounds when it's spoken.

The social structure of Thai society demands different registers of speech depending on who you're talking to. To make things simple we've chosen the correct form of speech appropriate to the context of each phrase. Thai is a logical language and despite some challenges, rattling off a meaningful phrase is easier than you might think. This phrasebook includes the script next to the pronunciation so that when all else fails you can open the book and point at what you want to say.

This book contains the useful words you'll need to get by as well as fun, spontaneous phrases that lead to a better understanding of Thailand and its people. The contact you make using Thai will make your travels unique. Local knowledge, new relationships and a sense of satisfaction are on the tip of your tongue, so don't just stand there – say something!

abbreviations used in this book

f	feminine
inf	informal
m	masculine
pl	plural
pol	polite

Just about all of the sounds in Thai exist in English. While some people may find it difficult to pronounce Thai words, persistence is the key. Locals will appreciate your efforts and often help you along. Smile, point and try again. You'll be surprised how much sense you can convey with just a few useful words.

vowel sounds

Thai vowel sounds are similar to those in the English words listed in this table. Accents above vowels (like à, é and ò) relate to the tones (see next page).

symbol	english equivalent	example
a	run	bàt
aa	bad	gàa
ah	father	gah
ai	aisle	jài
air	flair	wair-lah
e	bed	ben
i	bit	bit
ee	see	bee
eu	her or french bleu	beu
ew	new with rounded lips	néw
o	hot	bòt
oh	note	đoh
or	for	pôr

pronunciation

11

u	put	sùk
oo	moon	kôo
ou	o plus u, similar to the the **o** in old	láa·ou
ow	c**ow**	bow
oy	b**oy**	soy

tones

If you listen to someone speaking Thai you'll notice that some vowels are pronounced at a high or low pitch while others swoop or glide in a sing-song manner. This is because Thai, like a number of other Asian languages, uses a system of carefully pitched tones to make distinctions between words. There are five distinct tones in Thai: mid, low, falling, high and rising. The accent marks above the vowel remind you which to use. The mid tone has no accent.

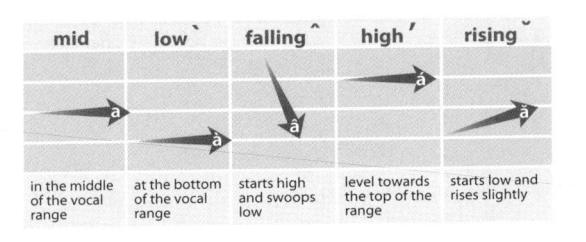

mid	low `	falling ^	high ´	rising ˇ
in the middle of the vocal range	at the bottom of the vocal range	starts high and swoops low	level towards the top of the range	starts low and rises slightly

consonant sounds

Most consonants in our phonetic system are pronounced the same as in English but Thai does has a few tricky consonants. Watch out for the b sound which is halfway between a 'b' and a 'p', and the d sound which is halfway between a 'd' and a 't'.

symbol	english equivalent	example
b	**b**ig	bòr
ɓ	rib-punch	ɓlah
ch	**ch**art	chìng
d	**d**og	dèk
đ	har**d-t**imes	đòw
f	**f**ull	fãh
g	**g**et	gài
h	**h**at	hèep
j	**j**unk	jahn
k	**k**ite	kài
l	**l**ike	ling
m	**m**at	máh
n	**n**ut	nŏo
ng	si**ng**	ngoo
p	**p**ush	pahn
r	**r**at	reu·a
s	**s**it	săh-lah
t	**t**ap	tów
w	**w**atch	wat
y	**y**es	yàhk

syllables

In this book we have used hyphens to separate syllables from each another. So the word ang-grit (English) is made up of two distinct syllables ang and grit.

In some words we have divided the syllables further with a dot · in order to help you separate vowel sounds and avoid mispronunciation. So the word kĕe·an is actually pronounced as one syllable with two separate vowel sounds.

pronunciation

You'll also occasionally come across commas in our phonetic guides. This just means you need to pause slightly to prevent a misinterpretation of the phrase.

plunge in!

Don't be discouraged if Thai seems difficult at first – this is only because we aren't used to pronouncing certain Thai sounds the way we do in English. Speak slowly and follow the coloured phonetic guides next to each phrase. If you absolutely can't make yourself understood, simply point to the Thai phrase and show it to the person you're speaking to. The most important thing is to laugh at your mistakes and keep trying. Remember, communicating in a foreign language is, above all, great fun.

This chapter contains a basic grammar of Thai explained in simple terms. It's arranged alphabetically to help you make your own sentences. We hope it will encourage you to explore beyond the territory of the phrases given in this phrasebook and to create your own adventures in communication. You should be encouraged by the fact that Thai grammar is really quite a simple and logical system.

a/an & the

In Thai there are no equivalents to the English articles a, an or the. Simply say the noun by itself. For example:

The radio doesn't work.
  วิทยุเสีย
                     wí-tá-yú sěe·a
                     (lit: radio ruined)

See also **nouns**.

adjectives & adverbs see describing things

be

The verb เ‎ben เป็น is the closest Thai equivalent to the English verb 'be' but with some important differences. It's used to join nouns or pronouns.

I am a teacher.
ผม/ดิฉันเป็นครู

pŏm/dì-chăn ben kroo **m/f**
(lit: I ben teacher)

This dog is a ridgeback.
หมานี้เป็นหมาหลังอาน

măh née ben măh lăng ahn
(lit: dog this ben dog ridgeback)

However, it can't be used to join nouns and adjectives – the adjective simply follows the noun directly, with no verb:

I am cold.
ผม/ดิฉันหนาว

pŏm/dì-chăn nŏw **m/f**
(lit: I cold)

The word ben also has other meanings, such as 'have' when describing a person's condition:

I have a fever.
ผม/ดิฉันเป็นไข้

pŏm/dì-chăn ben kâi **m/f**
(lit: I ben fever)

She has a cold.
เขาเป็นหวัด

kŏw ben wàt
(lit: she ben cold)

It can even be used to show ability:

She knows how to play guitar.
เขาเล่นกีตาร์เป็น

kŏw lên gee-đah ben
(lit: she play guitar ben)

One question you'll hear quite often in Thailand is:

Can you eat Thai food?
คุณทานอาหารไทยเป็นไหม

kun tahn ah-hăhn tai ben măi
(lit: you eat food Thai ben măi)

This ultimately means, 'Can you tolerate spicy food?' (see **questions and answers** for a description of măi).

See also **pointing something out** and **verbs**.

commands & requests

The word kŏr is used to make polite requests. Depending on the context, it's roughly equivalent to 'Please give me a …' or 'May I ask for a …'. Note that kŏr always comes at the beginning of a sentence and is often used in conjunction with the added 'polite' word nòy (a little), spoken with a low tone at the end of the sentence:

Can I have some rice?
ขอข้าวหน่อย

kŏr kôw nòy
(lit: kŏr rice nòy)

To ask someone to do something, preface the sentence with chôo·ay ช่วย. To invite someone to do something, use cheun เชิญ. The closest English equivalent is 'please':

Please close the window.
ช่วยปิดหน้าต่าง

chôo·ay bìt nâh-đàhng
(lit: chôo·ay close window)

Please sit down.
เชิญนั่ง

cheun nâng
(lit: cheun sit)

To express a greater sense of urgency, use sì สิ at the end of the sentence:

Close the door!
ปิดประตูสิ

bìt brà-đoo sì
(lit: close door sì)

comparing things

In Thai, there is a very simple formula for comparing one thing to another. For comparisons, add gwàh กว่า (roughly trans-lated as 'more') to the adjective. To say something is the best of its kind, add têe-sùt ที่สุด (roughly translated as 'the most').

good	ดี	dee
better	ดีกว่า	dee-gwàh
best	ดีที่สุด	dee têe-sùt

If, on the other hand, you are comparing something or some-one to a previous or later state, the terms kêun (ขึ้น, literally 'up') and long (ลง, literally 'down') are used instead of gwàh.

The room is getting hotter.
ห้องกำลังร้อนขึ้น   hôrng gam-lang rórn kêun
       (lit: room getting hot up)

The room is getting cooler.
ห้องกำลังเย็นลง   hôrng gam-lang yen long
       (lit: room getting cool down)

To say that two things are the same use měu·an gan เหมือนกัน (is/are the same) or měu·an gàp เหมือนกับ (is/are the same as):

Thai customs are the same.
ประเพณีไทยเหมือนกัน   brà-peh-nee tai měu·an gan
       (lit: custom Thai are-the-same)

That kind is the same as this kind.
อย่างนั้นเหมือนกับอย่างนี้   yàhng nán měu·an gàp yàhng née
       (lit: kind that is-the-same-as kind this)

counting things

Occasionally in English you can't just put a number with a noun – you use an extra word which 'classifies' the noun. These are also known as counters. For example, we would say 'three pairs of pants' instead of 'three pants'. The word 'pairs' not only classifies pants but also shoes, sunglasses, socks and so on. In Thai, you always need to use a classifier whenever you specify a number of objects in a given category. The classifier always goes after the noun and the number. For example:

Four houses.

บ้านสี่หลัง

bâhn sèe lăng
(lit: house four lang)

Here are some examples of classifiers in Thai:

animals, furniture, clothing	ตัว	đoo·a
books, candles	เล่ม	lêm
eggs	ฟอง	forng
glasses (of water, tea)	แก้ว	gâa·ou
houses	หลัง	lăng
letters, newspapers	ฉบับ	chà·bàp
monks, Buddha images	รูป	rôop
pieces, slices (cakes, cloth)	ชิ้น	chín
pills, seeds, small gems	เม็ด	mét
plates, glasses, pages	ใบ	bai
plates of food	จาน	jahn
rolls (toilet paper, film)	ม้วน	móo·an
royalty, stupas	องค์	ong
stamps, planets, stars	ดวง	doo·ang
small objects	อัน	an
trains	ขบวน	kà·boo·an
vehicles (bikes, cars, train carriages)	คัน	kan

If you don't know (or forget) the relevant classifier, the word an อัน may be used for almost any small object. Alternatively, Thais sometimes repeat the noun rather than use a classifier.

For more on classifiers see **numbers & amounts**, page 35.

describing things

To describe something in Thai, all you need to do is place the adjective after the thing you wish to describe:

big house	บ้านใหญ่	bâhn yài (lit: house big)
small room	ห้องเล็ก	hôrng lék (lit: room small)
delicious food	อาหารอร่อย	ah-hăhn à-ròy (lit: food delicious)

Adjectives that can logically be used to modify action may also function as adverbs in Thai. An adjective used adverbially is often doubled, and always follows the verb:

| slow horse | ม้าช้า | máh cháh (lit: horse slow) |

and

| drive slowly | ขับช้าๆ | kàp cháh-cháh (lit: drive slow-slow) |

See also **comparing things**.

future see **verbs**

gender

The pronoun 'I' will change depending on the gender of the speaker – so a man will refer to himself as pŏm ผม (I, me) while a woman will refer to herself as dì-chǎn ดิฉัน (I, me). When being polite to others, it's customary to add the word kráp ครับ (if you're a man) or kâ ค่ะ (if you're a woman) as a kind of a 'softener' to the end of questions and statements.

Often you'll see the symbol **m/f** in this book which stands for male/female. Whenever a sentence is marked with **m/f** you have to make a choice between pŏm and dì-chǎn or kráp and kâ depending on your gender. For example in the sentence:

I don't understand.
ผม/ดิฉันไม่เข้าใจ   pŏm/dì-chǎn mâi kôw jai **m/f**

A man would say 'pŏm mâi kôw jai' but a woman would say 'dì-chǎn mâi kôw jai'. Thai also has a neutral form of I, chǎn ฉัน, although we don't use it in this book as it is informal.

have

The verb 'have' is expressed by simply placing the word mee มี before the object:

I have a bicycle.
ผม/ดิฉันมีรถจักรยาน   pŏm/dì-chǎn mee
                                        rót-jàk-gà-yahn **m/f**
                                        (lit: I have bicycle)

Do you have fried noodles?
มีก๋วยเตี๋ยวผัดไหม   mee gŏo·ay-đĕe·o pàt măi
                                        (lit: have noodle fry not)

See also **possession**.

joining words

Use these conjunctions to join two phrases together:

and	และ	láa
because	เพราะว่า	pró wâh
but	แต่	đàa
or	หรือ	rěu
so that	เพื่อ	pêu·a
therefore	เพราะฉะนั้น	pró chà-nán
with	กับ	gàp (also 'and', as in 'rice and curry')

location

Location is indicated by using prepositions. These are words that show relationships between objects or people. Instead of just pointing, try using some of these useful terms:

adjacent to	ติดกับ	đìt gàp
around	รอบ	rôrp
at	ที่	têe
at the edge of	ริมกับ	rim gàp
from	จาก	jàhk
in	ใน	nai
inside	ภายใน	pai nai
under	ใต้	đâi
with	กับ	gàp

See also the section **directions**, page 61.

more than one see also numbers & amounts

Words in Thai do not change when they become plural:

The house is large.
The houses are large.
บ้านใหญ่   bâhn yài
                                 (lit: house large)

A 'classifier' or number before the object will help you
determine whether or not a word is plural.

For more about numbers see **classifiers** and the section
numbers & amounts, page 35.

my & your see possession

negative

The most common negative marker in Thai is mâi ไม่ (not).
Any verb or adjective may be negated by the insertion of mâi
immediately before it. You can also use ɓlòw เปล่า but only in
conjunction with questions that use the ɓlòw tag (see questions and answers).

He/She isn't thirsty.
เขาไม่หิวน้ำ   kŏw mâi hěw nám
                                 (lit: he/she not thirsty)

I don't have any cash.
ผม/ดิฉันไม่มีตางค์   pŏm/dì-chăn mâi mee đahng m/f
                                 (lit: I not have cash)

We're not French.
เราไม่เป็นคนฝรั่งเศส   row mâi ɓen kon fà-rang-sèt
                                 (lit: we not be person France)

John has never gone to Chiang Mai.

จอนไม่เคยไปเชียงใหม่   jon mâi keu·i bai chee·ang mài
(lit: John not ever go Chiang Mai)

We won't go to Ubon tomorrrow.

พรุ่งนี้เราจะไม่ไปอุบล   prûng-née row jà mâi bai ù-bon
(lit: tomorrow we will not go Ubon)

nouns

Nouns always remain the same whether or not they're singular or plural. They don't need to be introduced with articles such as 'a' or 'the'.

I'm a soldier.

ผม/ดิฉันเป็นทหาร   pŏm/dì-chăn ben tá-hăhn m/f
(lit: I be soldier)

We're soldiers.

เราเป็นทหาร   row ben tá-hăhn
(lit: we be soldier)

You can form nouns from verbs of physical action by adding gahn การ before the verb:

to travel	เดินทาง	deun tahng
travel	การเดินทาง	gahn deun tahng

You can form nouns from adjectives by adding kwahm ความ before the adjective:

hot	ร้อน	rórn
heat	ความร้อน	kwahm rórn

past see verbs

plural see **more than one**

pointing something out

If you want to say 'there is' or 'there are', to describe the existence of something somewhere else, the verb mee มี (have) is used instead of ฺben เป็น (see also **be**):

In Bangkok there are many cars.
ที่กรุงเทพฯมีรถยนต์มาก   têe grung têp mee rót-yon mâhk
                      (lit: in Bangkok mee car many)

At Wat Pho there is a large Buddha image.
ที่วัดโพธิ์มีพระพุทธรูปใหญ่   têe wát poh mee
                      prá-pút-tá-rôop yài
                      (lit: in Wat Pho mee Buddha
                      image large)

See also **have** and **this & that**.

polite forms see **pronouns**

possession

The word kŏrng ของ is used to denote possession and is roughly the same as 'of' or 'belongs to' in English:

| my bag | กระเป๋าของผม | grà-ฺbŏw kŏrng pŏm (lit: bag kŏrng me) |
| his/her seat | ที่นั่งของเขา | têe nâng kŏrng kŏw (lit: seat kŏrng him/her) |

Does this belong to you?
นี่ของคุณหรือเปล่า

               nêe kŏrng kun rĕu ฺblòw
               (lit: this kŏrng you or not)

present see **verbs**

pronouns

Personal pronouns (I, you, she, he etc) aren't used as frequently as they are in English, as the subject of a sentence is frequently omitted after the first reference, or when it's clear from the context. There's no distinction between subject and object pronouns – the word pŏm ผม means both 'I' and 'me' (for a man), and kŏw เขา means 'he/she/they' and 'him/her/them'.

I, me (m)	ผม	pŏm
I, me (f)	ดิฉัน	dì-chăn
I, me (m&f)	ฉัน	chăn
you	คุณ	kun
he, she	เขา	kŏw
they	เขา	kŏw

In Thai there are additional words for the personal pronoun 'you' depending on the level of politeness or informality required:

you (very polite – to monks, royalty)	ท่าน	tâhn
you (informal – to a child or lover)	เธอ	teu
you (very informal – to a small child)	หนู	nŏo
you (vulgar – to a close friend)	มึง	meung

Don't worry if you're not sure which one to choose. In this phrasebook we have always provided the appropriate form of 'you' demanded by the context of the phrase.

See also **gender**.

questions & answers

Thai has two ways of forming questions – through the use of question words like 'who', 'how' and 'what', or through the addition of a tag like 'isn't it?' to the end of a sentence.

To form a yes-or-no question in Thai, all you need to do is place măi ไหม (no literal translation) at the end of a statement:

Is the weather hot?

อากาศร้อนไหม

ah-gàht rórn măi
(lit: weather hot măi)

To say 'aren't you?' use châi măi ใช่ไหม:

You're a student, aren't you?

คุณเป็นนักเรียนใช่ไหม

kun ben nák ree·an châi măi
(lit: you be student châi măi)

The tag châi măi is also used to mean 'isn't it?'.

To answer a question, just repeat the verb, with or without the negative particle. The negative particles are măi, châi măi, blòw and yang. The word rĕu means 'or', and with a negative particle it means 'or not' – however often the negative isn't stated and the question simply ends with rĕu. Informally, a negative particle alone will do for a negative reply.

Do you want a beer?		
เอาเบียร์ไหม		ow bee·a măi (lit: want beer măi)
Yes.	เอา	ow (lit: want)
No.	ไม่เอา	mâi ow (lit: not want)
Are you angry?		
โกรธหรือเปล่า		gròht rĕu blòw (lit: angry rĕu blòw)
Yes.	โกรธ	gròht (lit: angry)
No.	เปล่า	blòw (lit: not)

question words

Many English speakers instinctively place a raised inflection to the end of a Thai question. Try to avoid doing this as it will usually interfere with the tones (see the section **pronunciation**, page 11). In Thai a question is formed by using 'question tags' at the beginning or end of a phrase:

what	อะไร	à-rai
What do you need?	คุณต้องการอะไร	kun đôrng gahn à-rai (lit: you want what)
how	อย่างไร	yàhng rai
How do you do it?	ทำอย่างไร	tam yàhng rai (lit: do how)
who	ใคร	krai
Who is sitting there?	ใครนั่งที่นั่น	krai nâng têe nán (lit: who sit there)
when	เมื่อไร	mêu·a-rai
When will you go to Chiang Mai?	เมื่อไรจะไปเชียงใหม่	mêu·a-rai jà bai chee·ang mài (lit: when will go Chiang Mai)
why	ทำไม	tam-mai
Why are you quiet?	ทำไมเงียบ	tam-mai ngêe·ap (lit: why quiet)
where	ที่ไหน	têe năi
Where is the bathroom?	ห้องน้ำอยู่ที่ไหน	hôrng nám yòo têe năi (lit: bathroom is where)
which	ไหน	năi
Which one do you like?	ชอบอันไหน	chôrp an năi (lit: like one which)

this & that

The words nêe นี่ (this) and nân นั่น (that) are spoken with a fall-ing tone when used alone as pronouns:

What's this?
นี่อะไร

nêe à-rai
(lit: this what)

How much is that?
นั่นเท่าไร

nân tôw rai
(lit: that how much)

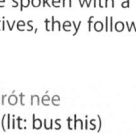

However, when used with a noun, they're spoken with a high tone (nán นั่น, née นี่) and like Thai adjectives, they follow the noun they refer to:

| this bus | รถนี้ | rót née (lit: bus this) |
| that plane | จานนั้น | jahn nán (lit: plane that) |

To say 'these' and 'those' add the word lòw เหล่า before née and nán and use a high tone:

these	เหล่านี้	lòw née
those	เหล่านั้น	lòw nán
these chickens	ไก่เหล่านี้	gài lòw née (lit: chicken these)

verbs

Thai verbs don't change according to tense. Thus the sentence kŏw gin gài เขากินไก่ can mean 'He/She **eats** chicken', 'He/She **ate** chicken' or 'He/She **has eaten** chicken'. Context will often tell you what time is being referred to. Otherwise you can do one of the following:

• specify the time with a word like wan-née วันนี้ (today) or mêu·a wahn née เมื่อวานนี้ (yesterday):

He/She ate chicken yesterday.

เมื่อวานนี้เขากินไก่　　　　mêu·a wahn née kŏw gin gài
　　　　　　　　　　　　(lit: yesterday he/she eat chicken)

• add one of the words explained below to indicate whether an action is **ongoing**, **completed** or **to-be-completed**:

ongoing action

The word gam-lang กำลัง is used before the verb to mark ongoing or progressive action, a bit like the English 'am/are/is doing'. However, it's not used unless the speaker feels it's absolutely necessary to express the continuity of an action:

I'm washing the clothes.

กำลังซักเสื้อผ้า　　　　　gam-lang sák sêu·a pâh
　　　　　　　　　　　　(lit: gam-lang wash clothes)

completed action

A common way of expressing completed action in Thai is by using the word láa·ou แล้ว (already) at the end of the sentence:

We have been to Bangkok.

เราไปกรุงเทพฯแล้ว　　　row bai grung têp láa·ou
　　　　　　　　　　　　(lit: we go Bangkok láa·ou)

I have spent the money.

ผม/ดิฉันจ่ายเงินแล้ว　　　pŏm/dì-chăn jài ngeun láa·ou m/f
　　　　　　　　　　　　(lit: I pay money láa·ou)

The word láa·ou can also refer to a current condition that began a short time ago:

I'm hungry already.

ผม/ดิฉันหิวแล้ว
pŏm/dì·chăn hĕw kôw láa·ou **m/f**
(lit: I hungry rice láa·ou)

The marker dâi ได้ shows past tense, but unlike láa·ou, never refers to a current condition. It immediately precedes the verb, and is often used in conjunction with láa·ou. It's more commonly used in negative statements than in the affirmative:

Our friends didn't go to Chiang Mai.

เพื่อนเราไม่ได้ไป
เชียงใหม่
pêu·an row mâi dâi bai
chee·ang mài
(lit: friend us not dâi go
Chiang Mai)

to-be-completed action

The word ja จะ is used to mark an action to be completed in the future. It always appears directly before the verb:

He/She will buy rice.

เขาจะซื้อข้าว
kŏw jà séu kôw
(lit: he/she jà buy rice)

word order

Generally speaking the word order follows the pattern of subject-verb-object like in English:

We eat rice.

เรากินข้าว
row gin kôw
(lit: we eat rice)

You study Thai.
คุณเรียนภาษาไทย   kun ree·an pah·săh tai
(lit: you study language Thai)

Sometimes the object is placed first to add emphasis:

I don't like that bowl
ชามนั้นผม/ดิฉันไม่ชอบ   chahm nán pŏm/dì·chăn
mâi chôrp **m/f**
(lit: bowl that I not like)

yes/no questions see questions

Do you speak English?
คุณพูดภาษาอังกฤษได้ไหม

kun pôot pah-săh ang-grìt dâi măi

Does anyone speak English?
มีใครพูดภาษาอังกฤษ
ได้บ้างไหม

mee krai pôot pah-săh ang-grìt dâi bâhng măi

Do you understand?
คุณเข้าใจไหม

kun kôw jai măi

Yes, I do.
ครับ/ค่ะ เข้าใจ

kráp/kâ, kôw jai m/f

No, I don't.
ไม่เข้าใจ

mâi kôw jai

I speak a little.
พูดได้นิดหน่อย

pôot dâi nít nòy

I (don't) understand.
ผม/ดิฉัน (ไม่) เข้าใจ

pŏm/dì-chăn (mâi) kôw jai m/f

How do you …?   … อย่างไร   … yàhng rai
  pronounce this   ออกเสียง   òrk sĕe·ang
  write 'Saraburi'   เขียนสระบุรี   kĕe·an sà-rà-bù-ree

What does 'anahkot' mean?
อนาคต แปลว่าอะไร

à-nah-kót blaa wâh à-rai

listen for …

kun pôot pah-săh tai dâi măi
คุณพูดภาษาไทยได้ไหม

Can you speak Thai?

Could you please ...?	... ได้ไหม	... dâi măi
repeat that	พูดอีกที	pôot èek tee
speak more slowly	พูดช้าๆ	pôot cháa cháa
write it down	เขียนลงให้	kĕe·an long hâi

---

thai with a twist

Thai people love to use colourful language to express themselves. Here are a couple of common sayings you could try out for effect:

To ride an elephant to catch a grasshopper.
(to go overboard)

ขี่ช้างจับตั๊กแตน   kèe cháhng jàp đák-gà-đaan

When you're fat, you smell good. When you're thin, you stink.
(Nobody loves you when you're down-and-out.)

เมื่อพีเนื้อหอม	mêu·a pee néu·a hŏrm
เมื่อผอมเนื้อเหม็น	mêu·a pŏrm néu·a mĕn

Feeling confident? See if you can impress a local with this Thai tongue twister:

tá-hăhn tĕu ƀeun ƀàak ƀoon ƀai ƀòhk đèuk

ทหารถือปืนแบกปูน	**(A soldier with his gun**
ไปโบกตึก	**carries cement to render**
	the building.)

cardinal numbers

เลขนับจำนวน

1	หนึ่ง	nèung
2	สอง	sŏrng
3	สาม	săhm
4	สี่	sèe
5	ห้า	hâh
6	หก	hòk
7	เจ็ด	jèt
8	แปด	bàat
9	เก้า	gôw
10	สิบ	sìp
11	สิบเอ็ด	sìp-èt
12	สิบสอง	sìp-sŏrng
13	สิบสาม	sìp-săhm
14	สิบสี่	sìp-sèe
15	สิบห้า	sìp-hâh
16	สิบหก	sìp-hòk
17	สิบเจ็ด	sìp-jèt
18	สิบแปด	sìp-bàat
19	สิบเก้า	sìp-gôw
20	ยี่สิบ	yêe-sìp
21	ยี่สิบเอ็ด	yêe-sìp-èt
22	ยี่สิบสอง	yêe-sìp-sŏrng
30	สามสิบ	săhm-sìp
40	สี่สิบ	sèe-sìp
50	ห้าสิบ	hâh-sìp
100	หนึ่งร้อย	nèung róy
200	สองร้อย	sŏrng róy
1,000	หนึ่งพัน	nèung pan
1,000,000	หนึ่งล้าน	nèung láhn

ordinal numbers

1st	ที่หนึ่ง	têe nèung
2nd	ที่สอง	têe sŏrng
3rd	ที่สาม	têe săhm
4th	ที่สี่	têe sèe
5th	ที่ห้า	têe hâh

classifiers

ลักษณนาม

Words of measure, or classifiers, are sometimes used in English with phrases such as 'three loaves of bread' (not 'three breads') and 'three sheets of paper' (and not 'three papers'). In Thai, whenever you specify a particular number of any noun, you must use a classifier.

For example, the question 'Can I have a bottle of beer?' (kŏr bee·a kòo·at nèung ขอเบียร์ขวดหนึ่ง) is literally 'Can I have beer one bottle?'.

For examples of classifiers and how to use them, see the **phrasebuilder**, page 15.

go figure

Just as in English we can use a figure, eg '7', instead of writing out the whole word, Thai also has a basic system for writing numbers. Use this chart to decipher numbers on street signs, shop doors and price tags:

1	๑	6	๖	11	๑๑	16	๑๖
2	๒	7	๗	12	๑๒	17	๑๗
3	๓	8	๘	13	๑๓	18	๑๘
4	๔	9	๙	14	๑๔	19	๑๙
5	๕	10	๑๐	15	๑๕	20	๒๐

telling the time

การบอกเวลา

Telling the time in Thai can be very challenging for an outsider to master. While the Western twelve-hour clock divides the day between two time periods, am and pm, the Thai system has four periods. The 24-hour clock is also commonly used by government and media. If you plan to stay in Thailand for a long time it's worth learning how to tell the time. Otherwise simply refer to the list below where each hour of the twelve-hour clock has been translated into the Thai system.

What time is it?	กี่โมงแล้ว	gèe mohng láa·ou
12 midnight	หกทุ่ม/เที่ยงคืน	hòk tûm/têe·ang keun
1am	ตีหนึ่ง	đee nèung
2am	ตีสอง	đee sŏrng
3am	ตีสาม	đee săhm
4am	ตีสี่	đee sèe
5am	ตีห้า	đee hâh
6am	หกโมงเช้า	hòk mohng chów
7am	หนึ่งโมงเช้า	nèung mohng chów
11am	ห้าโมงเช้า	hâh mohng chów
12 noon	เที่ยง	têe·ang
1pm	บ่ายโมง	bài mohng
2pm	บ่ายสองโมง	bài sŏrng mohng
4pm	บ่ายสี่โมง	bài sèe mohng
4pm	สี่โมงเย็น	sèe mohng yen
6pm	หกโมงเย็น	hòk mohng yen
7pm	หนึ่งทุ่ม	nèung tûm
8pm	สองทุ่ม	sŏrng tûm
9pm	สามทุ่ม	săhm tûm
10pm	สี่ทุ่ม	sèe tûm
11pm	ห้าทุ่ม	hâh tûm

To give times after the hour, just add the number of minutes following the hour.

4.30pm

บ่ายสี่โมงครึ่ง   bài sèe mohng krêung
                (lit: four afternoon hours
                half)

4.15pm

บ่ายสี่โมงสิบห้านาที   bài sèe mohng sìp-hâh nah-tee
                   (lit: four afternoon hours
                   fifteen)

To give times before the hour, add the number of minutes beforehand.

3.45pm

อีกสิบห้านาทีบ่ายสี่โมง   èek sìp-hâh nah-tee bài sèe mohng
                   (lit: another fifteen minutes
                   four afternoon hours)

Thai time

In Thailand you may hear a person who arrives late for an appointment joke about being on 'Thai time' as punctuality is generally a more fluid concept than some Westerners are used to. But there is a specifically Thai way of telling the time which you'll need to learn if you want to avoid being late yourself.

The day is broken up into four periods. From midnight to six in the morning times begin with the word đee ต (strike), from six in the morning until midday they end with the word chów เช้า (morning), from midday to six in the evening they begin with the word bai บ่าย (afternoon) and from six in the evening until midnight they end with the word tûm ทุ่ม (thump).

So 3am is đee sǎhm ตีสาม (lit: strike three) and 9pm is sǎhm tûm สามทุ่ม (lit: three thumps).

days of the week

Monday	วันจันทร์	wan jan
Tuesday	วันอังคาร	wan ang-kahn
Wednesday	วันพุธ	wan pút
Thursday	วันพฤหัสบดี	wan pá-réu-hàt
Friday	วันศุกร์	wan sùk
Saturday	วันเสาร์	wan sŏw
Sunday	วันอาทิตย์	wan ah-tít

the calendar

เดือน

months

January	เดือนมกราคม	deu·an má-gà-rah-kom
February	เดือนกุมภาพันธ์	deu·an gum-pah-pan
March	เดือนมีนาคม	deu·an mee-nah-kom
April	เดือนเมษายน	deu·an mair-săh-yon
May	เดือนพฤษภาคม	deu·an préut-sà-pah-kom
June	เดือนมิถุนายน	deu·an mí-tù-nah-yon
July	เดือนกรกฎาคม	deu·an gà-rák-gà-dah-kom
August	เดือนสิงหาคม	deu·an sĭng-hăh-kom
September	เดือนกันยายน	deu·an gan-yah-yon
October	เดือนตุลาคม	deu·an đù-lah-kom
November	เดือนพฤศจิกายน	deu·an préut-sà-jì-gah-yon
December	เดือนธันวาคม	deu·an tan-wah-kom

time & dates

dates

What date is it today?

วันนี้วันที่เท่าไร wan née wan têe tôw-rai

It's (27 September).

วันที่ (ยี่สิบเจ็ดเดือนกันยายน) wan têe (yêe-sìp-jèt deu·an gan-yah-yŏn)

seasons

dry season (November to March)	หน้าแล้ง	nâh láang
rainy season (June to September)	หน้าฝน	nâh fŏn
cool season (winter)	หน้าหนาว	nâh nŏw
hot season (summer)	หน้าร้อน	nâh rórn
moonsoon	หน้ามรสุม	nâh mor-rá-sŭm

For more on the weather, see **outdoors**, page 147.

present

ปัจจุบัน

now	เดี๋ยวนี้	dĕe·o née
this ...	... นี้	... née
afternoon	บ่าย	bài
month	เดือน	deu·an
morning	เช้า	chów
week	อาทิตย์	ah-tít
year	ปี	bee
today	วันนี้	wan née
tonight	คืนนี้	keun née

past

(three days) ago	(สามวัน) ทีแล้ว	(sǎhm wan) tee láa·ou
day before yesterday	เมื่อวานซืน	mêu·a wahn seun
last ...	... ทีแล้ว	... tee láa·ou
month	เดือน	deu·an
week	อาทิตย์	ah-tít
year	ปี	ƀee
last night	เมื่อคืนนี้	mêu·a keun née
since (May)	ตั้งแต่ (พฤษภาคม)	ƀâng ɗàa (préut-sà-pah-kom)
yesterday ...	... เมื่อวาน	... mêu·a wahn
afternoon	บ่าย	bài
evening	เย็น	yen
morning	เช้า	chów

future

day after tomorrow	วันมะรืน	wan má-reun
in (six days)	อีก (หกวัน)	èek (hòk wan)
next ...	... หน้า	... nâh
month	เดือน	deu·an
week	อาทิตย์	ah-tít
year	ปี	ƀee
tomorrow ...	พรุ่งนี้ ...	prûng née ...
afternoon	บ่าย	bài
evening	เย็น	yen
morning	เช้า	chów
until (June)	จนถึง (มิถุนายน)	jon tĕung (mí-tù-nah-yon)

time & dates

41

during the day

afternoon	บ่าย	bài
dawn	อรุณ	à-run
day	วัน	wan
evening	เย็น	yen
midday	เที่ยงวัน	têe·ang wan
midnight	เที่ยงคืน	têe·ang keun
morning	เช้า	chów
night	ตอนคืน	đorn keun
sunrise	ตะวันขึ้น	đà-wan kêun
sunset	ตะวันตก	đà-wan đòk

How much is it?
ราคาเท่าไร
rah-kah tôw rai

Can you write down the price?
เขียนราคาลงให้ได้ไหม
kěe·an rah-kah long hâi
dâi măi

Can you count it out for me?
นับให้ดูได้ไหม
náp hâi doo dâi măi

Can I have smaller notes?
ขอใบย่อยได้ไหม
kŏr bai yôy dâi măi

Do you accept …?	รับ … ไหม	ráp … măi
credit cards	บัตรเครดิต	bàt krair-dìt
debit cards	บัตรธนาคาร	bàt tá-nah-kahn
travellers cheques	เช็คเดินทาง	chék deun tahng
I'd like …, please.	ขอ … หน่อย	kŏr … nòy
my change	เงินทอน	ngeun torn
a refund	เงินคืน	ngeun keun
a receipt	ใบเสร็จ	bai sèt
to return this	เอามาคืน	ow mah keun
I'd like to …	ผม/ดิฉัน อยากจะ …	pŏm/dì-chăn yàhk jà … m/f
cash a cheque	ขึ้นเช็ค	kêun chék
change a travellers cheque	แลกเช็คเดินทาง	lâak chék deun tahng
change money	แลกเงิน	lâak ngeun
get a cash advance	รูดเงินจากบัตรเครดิต	rôot ngeun jàhk bàt krair-dìt
withdraw money	ถอนเงิน	tŏrn ngeun

Where's ...?	... อยู่ที่ไหน	... yòo têe năi
an ATM	ตู้เอทีเอม	đôo air tee em
a foreign	ที่แลกเงินต่าง	têe lâak ngeun
exchange office	ประเทศ	đàhng ʾbrà-têt

What's the ...?	... เท่าไร	... tôw rai
charge	ค่าธรรมเนียม	kâh tam·nee·am
exchange rate	อัตราแลกเปลี่ยน	àt-ɖrah lâak
		ʾblèe·an

It's ...		
free	ไม่มีค่าธรรมเนียม	mâi mee kâh
		tam·nee·am
(12) baht	(สิบสอง) บาท	(sìp sŏrng) baht

talking *kráp*

Adopting the proper niceties in Thailand is a good practical habit to get into. You'll notice that some of the phrases in this book end with the word kráp ครับ for a male speaker or kâ ค่ะ for a female speaker.

These are used at the end of a sentence in situations that require a verbal softener. For instance, the question kun ʾbai năi คุณไปไหน (Where are you going?) could sound very abrupt. A more polite way to say it would be kun ʾbai năi kráp คุณไปไหนครับ if you are a man or kun ʾbai năi kâ คุณไปไหนค่ะ if you are a woman.

getting around

การเดินทาง

Which boat goes to (Ayuthaya)?
เรือลำไหนไป · reu·a lam năi bai
(อยุธยา) · (à-yút-tá-yah)

Which bus/*songthaew* goes to (Ayuthaya)?
รถเมล์/สองแถว คัน · rót mair/sŏrng-tăa·ou kan
ไหนไป (อยุธยา) · năi bai (à-yút-tá-yah)

Which train goes to (Ayuthaya)?
รถไฟ ขบวนไหนไป · rót fai kà-buan năi bai
(อยุธยา) · (à-yút-tá-yah)

Is this the ... to (Chiang Mai)?	อันนี้เป็น ...ไป (เชียงใหม่) ใช่ไหม	an née ben ... bai (chee·ang mài) châi măi
boat	เรือ	reu·a
bus	รถเมล์	rót mair
train	รถไฟ	rót fai

When's the ... bus?	รถเมล์ คัน ... มาเมื่อไร	rót mair kan ... mah mêu·a rai
first	แรก	râak
last	สุดท้าย	sùt tái
next	ต่อไป	dòr bai

What time does it leave?
ออกกี่โมง · òrk gèe mohng

What time does it get to (Chiang Mai)?
ถึง (เชียงใหม่) กี่โมง · tĕung (chee·ang mài) gèe mohng

How long will it be delayed?
จะเสียเวลานานเท่าไร · jà sĕe·a wair-lah nahn tôw-rai

Excuse me, is this seat free?
ขอโทษ ครับ/ค่ะ ที่นั่งนี้ว่างไหม
kŏr tôht kráp/kâ têe
nâng née wâhng măi **m/f**

That's my seat.
นั่นที่นั่งของ ผม/ดิฉัน
nân têe nâng kŏrng
pŏm/dì-chăn **m/f**

Please tell me when we get to (Chiang Mai).
เมื่อถึง (เชียงใหม่)
กรุณาบอกด้วย
mêu·a tĕung (chee·ang mài)
gà-rú-nah bòrk dôo·ay

Please stop here.
ขอจอดที่นี้
kŏr jòrt têe née

How long do we stop here?
เราจะหยุดที่นี้นานเท่าไร
row jà yùt têe née
nahn tôw-rai

tickets

ตั๋ว

Where do I buy a ticket?
ต้องซื้อตั๋วที่ไหน
đôrng séu đŏo·a têe năi

Do I need to book?
ต้องจองล่วงหน้าหรือเปล่า
đôrng jorng lôo·ang nâh
rĕu ɓlòw

Can I have a ... ticket (to Chiang Mai)?	ขอตั๋ว ...ไป (เชียงใหม่)	kŏr đŏo·a ...ɓai (chee·ang mài)
1st-class	ชั้นหนึ่ง	chán nèung
2nd-class	ชั้นสอง	chán sŏrng
3rd-class	ชั้นสาม	chán săhm
child's	สำหรับเด็ก	săm-ràp dèk
one-way	เที่ยวเดียว	têe·o dee·o
return	ไปกลับ	ɓai glàp
student's	สำหรับนักศึกษา	săm-ràp nák sèuk-săh

an nán	อันนั้น	that one
an née	อันนี้	this one
bor-rí-sàt tôrng têe·o	บริษัทท่องเที่ยว	travel agent
cháh wair-lah	ช้าเวลา	delayed
chan-chah-lah	ชานชาลา	platform
chôrng kǎi đŏo·a	ช่องขายตั๋ว	ticket window
đah-rahng wair-lah	ตารางเวลา	timetable
đem	เต็ม	full
yók lêrk	ยกเลิก	cancelled

I'd like	ต้องการที่นั่ง ...	đôrng gahn
a/an ... seat.		têe nâng ...
aisle	ติดทางเดิน	đìt tahng deun
nonsmoking	ในเขตห้ามสูบบุหรี่	nai kèt hâhm sòop bù-rèe
smoking	ในเขตสูบบุหรี่ได้	nai kèt sòop bù-rèe dâi
window	ติดหน้าต่าง	đìt nâh đàhng

Is there (a) ...?	มี ... ไหม	mee ... mǎi
air-conditioning	ปรับอากาศ	ɓràp ah-gàht
blanket	ผ้าห่ม	páh hòm
sick bag	ถุงขยะ	tǔng kà-yà
toilet	ส้วม	sôo·am

How much is it?
ราคาเท่าไร
rah-kah tôw-rai

How long does the trip take?
การเดินทางใช้เวลานานเท่าไร
gahn deun tahng chái wair-lah nahn tôw-rai

Is it a direct route?
เป็นทางตรงไหม
ɓen tahng đrong mǎi

Can I get a stand-by ticket?
จะซื้อที่นั่งสำรองได้ไหม
jà séu têe nâng sǎm-rorng dâi mǎi

Can I get a sleeping berth?
จะจองที่นอนได้ไหม jà jorng têe norn dâi măi

What time should I check in?
จะต้องมากี่โมง jà đôrng mah gèe mohng

I'd like to … my	ผม/ดิฉัน อยาก	pŏm/dì-chăn yàhk
ticket, please.	จะขอ … ตั๋ว	jà kŏr … đŏo·a **m/f**
cancel	ยกเลิก	yók lêuk
change	เปลี่ยน	ʰlèe·an
confirm	ยืนยัน	yeun yan

luggage

สัมภาระ

Where can I find …?	จะหา … ได้ที่ไหน	jà hăh … dâi têe năi
the baggage claim	ที่รับกระเป๋า	têe ráp grà-ʰŏw
the left-luggage office	ห้องฝากกระเป๋า	hôrng fàhk grà-ʰŏw
a luggage locker	ตู้ฝากกระเป๋า	đôo fàhk grà-ʰŏw
a trolley	รถเข็น	rót kĕn

My luggage	กระเป๋าของ	grà-ʰŏw kŏrng
has been …	ผม/ดิฉัน	pŏm/dì-chăn
	โดน … แล้ว	dohn … láa·ou **m/f**
damaged	เสียหาย	sĕe·a hăi
lost	หายไป	hăi ʰai
stolen	ขโมย	kà-moy

That's (not) mine.
นั่น (ไม่) ใช่ของ ผม/ดิฉัน nân (mâi) châi kŏrng pŏm/
dì-chăn **m/f**

---

listen for …

| grà-ʰŏw đìt đoo·a | กระเป๋าติดตัว | **carry-on baggage** |
| nám-nàk geun | น้ำหนักเกิน | **excess baggage** |

plane

เครื่องบิน

Where does flight (TG 132) arrive/depart?
เที่ยวบิน (ทีจี หนึ่งสามสอง)　têe·o bin (tee jee nèung
เข้า/ออก ที่ไหน　sähm sörng) kôw/òrk têe năi

Where's ...?	... อยู่ที่ไหน	... yòo têe năi
the airport shuttle	รถบัสสนามบิน	rót bàt sà-nähm bin
arrivals	เที่ยวบินขาเข้า	têe·o bin käh kôw
departures	เที่ยวบินขาออก	têe·o bin käh òrk
the duty-free	ที่ขายของปลอดภาษี	têe käi körng blòrt pah-sěe
gate (12)	ประตูที่ (สิบสอง)	brà-đoo têe (sìp-sörng)

bus, coach & train

รถเมล์รถทัวร์ และ รถไฟ

How often do buses come?
รถบัสมาบ่อยเท่าไร　rót bàt mah bòy tôw-rai

Does it stop at (Saraburi)?
รถจอดที่ (สระบุรี) ไหม　rót jòrt têe (sà-rà-bù-ree) măi

What's the next stop?
ที่จอดต่อไปคือที่ไหน　têe jòrt đòr pai keu têe năi

transport

49

I'd like to get off at (Saraburi).

ขอลงที่ (สระบุรี) kŏr long têe (sà-rà-bù-ree)
ครับ/ค่ะ kráp/kâ **m/f**

air-conditioned bus	รถปรับอากาศ	rót bràp ah-gàht
city bus	รถเมล์	rót mair
1st-class bus	รถชั้นหนึ่ง	rót chán nèung
government bus	รถ บ.ข.ส.	rót bor kŏr sŏr
intercity bus	รถบัส	rót bàt
ordinary bus	รถธรรมดา	rót tam-má-dah
VIP bus	รถวีไอพี	rót wee ai pee

What station is this?
ที่นี่สถานีไหน têe née sà-tăh-nee năi

What's the next station?
สถานีต่อไปคือสถานีไหน sà-tăh-nee dòr bai keu
  sà-tăh-nee năi

Does it stop at (Kaeng Koi)?
จอดอยู่ที่ (แก่งคอย) jòrt yòo têe (gàang koy)
ไหม măi

Do I need to change?
ต้องเปลี่ยนรถไหม dôrng plèe·an rót măi

Is it ...?	... หรือเปล่า	... rĕu plòw
direct	สายตรง	săi drong
express	รถด่วน	rót dòo·an

Which carriage is (for) ...?	ตู้ไหนสำหรับ ...	đôo năi săm-ràp ...
(Kaeng Koi)	(แก่งคอย)	(gàang koy)
1st class	ชั้นหนึ่ง	chán nèung
the dining car	ตู้ทานอาหาร	đôo tahn ah-hăhn
the sleeping car	ตู้นอน	đôo norn

I'd like a/an ...	ต้องการ ...	đôrng gahn ...
upper berth	ที่นอนชั้นบน	têe norn chán bon
lower berth	ที่นอนชั้นล่าง	têe norn chán lâhng

train	รถไฟ	rót fai
express train	รถไฟด่วน	rót fai dòo·an
sky train	รถไฟฟ้า	rót fai fáh
ordinary train	รถธรรมดา	rót tam·má·dah
rapid train	รถเร็ว	rót re·ou

boat

เรือ

What's the sea like today?
วันนี้สภาพน้ำเป็นอย่างไร
wan née sà·pâhp nám
ben yàhng rai

Are there life jackets?
มีเสื้อชูชีพไหม
mee sêu·a choo chêep măi

What island is this?
นี่คือเกาะไหน
nêe keu gò năi

What beach is this?
นี่คือชายหาดไหน
nêe keu chai hàht năi

I feel seasick.
รู้สึกเมาคลื่น
róo·sèuk mow klêun

cabin	ห้องนอน	hôrng norn
canal	คลอง	klorng
captain	นายเรือ	nai reu·a
car deck	ดาดฟ้าสำหรับรถ	dàht fáh săm·ràp rót
Chinese junk	เรือสำเภา	reu·a săm·pow
cross-river ferry	เรือข้ามฟาก	reu·a kâhm fâhk
deck	ดาดฟ้า	dàht fáh
express boat	เรือด่วน	reu·a dòo·an
ferry	เรือข้ามฟาก	reu·a kâhm fâhk
hammock	เปลญวน	blair yoo·an

hire boat	เรือรับจ้าง	reu·a ráp jâhng
life jacket	เสื้อชูชีพ	sêu·a choo chêep
lifeboat	เรือชูชีพ	reu·a choo chêep
longtail boat	เรือหางยาว	reu·a hăhng yow
sampan	เรือสำปั้น	reu·a săm-bân
yacht	เรือยอชต์	reu·a yôrt

taxi, *samlor* & *túk-túk*

แท็กซี่สามล้อและตุ๊กๆ

A fun way to travel short distances in Thailand is by *samlor* (săhm lór สามล้อ) which are three-wheeled bicycle-rickshaws powered by an energetic chauffeur. In city districts that are too congested or chaotic for a săhm lór get a ride with a mor-đeu-sai ráp jâhng มอเตอร์ไซค์รับจ้าง or motorcyle taxi. Almost emblematic of Thailand's cities is the *túk-túk* (đúk đúk ตุ๊กๆ), a name suggestive of the sound these three-wheeled taxis make as they buzz through the traffic. Bargain hard for all of these transport options, but be sure to offer a tip to any *samlor* driver who works up a worthy sweat .

I'd like a taxi ...	ต้องการรถแท็กซี่ ...	đôrng gahn rót - táak sêe ...
at (9am)	เมื่อ (สามโมงเช้า)	mêu·a (săhm mohng chów)
now	เดี๋ยวนี้	dĕe·o née
tomorrow	พรุ่งนี้	prûng née
Is this ... free?	... อันนี้ฟรีหรือเปล่า	... an née free rĕu blòw
motorcycle	มอเตอร์ไซค์	mor-đeu-sai
taxi	รับจ้าง	ráp jâhng
samlor	สามล้อ	săhm lór
taxi	แท็กซี่	táak-sêe
túk-túk	ตุ๊กๆ	đúk đúk

Please ...	ขอ ...	kŏr ...
slow down	ให้ช้าลง	hâi cháh long
stop here	หยุดตรงนี้	yùt đrong née
wait here	คอยอยู่ที่นี้	koy yòo têe née

Where's the taxi rank?
ที่ขึ้นรถแท็กซี่อยู่ที่ไหน

têe kêun rót táak-sêe
yòo têe nǎi

Is this a metered taxi?
แท็กซี่คันนี้มีมิเตอร์ไหม

táak-sêe kan née mee
mí-đeu mǎi

Please put the meter on.
ขอเปิดมิเตอร์ด้วย

kŏr bèut mí-đeu dôo·ay

How much is it to ...?
ไป ... เท่าไร

pai ... tôw-rai

Please take me to (this address).
ขอพาไป (ที่นี้)

kŏr pah bai (têe née)

How much is it?
ราคาเท่าไร

rah-kah tôw-rai

That's too expensive. How about ... baht?
แพงไป ... บาทได้ไหม

paang bai ... bàht dâi mǎi

car & motorbike

รถยนต์และรถมอเตอร์ไซค์

car & motorbike hire

How much	ค่าเช่า ...	kâh chôw ...
for ... hire?	ละเท่าไร	lá tôw-rai
daily	วัน	wan
weekly	อาทิตย์	ah-tít

Do I need to leave a deposit?
จะต้องมีเงินฝากด้วยไหม

jà đôrng mee ngeun fàhk
dôo·ay mǎi

I'd like to hire a/an ...	อยากจะเช่า ...	yàhk jà chôw ...
4WD	รถโฟร์วีล	rót foh ween
automatic	รถเกียร์ออโต	rót gee·a or-đoh
car	รถเก๋ง	rót gĕng
jeep	รถจี๊ป	rót jéep
manual	รถเกียร์ธรรมดา	rót gee·a tam-má-dah
motorbike	รถมอเตอร์ไซค์	rót mor-đeu-sai
motorbike with driver	รถมอเตอร์ไซค์ รับจ้าง	mor-đeu-sai ráp jâhng
scooter	รถสกู๊ตเตอร์	rót sa-góot-đeu
van	รถตู้	rót đôo

With ...	กับ ...	gàp ...
air-conditioning	แอร์	aa
a driver	คนขับ	kon kàp

Does that include insurance?
รวมประกันด้วยไหม
roo·am bprà-gan dôo·ay măi

Does that include mileage?
รวมระยะทางด้วยไหม
roo·am rá-yá tahng dôo·ay măi

Do you have a road map?
มีแผนที่ถนนไหม
mee păn têe tà-nŏn măi

Can I have a helmet?
ขอหมวกกันน็อกด้วย
kŏr mòo·ak gan nórk dôo·ay

How many cc's is it?
เครื่องขนาดกี่ซีซี
krêu·ang kà-nàht gèe see-see

When do I need to return it?
จะต้องเอามาคืนเมื่อไร
jà đôrng ow mah keun mêu·a rai

on the road

What's the speed limit?

กฎหมายกำหนดความเร็วเท่าไร · gòt-măi gam-nòt kwahm
re·ou tôw-rai

Is this the road to (Ban Bung Wai)?

ทางนี้ไป (บ้านบุ่งหวาย) ไหม · tahng née bai (bâhn
bùng wăi) măi

Where's a petrol station?

ปั๊มน้ำมันอยู่ที่ไหน · bâm nám man yòo têe năi

Please fill it up.

เติมให้เต็ม · đeum hâi đem

I'd like ... litres.

เอา ... ลิตร · ow ... lít

diesel	น้ำมันโซล่าร์	nám man soh-lâh
LPG	ก๊าซ	gáht
premium unleaded	ชนิดพิเศษ	chá-nít pí-sèt
regular unleaded	ชนิดธรรมดา	chá-nít tam-má-dah

Can you check the ...?	ตรวจ ... ด้วยหน่อย	đròo·at ... dôo·ay nòy
oil	น้ำมันเครื่อง	nám man krêu·ang
tyre pressure	ลม	lom
water	น้ำ	nám

Can I park here?

จอดที่นี่ได้ไหม · jòrt têe née dâi măi

ทางเข้า	tahng kôw	**Entrance**
ทางออก	tahng òrk	**Exit Freeway**
ให้ทาง	hâi tahng	**Give Way**
ห้ามเข้า	hâhm kôw	**No Entry**
ทางเดียว	tahng dee·o	**One-way**
หยุด	yùt	**Stop**
ค่าผ่าน	kâh pàhn	**Toll**

How long can I park here?
จอดที่นี่ได้นานเท่าไร   jòrt têe née dâi nahn tôw-rai

Do I have to pay?
ต้องเสียเงินไหม   đôrng sěe·a ngeun măi

drivers licence	ใบขับขี่	bai kàp kèe
kilometres	กิโลเมตร	gì-loh-mét
parking meter	มิเตอร์จอดรถ	mí-đeu jòrt rot
petrol (gasoline)	เบนซิน	ben-sin

problems

I need a mechanic.
ต้องการช่างรถ   đôrng gahn châhng rót

I've had an accident.
มีอุบัติเหตุ   mee ù-bàt-đì-hèt

The vehicle has broken down (at Kaeng Koi).
รถเสียแล้ว (ที่แก่งคอย)   rót sěe·a láa·ou
(têe gàang koy)

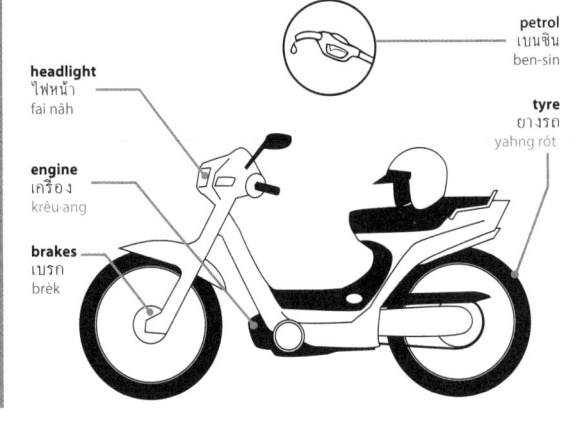

petrol
เบนซิน
ben-sin

headlight
ไฟหน้า
fai nâh

tyre
ยางรถ
yahng rót

engine
เครื่อง
krêu·ang

brakes
เบรก
brèk

The vehicle won't start.		
รถสตาร์ดไม่ติด		rót sà-đáht mâi đìt
I have a flat tyre.		
ยางแบน		yahng baan
I've lost my car keys.		
ทำกุญแจรถหาย		tam gun-jaa rót hăi
I've locked the keys inside.		
ปิดกุญแจรถข้างในรถ		bìt gun-jaa rót kâhng nai rót
I've run out of petrol.		
หมดน้ำมัน		mòt nám man
Can you fix it (today)?		
ซ่อม(วันนี้) ได้ไหม		sôrm (wan née) dâi măi
How long will it take?		
จะใช้เวลานานเท่าไร		jà chái wair-lah nahn tôw-rai

bicycle

รถจักรยาน

I'd like ...	ต้องการ ...	đôrng gahn ...
my bicycle repaired	ซ่อมรถจักรยาน	sôrm rót jàk-gà-yahn
to buy a bicycle	ซื้อรถจักรยาน	séu rót jàk-gà-yahn
to hire a bicycle	เช่ารถจักรยาน	chôw rót jàk-gà-yahn

I'd like a ... bike.	ต้องการรถจักรยาน ...	đôrng gahn rót jàk-gà-yahn ...
mountain	ภูเขา	poo kŏw
racing	แข่ง	kàang
second-hand	มือสอง	meu sŏrng

How much is it per ...?	... ละเท่าไร	... lá tôw-rai
day	วัน	wan
hour	ชั่วโมง	chôo·a mohng

Do I need a helmet?

ต้องใช้หมวกกันน็อกไหม

đôrng chái mòo·ak gan nórk măi

I have a puncture.

ยางแตกแล้ว

yahng đàak láa·ou

I'm ...	ผม/ดิฉัน ...	pŏm/dì-chăn ... **m/f**
in transit	เดินทางผ่าน	deun tahng pàhn
on business	มาธุระ	mah tú-rá
on holiday	มาพักผ่อน	mah pák pòrn

I'm here for ...	ผม/ดิฉัน มาพักที่นี่ ...	pŏm/dì-chăn mah pák têe née ... **m/f**
(10) days	(สิบ) วัน	(sìp) wan
(two) months	(สอง) เดือน	(sŏrng) deu·an
(three) weeks	(สาม) อาทิตย์	(săhm) ah-tít

I'm going to (Ayuthaya).

ผม/ดิฉัน กำลังไป (อยุธยา) pŏm/dì-chăn gam-lang bai
(à-yút-tá-yah) **m/f**

I'm staying at the (Bik Hotel).

พักอยู่ที่ (โรงแรมบิ๊ก) pák yòo têe (rohng raam bík)

The children are on this passport.

ลูกอยู่ในหนังสือเดินทาง เล่มนี้ lôok yòo nai năng-sĕu
deun tahng lêm née

listen for ...

kon dee·o	คนเดียว	**alone**
krôrp kroo·a	ครอบครัว	**family**
ká-ná	คณะ	**group**
năng-sĕu deun tahng	หนังสือเดินทาง	**passport**
wee-sâh	วีซ่า	**visa**

I have nothing to declare.
ไม่มีอะไรที่จะแจ้ง · mâi mee à-rai têe jà jâang

I have something to declare.
มีอะไรที่จะต้องแจ้ง · mee à-rai têe jà đôrng jâang

Do I have to declare this?
อันนี้ต้องแจ้งไหม · an née đôrng jâang măi

That's (not) mine.
นั่น (ไม่ใช่) ของ ผม/ดิฉัน · nân (mâi châi) kŏrng pŏm/dì-chăn **m/f**

I didn't know I had to declare it.
ไม่รู้ว่าต้องแจ้งอันนี้ด้วย · mâi róo wâh đôrng jâang an née dôo·ay

I have an export permit for this.
ผม/ดิฉัน มีใบอนุญาตส่งออก · pŏm/dì-chăn mee bai à-nú-yâht sòng òrk **m/f**

These are for personal use, not resale.
สิ่งเหล่านี้สำหรับการใช้ส่วนตัว ไม่ใช่เพื่อขาย · sìng lòw née săm-ràp gahn chái sòo·an đoo·a, mâi châi pêu·a kăi

Where's (the tourist office)?
(สำนักงานท่องเที่ยว) อยู่ที่ไหน (săm-nák ngahn tôrng têe·o) yòo têe năi

How far is it?
อยู่ไกลเท่าไร yòo glai tôw-rai

It's ...	อยู่ ...	yòo ...
behind ...	ที่หลัง ...	têe lăng ...
diagonally opposite	เยื้อง	yéu·ang
in front of ...	ตรงหน้า ...	đrong nâh ...
near ...	ใกล้ ๆ ...	glâi glâi ...
next to ...	ข้าง ๆ ...	kâhng kâhng ...
on the corner	ตรงหัวมุม	đrong hŏo·a mum
opposite ...	ตรงกันข้าม ...	đrong gan kâhm ...
straight ahead	ตรงไป	đrong bai

north	ทิศเหนือ	tít něu·a
south	ทิศใต้	tít đâi
east	ทิศตะวันออก	tít đà-wan òrk
west	ทิศตะวันตก	tít đà-wan đòk

Turn ...	เลี้ยว ...	lée·o ...
at the corner	ตรงหัวมุม	đrong hŏo·a mum
left	ซ้าย	sái
right	ขวา	kwăh

listen for ...

... gì-loh-mét	... กิโลเมตร	**... kilometres**
... mét	... เมตร	**... metres**
... nah-tee	... นาที	**... minutes**

By ...	โดย ...	doy ...
bus	รถเมล์	rót mair
samlor	สามล้อ	săhm lór
taxi	แท็กซี่	táak-sêe
túk-túk	ตุ๊กๆ	đúk đúk
On foot.	เดินไป	deun bai

typical addresses

What's the address?	ที่อยู่คืออะไร	têe yòo keu à-rai
city	เมือง	meu·ang
district	อำเภอ	am-peu
hamlet	ตำบล	đam-bon
lane	ซอย	soy
stream	ห้วย	hôo·ay
street	ถนน	tà-nŏn
village	หมู่บ้าน	mòo bâhn

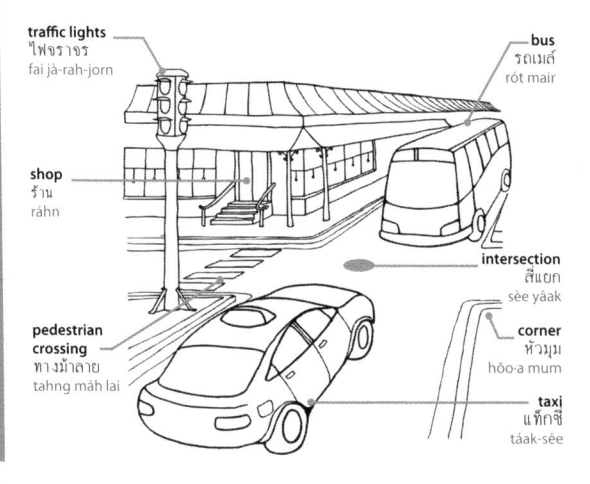

traffic lights
ไฟจราจร
fai jà-rah-jorn

shop
ร้าน
ráhn

pedestrian crossing
ทางม้าลาย
tahng máh lai

bus
รถเมล์
rót mair

intersection
สี่แยก
sèe yâak

corner
หัวมุม
hŏo·a mum

taxi
แท็กซี่
táak-sêe

finding accommodation

การหาที่พัก

Where's a ...?	... อยู่ที่ไหน	... yòo têe nǎi
camping ground	ค่ายพักแรม	kâi pák raam
beach hut	กระท่อมชายหาด	grà-tôm chai hàht
bungalow	บังกะโล	bang-gà-loh
guesthouse	บ้านพัก	bâhn pák
hotel	โรงแรม	rohng raam
temple lodge	วัด	wát
youth hostel	บ้านเยาวชน	bâhn yow-wá-chon

Can you	แนะนำที่ ...	náa nam
recommend	ได้ ไหม	têe ... dâi mǎi
somewhere ...?		
cheap	ราคาถูก	rah-kah tòok
good	ดี ๆ	dee dee
luxurious	หรูหรา	rǒo-rǎh
nearby	ใกล้ ๆ	glâi glâi
romantic	โรแมนติก	roh-maan-đik

What's the address?
ที่อยู่คืออะไร   têe yòo keu à-rai

Do you offer homestay accommodation?
มีการพักในบ้านคนไหม   mee gahn pák nai
                              bâhn kon mǎi

For phrases on how to get there, see **directions**, page 61.

For phrases on how to get there, see **directions**, page 61.

local talk

dive	ที่เลว	têe le·ou
rat-infested	ที่สกปรก	têe sòk-gà-bròk
top spot	ที่ที่เยี่ยม	têe têe yêe·am

booking ahead & checking in

I'd like to book a room, please.
ขอจองห้องหน่อย   kŏr jorng hôrng nòy

I have a reservation.
จองห้องมาแล้ว   jorng hôrng mah láa·ou

My name's ...
ชื่อ ...   chêu ...

listen for ...

đem láa·ou	เต็มแล้ว	**full**
gèe keun	กี่คืน	**How many nights?**
năng-sĕu deun tahng	หนังสือเดินทาง	**passport**

For (three) nights/weeks.
เป็นเวลา (สาม) คืน/อาทิตย์ ben wair-lah (săhm) keun/ah-tít

From ... to ....
จากวันที่ ... ถึงวันที่ ... jàhk wan têe ... tĕung wan têe ...

Do I need to pay upfront?
ต้องจ่ายเงินล่วงหน้าไหม đôrng jài ngeun lôo·ang nâh măi

How much is it per ...?	... ละเท่าไร	... lá tôw-rai
night	คืน	keun
person	คน	kon
week	อาทิตย์	ah-tít

Can I pay by ...?	จ่ายเป็น ... ได้ไหม	jài ben ... dâi măi
credit card	บัตรเครดิต	bàt krair-dìt
travellers cheque	เช็คเดินทาง	chék deun tahng

PRACTICAL

64

Do you have a/an ... room?	มีห้อง ... ไหม	mee hôrng ... măi
air-conditioned	แอร์	aa
double	เตียงคู่	đee·ang kôo
single	เดี่ยว	dèe·o
twin	สองเตียง	sŏrng đee·ang

Do you have a room with a fan?
มีห้องพัดลมไหม   mee hôrng pát lom măi

Does the price include breakfast?
ราคาห้องรวมค่า   rah-kâh hôrng roo·am kâh
อาหารเช้าด้วยไหม   ah-hăhn chów dôo·ay măi

That's too expensive.
แพงไป   paang bai

Can you lower the price?
ลดราคาได้ไหม   lót rah-kah dâi măi

Can I see it?
ดูได้ไหม   doo dâi măi

I'll take it.
เอา   ow

requests & queries

การขอและสอบถาม

When is breakfast served?
อาหารเช้าจัดกี่โมง   ah-hăhn chów jàt gèe
                               mohng

Where is breakfast served?
อาหารเช้าจัดที่ไหน   ah-hăhn chów jàt
                               têe năi

Please wake me at (seven).

กรุณาปลุกให้เวลา   gà-rú-nah bplùk hâi wair-lah
(เจ็ด) นาฬิกา   (jèt) nah-lí-gah

For time expressions see **times & dates**, page 37.

Can I use the …?	ใช้ … ได้ไหม	chái … dâi măi
kitchen	ห้องครัว	hôrng kroo·a
laundry	ห้องซักผ้า	hôrng sák pâh
telephone	โทรศัพท์	toh-rá-sàp
Do you have a/an …?	มี … ไหม	mee … măi
elevator	ลิฟท์	líp
laundry service	บริการซักผ้า	bor-rí-gahn sák pâh
safe	ตู้เซฟ	đôo sép
swimming pool	สระว่ายน้ำ	sà wâi nám
Do you … here?	ที่นี่ … ไหม	têe née … măi
arrange tours	จัดนำเที่ยว	jàt nam têe·o
change money	แลกเงิน	lâak ngeun

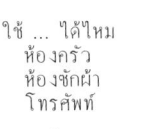

Could I have …, please?	ขอ … หน่อย	kŏr … nòy
an extra blanket	ผ้าห่มอีกผืนหนึ่ง	pâh hòm èek pĕun nèung
the key	กุญแจห้อง	gun-jaa hôrng
a mosquito coil	ยาจุดกันยุง	yah jùt gan yung
a mosquito net	มุ้ง	múng
a receipt	ใบเสร็จ	bai sèt
some soap	สบู่ก้อนหนึ่ง	sà-bòo gôrn nèung
a towel	ผ้าเช็ดตัว	pâh chét đoo·a

Is there a message for me?
มีข้อความฝากให้ ผม/ดิฉัน ไหม   mee kôr kwahm fàhk hâi
                                           pŏm/dì-chăn măi m/f

Can I leave a message for someone?
ฝากข้อความให้คนได้ไหม   fàhk kôr kwahm hâi kon
                                           dâi măi

I'm locked out of my room.
ห้อง ผม/ดิฉัน ปิดกุญแจ   hôrng pŏm/dì-chăn bìt
ไว้ เข้าไม่ได้   gun-jaa wái, kôw mâi dâi m/f

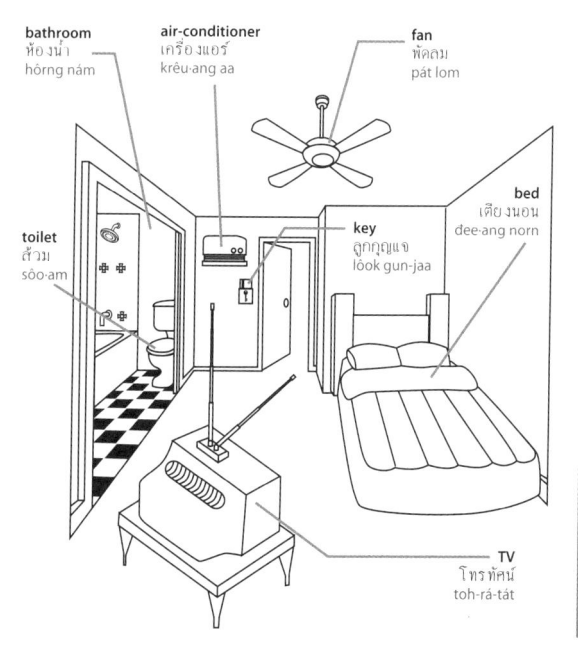

bathroom
ห้องน้ำ
hôrng nám

air-conditioner
เครื่องแอร์
krêu·ang aa

fan
พัดลม
pát lom

toilet
ส้วม
sôo·am

key
ลูกกุญแจ
lôok gun-jaa

bed
เตียงนอน
dee·ang norn

TV
โทรทัศน์
toh-rá-tát

complaints

It's too ...	... เกินไป	... geun bai
bright	สว่าง	sà-wàhng
cold	หนาว	nŏw
dark	มืด	mêut
expensive	แพง	paang
noisy	เสียงดัง	sĕe·ang dang
small	เล็ก	lék

The ... doesn't work.	... เสีย	... sĕe·a
air-conditioning	แอร์	aa
fan	พัดลม	pát lom
toilet	ส้วม	sôo·am

Can I get another (blanket)?
ขอ (ผ้าห่ม) อีกผืนได้ไหม
kŏr (pâh hòm) èek pĕun dâi măi

This (pillow) isn't clean.
(หมอนใบ) นี้ไม่สะอาด
(mŏrn bai) née mâi sà-àht

There's no hot water.
ไม่มีน้ำร้อน
mâi mee nám rórn

a knock at the door ...

Who is it?	ใคร ครับ/คะ	krai kráp/kâ m/f
Just a moment.	รอเดี๋ยว	ror dĕe·o
Come in.	เข้ามาได้	kôw mah dâi
Come back later, please.	กลับมาทีหลังได้ไหม	glàp mah tee lăng dâi măi

checking out

What time is checkout?
ต้องออกห้องกี่โมง

đôrng òrk hôrng gèe mohng

Can I have a late checkout?
ออกห้องสายหน่อยได้ไหม

òrk hôrng săi nòy dâi măi

Can you call a taxi for me (for 11 am)?
เรียกแท็กซี่ให้ (เวลา สิบเอ็ดโมง) ได้ไหม

rêe·ak táak-sêe hâi (wair-lah sìp-èt mohng) dâi măi

I'm leaving now.
จะออกห้องเดี๋ยวนี้

jà òrk hôrng dĕe·o née

Can I leave my bags here?
ฝากกระเป๋าไว้ที่นี่ได้ไหม

fàhk grà-b̌ow wái têe née dâi măi

There's a mistake in the bill.
บิลใบนี้ผิดนะ ครับ/ค่ะ

bin bai née pìt ná kráp/kâ m/f

Could I have my ..., please?	ขอ ... หน่อย	kŏr ... nòy
deposit	เงินมัดจำ	ngeun mát jam
passport	หนังสือเดินทาง	năng-sĕu deun tahng
valuables	ของมีค่า	kŏrng mee kâh

I had a great stay, thank you.
พักที่นี่สนุกมาก ขอบคุณ

pák têe née sà-nùk mâhk kòrp kun

I'll recommend it to my friends.
จะแนะนำที่นี่ให้เพื่อนด้วย   jà náa-nam têe née hâi
pêu·an dôo·ay

I'll be back ...	จะกลับมา ...	jà glàp mah ...
in (three) days	อีก (สาม) วัน	èek (săhm) wan
on (Tuesday)	เมื่อ(วันอังคาร)	mêu·a (wan ang-kahn)

camping

Do you have ...?	มี ... ไหม	mee ... măi
electricity	ไฟฟ้า	fai fáh
a laundry	ห้องซักผ้า	hôrng sák pâh
shower facilities	ที่อาบน้ำฝักบัว	têe àhp nám fàk boo·a
a site	ที่ปักเต็นท์	têe bàk đen
tents for hire	เต็นท์ให้เช่า	đen hâi chôw

How much is it per ...?	... ละเท่าไร	... lá tôw-rai
person	คน	kon
tent	เต็นท์ที่	đen
vehicle	รถคัน	rót kan

Is the water drinkable?
น้ำดื่มได้ไหม   nám dèum dâi măi

Is it coin-operated?
ต้องหยอดเหรียญไหม   đôrng yòrt rěe·an măi

Can I ...?	... ได้ไหม	... dâi măi
camp here	พักแรมที่นี่	pák raam têe née
park next to my tent	จอดรถข้างๆ เต็นท์	jòrt rót kâhng kâhng đen

Who do I ask to stay here?
ถ้าจะพักที่นี่จะต้องถามใคร   tâh jà pák têe née jà đôrng tăhm krai

renting

Do you have a/an ... for rent?	มี ... ให้เช่าไหม	mee ... hâi chôw măi
apartment	ห้องชุด	hôrng chút
cabin	บ้านพัก	bâhn pák
house	บ้าน	bâhn
room	ห้อง	hôrng

staying with locals

Can I stay at your place?
พักที่บ้านคุณได้ไหม   pák têe bâhn kun dâi măi

Is there anything I can do to help?
มีอะไรที่จะให้ช่วยไหม   mee à-rai têe jà hâi
                                 chôo·ay măi

I have my own ...	ผม/ดิฉัน มี ...	pŏm/dì-chăn mee ...
	ของตัวเอง	kŏrng đoo·a eng m/f
mattress	ฟูก	fôok
sleeping bag	ถุงนอน	tŭng norn
Can I ...?	จะให้ฉัน ... ไหม	ja hâi chăn ... măi
bring anything for the meal	เอาอาหาร อะไรมาช่วย	ow ah-hăhn à-rai mah chôo·ay
do the dishes	ช่วยล้างจาน	chôo·ay láhng jahn
set/clear the table	ช่วย ตั้ง/เก็บ โต๊ะ	chôo·ay đâng/gèp đó
take out the rubbish	ช่วยเก็บขยะ ออกไป	chôo·ay gèp kà-yà òrk bai

accommodation

71

Thanks for your (warm) hospitality.

ขอบคุณมากสำหรับ   korp kun mâhk săm-ràp
การต้อนรับ(ที่อบอุ่น)   gahn đôrn ráp (têe òp-ùn)

For dining-related expressions, see **food**, page 153.

body language

In Thailand it's important to be aware of your body. Close physical proximity, except in special circumstances such as a crowded Bangkok bus, can be discomforting to Thai people. Thus, you should avoid standing over people or encroaching too much on their personal space.

The head is considered the most sacred part of the body, while the feet are seen as vulgar. Never point at things with your feet nor intentionally touch another person with your feet. Neither should you sit with your feet pointing at someone or at an object of worship, such as a shrine, a picture of the king or Buddha statue. Equally, you should never touch or reach over another person's head. If it's necessary to reach over someone, such as when getting something from a luggage compartment on a bus or train, it's customary to say kŏr tôht ขอโทษ ('Excuse me') first.

looking for ...

Where's ...?	... อยู่ที่ไหน	... yòo têe nǎi
a department store	ห้างสรรพสินค้า	hâhng sàp-pá-sǐn-káh
a floating market	ตลาดน้ำ	đà-làht nám
a market	ตลาด	đà-làht
a supermarket	ซูเปอร์มาร์เก็ต	soo-ƀeu-mah-gèt

Where can I buy (a padlock)?
จะซื้อ (แม่กุญแจ) ได้ที่ไหน jà séu (mâa gun-jaa) dâi têe nǎi

For phrases on directions, see **directions**, page 61.

making a purchase

I'm just looking.
ดูเฉย ๆ doo chěu·i chěu·i

I'd like to buy (an adaptor plug).
อยากจะซื้อ (ปลั๊กต่อ) yàhk jà séu (ƀlák đòr)

How much is it?
เท่าไรครับ/คะ tôw-rai kráp/ká m/f

Can you write down the price?
เขียนราคาให้หน่อยได้ไหม kěe·an rah-kah hâi nòy dâi mǎi

Do you have any others?
มีอีกไหม mee èek mǎi

Can I look at it?
ขอดูได้ไหม kǒr doo dâi mǎi

73

Do you accept ...?	รับ ... ไหม	ráp ... măi
credit cards	บัตรเครดิต	bàt krair-dìt
debit cards	บัตรธนาคาร	bàt tá-nah-kahn
travellers cheques	เช็คเดินทาง	chék deun tahng

Could I have a ..., please?	ขอ ... ด้วย	kŏr ... dôo·ay
bag	ถุง	tŭng
receipt	ใบเสร็จ	bai sèt

Could I have it wrapped?
ห่อให้ได้ไหม — hòr hâi dâi măi

Does it have a guarantee?
มีรับประกันด้วยไหม — mee ráp bra-gan dôo·ay măi

Can I have it sent overseas?
จะส่งเมืองนอกให้ได้ไหม — jà sòng meu·ang nôrk hâi dâi măi

Can you order it for me?
สั่งให้ได้ไหม — sàng hâi dâi măi

Can I pick it up later?
จะกลับมารับทีหลังได้ไหม — jà glàp mah ráp tee lăng dâi măi

It's faulty.
มันบกพร่อง — man bòk prôrng

It's a fake.
เป็นของปลอม — ben kŏrng blorm

I'd like ..., please.	อยากจะ ... ครับ/ค่ะ	yàhk jà ... kráp/kâ m/f
a refund	ได้เงินคืน	dâi ngeun keun
my change	ได้เงินทอน	dâi ngeun torn
to return this	เอามาคืน	ow mah keun

signs

bargain	ราคาย่อมเยา	rah-kah yôrm yow
rip-off	ราคาขี้โกง	rah-kah kêe gohng
specials	ของลดราคา	kŏrng lót rah-kah
sale	ขายลดราคา	kăi lót rah-kah

PRACTICAL

74

bargaining

That's too expensive.
แพงไป paang bai

Can you lower the price?
ลดราคาได้ไหม lót rah-kah dâi măi

I don't have much money.
มีเงินไม่มากเท่าไร mee ngeun mâi mâhk
tôw-rai

Do you have something cheaper?
มีถูกกว่านี้ไหม mee tòok gwàh née măi

I'll give you (five baht).
จะให้ (ห้าบาท) jà hâi (hâh bàht)

I won't give more than … baht.
จะให้ไม่เกิน … บาท jà hâi mâi geun … bàht

What's your lowest price?
เท่าไรราคาต่ำสุด tôw-rai rah-kah đàm sùt

The quality isn't very good.
คุณภาพไม่ดีเท่าไร kun-ná-pâhp mâi dee
tôw-rai

---

little gems

diamond	เพชร	pét
emerald	แก้วมรกต	gâa·ou mor-rá-gòt
gems	เพชรพลอย	pét ploy
gold	ทอง	torng
gold-plated	เคลือบทอง	klêu·ap torng
jade	หยก	yòk
necklace	สร้อยคอ	sôy kor
ring	แหวน	wăan
ruby	ทับทิม	táp-tim
sapphire	นิล	nin
silver	เงิน	ngeun

clothes

My size is ...	ฉันใช้ขนาด ...	chăn chái kà-nàht ...
(32)	เบอร์	beu
	(สามสิบสอง)	(săhm sìp sŏrng)
large	ใหญ่	yài
medium	กลาง	glahng
small	เล็ก	lék

Can I try it on?
ลองได้ไหม   lorng dâi măi

It doesn't fit.
ไม่ถูกขนาด   mâi tòok kà-nàht

I'm looking for fisherman's pants.
มีกางเกงขากวยไหม   mee gahng geng kăh
goo·ay măi

Can you make ...?
ทำ ... ได้ไหม   tam ... dâi măi

The arms/legs	แขน/ขา ... เกินไป	kăan/kăh ... geun
are too ...		bai
short	สั้น	sân
long	ยาว	yow

For clothing items, see the **dictionary**.

hairdressing

I'd like (a) ...	ต้องการ ...	đôrng gahn ...
blow wave	เป่าผมสวย	bòw pŏm sà-lŏo·ay
colour	ย้อมผม	yórm pŏm
haircut	ตัดผม	đàt pŏm
my beard trimmed	ตกแต่งหนวด	đòk đàang nòo·at
shave	โกนหนวด	gohn nòo·at
trim	เล็ม	lem

Don't cut it too short.
อย่าตัดให้สั้นเกินไป　　　　yàh đàt hâi sân geun bai

Is this a new blade?
ใบมีดนี้ใหม่หรือเปล่า　　　　bai mêet née mài rěu blòw

Shave it all off!
โกนให้หมดเลย　　　　gohn hâi mòt leu·i

I should never have let you near me!
ไม่น่าจะให้คุณแตะต้องฉันเลย　　mâi nâh jà hâi kun đàa
　　　　đôrng chăn leu·i

For colours, see the **dictionary**.

repairs

Can I have my ...	ที่นี่ช่อม ... ได้ไหม	têe née sôrm ...
repaired here?		dâi mǎi
When will	จะช่อม...เสร็จ	jà sôrm ... sèt
my ... be ready?	เมื่อไร	mêu·a rai
backpack	เป้	bâir
camera	กล้องถ่ายรูป	glôrng tài rôop
(sun)glasses	แว่นตา (กันแดด)	wâan đah (gan
		dàat)
shoes	รองเท้า	rorng tów

books & reading

Do you have a book by (Sulak Sivarak)?
มีหนังสือโดย (อาจารย์　　mee năng-sěu doy (ah-jahn
สุลักษณ์ ศิวรักษ์) ไหม　　sù-lák sì-wá-rák) mǎi

Do you have an entertainment guide?
มีคู่มือการบันเทิง ไหม　　mee kôo meu gahn
　　　　ban-teung mǎi

Is there an English-language ...?	มี ... ภาษาอังกฤษ ไหม	mee ... pah-săh ang-grìt măi
bookshop	ร้านขายหนังสือ	ráhn kăi năng-sěu
section	แผนก	pà-nàak

I'd like a ...	ต้องการ ...	đôrng gahn ...
dictionary	พจนานุกรม	pót-jà-nah-nú-grom
newspaper (in English)	หนังสือพิมพ์ (ภาษาอังกฤษ)	năng-sěu pim (pah-săh ang-grìt)
notepad	สมุดบันทึก	sà-mùt ban-téuk

Can you recommend a book to me?
แนะนำหนังสือดีๆ ได้ไหม

náa-nam năng-sěu dee dee dâi măi

Do you have Lonely Planet guidebooks?
มีคู่มือท่องเที่ยว โลน ลี พลาเนต ไหม

mee kôo meu tôrng têe·o lohn-lee plah-nét măi

music

คนตรี

I'd like a ...	ต้องการ ...	đôrng gahn ...
blank tape	ม้วนเทปเปล่า	móo·an tép blòw
CD	แผ่นซีดี	pàan see-dee
DVD	แผ่นดีวีดี	pàan dee-wee-dee
VCD	แผ่นวีซีดี	pàan wee-see-dee

I'm looking for something by (Carabao).

กำลังหาชุดเพลง   gam-lang häh chút pleng
(วงคาราบาว)   (wong kah-rah-bow)

What's their best recording?

เพลงชุดไหนเป็นชุด   pleng chút năi ben chút
ที่ดีที่สุดของเขา   têe dee têe sùt kŏrng kŏw

Can I listen to this?

ฟังได้ไหม   fang dâi măi

photography

การถ่ายรูป

Can you …?	… ได้ไหม	… dâi măi
develop this film	ล้างฟิล์มนี้	láhng fim née
load my film	ใส่ฟิล์มให้	sài fim hâi

When will it be ready?

จะเสร็จเมื่อไร   jà sèt mêu·a-rai

How much is it?

ราคาเท่าไร   rah-kah tôw-rai

I need … film	ต้องการฟิล์ม …	đôrng gahn fim …
for this camera.	สำหรับกล้องนี้	săm-ràp glôrng née
B&W	ขาวดำ	kŏw dam
colour	สี	sĕe
slide	สไลด์	sà-lai
(200) speed	มีความไว	mee kwahm wai
	(๒๐๐)	(sŏrng róy)

I need a passport photo taken.
   ต้องการถ่ายภาพ   đôrng gahn tài pâhp săm-
   สำหรับหนังสือเดินทาง   ràp năng-sĕu deun tahng

I'm not happy with these photos.
   ผม/ดิฉันไม่พอใจภาพนี้เลย   pŏm/dì-chăn mâi por jai
                                  pâhp née leu·i **m/f**

I don't want to pay the full price.
   ไม่อยากจ่ายราคาเต็ม   mâi yàhk jài rah-kah đem

gender benders

There are two words for the pronoun 'I' in Thai. Male speakers refer to themselves as pŏm ผม and female speakers refer to themselves as dì-chăn ดิฉัน. Wherever you see an **m/f** symbol in this book it means you have to make a choice depending on your gender. This also goes for the polite softeners kráp ครับ (for a man) and kâ ค่ะ (for a woman). See page 21 for an explanation of softeners.

post office

ที่ทำการไปรษณีย์

I want to send a ...	ผม/ดิฉัน อยาก จะส่ง ...	pŏm/dì-chăn yàhk jà sòng ... m/f
fax	แฟกซ์	fàak
letter	จดหมาย	jòt-măi
parcel	พัสดุ	pát-sà-dù
postcard	ไปรษณียบัตร	brai-sà-nee-yá-bàt

I want to buy ...	ผม/ดิฉัน ยากจะซื้อ ...	pŏm/dì-chăn yàhk jà séu ... m/f
an aerogramme	จดหมายอากาศ	jòt-măi ah-gàht
an envelope	ซอง จดหมาย	sorng jòt-măi
a stamp	แสตมป์	sà-đaam

May I have a registered receipt?
ขอใบเสร็จการลงทะเบียนด้วย kŏr bai sèt gahn long tá-bee·an dôo·ay

customs declaration	ใบแจ้งศุลกากร	bai jâang sŭn-lá-gah-gorn
domestic	ภายในประเทศ	pai nai brà-têt
fragile	ระวังแตก	rá-wang đàak
international	ระหว่างประเทศ	rá-wàhng brà-têt
mail	ไปรษณีย์	brai-sà-nee
mailbox	ตู้ไปรษณีย์	đôo brai-sà-nee
postcode	รหัสไปรษณีย์	rá-hàt brai-sà-nee

airmail	ไปรษณีย์อากาศ	ɓrai-sà-nee ah-gàht
express mail	ไปรษณีย์ด่วน	ɓrai-sà-nee dòo·an
registered mail	ลงทะเบียน	long tá-bee·an
sea mail	ไปรษณีย์ทางทะเล	ɓrai-sà-nee tahng tá-lair
surface mail	ไปรษณีย์ทางธรรมดา	tahng tam-má-dah

Please send it by airmail to (Australia).
ขอส่งทาง อากาศ
ไปประเทศ (ออสเตรเลีย)
kŏr sòng tahng ah-gàht ɓai ɓrà-têt (or-sà-đrair-lee·a)

Please send it by surface mail to (Australia).
ขอส่งทาง ธรรมดา
ไปประเทศ (ออสเตรเลีย)
kŏr sòng tahng tam-má-dah ɓai ɓrà-têt (or-sà-đrair-lee·a)

It contains (souvenirs).
ข้างในมี (ของที่ระลึก)
kâhng nai mee (kŏrng têe rá-léuk)

Is there any mail for me?
มีจดหมายของ ผม/ดิฉัน ด้วยไหม
mee jòt-măi kŏrng pŏm/ dì-chăn dôo·ay măi m/f

phone

What's your phone number?
เบอร์โทรของคุณคืออะไร
beu toh kŏrng kun keu à-rai

Where's the nearest public phone?
ตู้โทรศัพท์ที่ใกล้เคียง อยู่ที่ไหน
đôo toh-rá-sàp têe glâi kee·ang yòo têe năi

Can I look at a phone book?
ขอดูสมุดโทรศัพท์ได้ไหม
kŏr doo sà-mùt toh-rá-sàp dâi măi

Can you help me find the number for …?
ช่วยหาเบอร์ของ … ให้หน่อย · chôo·ay hǎh beu
körng … hâi nòy

I'd like to speak for (10) minutes.
อยากจะพูดเป็นเวลา · yàhk jà pôot ben wair-lah
(สิบ) นาที · (sìp) nah-tee

I want to … · อยากจะ … · yàhk jà …
buy a phonecard	ซื้อบัตรโทรศัพท์	séu bàt toh-rá-sàp
call (Singapore)	โทรไปประเทศ	toh bai bra-têt
	(สิงคโปร์)	(sǐng-ká-boh)
make a (local) call	โทร(ภายใน	toh (pai nai jang-
	จังหวัดเดียวกัน)	wàt dee·o gan)
reverse the charges	โทรเก็บปลายทาง	toh gèp blai tahng
speak for	พูดเป็นเวลา	pôot ben wair-lah
(three) minutes	(สาม) นาที	(sǎhm) nah-tee

How much · … คิดเงินเท่าไร · … kít ngeun tôw-rai
does … cost?
a (three)-minute call	โทร (สาม) นาที	toh (sǎhm) nah-tee
each extra minute	ทุกนาทีต่อไป	túk nah-tee dòr bai

The number is …
เบอร์ก็คือ … · beu gôr keu …

What's the country code for (New Zealand)?
รหัสประเทศ · rá-hàt bra-têt
(นิวซีแลนด์) คืออะไร · (new see-laan) keu à-rai

It's engaged.
โทรศัพท์ไม่ว่าง · toh-rá-sàp mâi wâhng

I've been cut off.
สายขาดแล้ว · sǎi kàht láa·ou

The connection's bad.
สายไม่ดี · sǎi mâi dee

Hello.
ฮัลโหล · han-lǒh

Can I speak to …?
ขอเรียนสาย … หน่อยนะ · kǒr ree·an sǎi … nòy ná
ครับ/ค่ะ · kráp/ká m/f

| It's ... | นี่คือ ... | nêe keu ... |
| Is ... there? | ... อยู่ไหม | ... yòo măi |

Please say I called.
กรุณาบอกเขาด้วย
ว่าผม/ดิฉันโทรมา
gà-rú-nah bòrk kŏw dôo·ay
wâh pŏm/dì-chăn toh mah m/f

Can I leave a message?
ฝากข้อความได้ไหม
fàhk kôr kwahm dâi măi

My number is ...
เบอร์ของผม/ดิฉันคือ ...
beu kŏrng pŏm/dì-chăn keu ... m/f

I don't have a contact number.
ผม/ดิฉันไม่มีเบอร์ติดต่อ
pŏm/dì-chăn mâi mee beu
dìt-dòr m/f

I'll call back later.
จะโทรอีกทีทีหลัง
jà toh èek tee têe lăng

listen for ...

toh pìt	โทรผิด	**Wrong number.**
krai toh	ใครโทร	**Who's calling?**
jà ree·an săi	จะเรียน	**Who do you want**
gàp krai	สายกับใคร	**to speak to?**
sàk krôo	สักครู่	**One moment.**
kŏw mâi yòo	เขาไม่อยู่	**He/She is not here.**

mobile/cell phone

โทรศัพท์มือถือ

I'd like a ...	ต้องการ ...	đôrng gahn ...
charger for	เครื่องชาร์จ	krêu·ang cháht
my phone	โทรศัพท์	toh-rá-sàp
mobile/cell phone	เช่าโทรศัพท์	chôw toh-rá-sàp
for hire	มือถือ	meu tĕu
prepaid mobile/	โทรศัพท์มือถือ	toh-rá-sàp meu tĕu
cell phone	แบบจ่ายล่วงหน้า	bàap jài lôo·ang nâh
SIM card	บัตรซิม	bàt sim

What are the rates?
อัตราการใช้เท่าไร

àt-đrah gahn chái tôw-rai

(Three baht) per minute.
(สามบาท) ต่อหนึ่ง นาที

(săhm bàht) đòr nèung
nah-tee

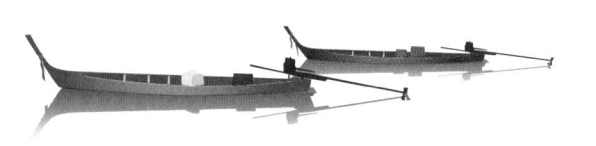

the internet

Where's the local Internet café?
ที่ไหนร้านอินเตอร์เนต
ที่ใกล้เคียง

têe năi ráhn in-đeu-nét
têe glâi kee·ang

I'd like to …	อยากจะ …	yàhk jà …
check my	ตรวจอีเมล	đròo·at
email		ee-mairn
get Internet	ติดต่อทาง	đit đòr tahng
access	อินเตอร์เนต	in-đeu-nét
use a printer	ใช้เครื่องพิมพ์	chái krêu·ang pim
use a scanner	ใช้เครื่องสแกน	chái krêu·ang
		sà-gaan

Do you have …?	มี … ไหม	mee … măi
Macs	เครื่องแม็ก	krêu·ang máak
PCs	เครื่องพีซี	krêu·ang pee-see
a Zip drive	ซิปไดรว์	síp drai

How much per …?	คิด … ละเท่าไร	kít … lá tôw-rai
hour	ชั่วโมง	chôo·a mohng
(five)-minutes	(ห้า) นาที	(hâh) nah-tee
page	หน้า	nâh

How do I log on?
ต้องล็อกอินอย่างไร · đôrng lórk-in yàhng rai

Please change it to the English-language setting.
ช่วยเปลี่ยนเป็นระบบ · chôo·ay bplèe·an bpen rá-bòp
ภาษาอังกฤษหน่อย · pah-săh ang-grìt nòy

This computer is too slow.
เครื่องนี้ช้าไป · krêu·ang née cháh bai

Can I change computers?
เปลี่ยนเครื่องได้ไหม · bplèe·an krêu·ang dâi măi

It's crashed.
เครื่องแฮ้งแล้ว · krêu·ang háang láa·ou

I've finished.
เสร็จแล้ว · sèt láa·ou

bank

ธนาคาร

Automated teller machines – ATMs – (đôo air-tee-em ตู้เอทีเอ็ม) are widely available in regional towns, even small ones, as long as they have a bank, but you won't find them in villages. Credit cards (bàt krair-dìt บัตรเครดิต) are generally used in large towns, but don't count on them being accepted in small towns. Travellers cheques (chék deun tahng เช็คเดินทาง) can be changed in banks that have a Foreign Exchange (lâak ngeun đàhng ฟรà-têt แลกเงินต่างประเทศ) sign on them.

What time does the bank open?

ธนาคารเปิดกี่โมง | tá-nah-kahn bèut gèe mohng

Where can I ...?	... ได้ที่ไหน	... dâi têe năi
I'd like to ...	อยากจะ ...	yàhk jà ...
cash a cheque	ขึ้นเช็ค	kêun chék
change a travellers cheque	แลกเช็คเดินทาง	lâak chék deun tahng
change money	แลกเงิน	lâak ngeun
get a cash advance	รูดเงินจาก บัตรเครดิต	rôot ngeun jàhk bàt krair-dìt
withdraw money	ถอนเงิน	tŏrn ngeun

Where's ...?	... อยู่ที่ไหน	... yòo têe năi
an ATM	ตู้เอทีเอ็ม	đôo air-tee-em
a foreign exchange office	ที่แลกเงินต่าง ประเทศ	têe lâak ngeun đàhng brà-têt

The ATM took my card.

ตู้เอทีเอ็มกินบัตรของผม/ดิฉัน | đôo air-tee-em gin bàt kŏrng pŏm/dì-chăn m/f

I've forgotten my PIN.

ผม/ดิฉัน ลืมรหัสบัตรเอทีเอ็ม   pŏm/dì-chăn leum rá-hàt bàt air-tee-em m/f

Can I use my credit card to withdraw money?

ใช้บัตรเครดิตถอนเงินได้ไหม   chái bàt krair-dìt tŏrn ngeun dâi măi

Can I have smaller notes?

เอาเป็นใบย่อยกว่านี้ได้ไหม   ow ben bai yôy gwàh née dâi măi

Has my money arrived yet?

เงินของ ผม/ดิฉัน มาถึงหรือยัง   ngeun kŏrng pŏm/dì-chăn mah tĕung rĕu yang m/f

How long will it take to arrive?

อีกนานเท่าไรจึงจะมา   èek nahn tôw-rai jeung jà mah

What's the ...?	... เท่าไร	... tôw-rai
charge for that	ค่าธรรมเนียม	kâh tam-nee-am
exchange rate	อัตราแลกเปลี่ยน	àt-đrah lâak blèe-an

---

listen for ...

làk tăhn	หลักฐานส่วนตัว	identification
năng-sĕu deun tahng	หนังสือเดินทาง	passport
long chêu têe née	ลงชื่อที่นี่	Sign here.
mee ban-hăh	มีปัญหา	There's a problem.
mâi mee ngeun lĕu·a láa·ou	ไม่มีเงินเหลือแล้ว	You have no funds left.
tam mâi dâi	ทำไม่ได้	We can't do that.

I'd like …	ผม/ดิฉัน ต้อง การ …	pŏm/dì-chăn đôrng gahn m/f
an audio set	ชุดเทปนำเที่ยว	chút tép nam têe·o
a catalogue	คู่มือแนะนำ	kôo meu náa nam
a guide	ไกด์	gai
a guidebook	คู่มือนำเที่ยว	kôo meu nam têe·o
in English	เป็นภาษาอังกฤษ	ben pah-săh ang-grìt
a (local) map	แผนที่ (ท้อง ถิ่น)	păn têe (tórng tìn)
Do you have information on … sights?	มีข้อมูลเกี่ยว กับแหล่ง ท่อง เที่ยว … ไหม	mee kôr moon gèe·o gàp làang tôrng têe·o … măi
cultural	ทาง วัฒนธรรม	tahng wát-tá-ná-tam
historical	ทาง ประวัติศาสตร์	tahng brà-wàt-đì-sàht
religious	ทาง ศาสนา	tahng sàht-sà-năh

I'd like to see …
ผม/ดิฉัน อยากจะดู …
pŏm/dì-chăn yàhk jà doo … m/f

What's that?
นั่นคืออะไร
nân keu à-rai

Who made it?
ใครสร้าง
krai sâhng

How old is it?
เก่าเท่าไร
gòw tôw-rai

Can we take photos?
ถ่ายรูปได้ไหม   tài rôop dâi măi

Could you take a photo of me?
ถ่ายรูปให้ผม/ดิฉันหน่อยได้ไหม   tài rôop hâi pŏm/dì-chăn
                                                       nòy dâi măi m/f

Can I take a photo (of you)?
ถ่ายรูป (คุณ) ได้ไหม   tài rôop (kun) dâi măi

I'll send you the photo.
จะส่งภาพมาให้   jà sòng pâhp ma hâi

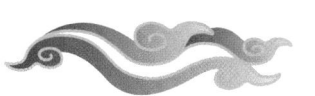

Buddhist temple	วัด	wát
statue	รูปหล่อ	rôop lòr
temple ruins	ซากวัดโบราณ	sâhk wát boh-rahn

getting in

Is there a	ลดราคาสำหรับ ...	lót rah-kah
discount for ...?	ไหม	săm-ràp ... măi
children	เด็ก	dèk
families	ครอบครัว	krôrp kroo·a
groups	คณะ	ká-ná
older people	คนสูงอายุ	kon sŏong ah-yú
pensioners	คนกินเงินบำนาญ	kon gin ngeun
		bam-nahn
students	นักศึกษา	nák sèuk-săh

What time does it open/close?
เปิด/ปิด กี่โมง   bèut/bìt gèe mohng

What's the admission charge?
ค่าเข้าเท่าไร   kâh kôw tôw-rai

Shoes are always removed when entering a house and this also applies to religious buildings. Dress code requirements for entering temples vary, from fairly casual in a rural *wat* to the strictly-enforced no-sandals policy for entering the grounds at Wat Phra Kaew in Bangkok. Listen for officials using this phrase:

gà-rú-nah tòrt rorng tów
กรุณาถอดรองเท้า   **Please take off your shoes.**

tours

ทัวร์

Can you recommend a …?	แนะนำ … ได้ไหม	náa-nam … dâi măi
When's the next …?	… ต่อไปออกกี่โมง	… dòr bai òrk gèe mohng
boat-trip	เที่ยวเรือ	têe·o reu·a
day trip	เที่ยวรายวัน	têe·o rai wan
tour	ทัวร์	too·a
Is … included?	รวม … ด้วยไหม	roo·am … dôo·ay măi
accommodation	ค่าพัก	kâh pák
food	ค่าอาหาร	kâh ah-hăhn
transport	ค่าการขนส่ง	kâh gahn kŏn sòng

The guide will pay.
ไกด์จะจ่ายให้   gai jà jài hâi

The guide has paid.
ไกด์จ่ายไปแล้ว   gai jài bai láa·ou

How long is the tour?
การเที่ยวใช้เวลานานเท่าไร   gahn têe·o chái wair-lah
nahn tôw-rai

sightseeing

91

What time should we be back?

ควรจะกลับมากี่โมง

koo·an jà glàp mah gèe mohng

I'm with them.

ผม/ดิฉัน อยู่กับเขา

pŏm/dì·chăn yòo gàp kŏw m/f

I've lost my group.

ผม/ดิฉัน หล งคณะอยู่

pŏm/dì·chăn lŏng ká·ná yòo m/f

who's who in the zoo

Ever wonder how a rooster says 'cock-a-doodle-do' in a foreign land? If you find yourself face-to-face with a friendly-looking creature, make sure you adopt the correct forms of address. Accidently greeting a dog as a cat can have embarrassing consequences so refer to the chart below if you are unsure:

bird	จิ๊บๆ	jíp jíp	*tweet-tweet*
cat	เหมียว	mĕe·o	*miao*
chick	เจี๊ยบ ๆ	jée·ap jée·ap	*cheep-cheep*
cow	มอ	mor	*moo*
dog	โฮ่งๆ	hôhng hôhng	*woof woof*
duck	ก๊าบๆ	gáhp gáhp	*quack quack*
elephant	แปร๊นแปร๊	ʉ̀râan ʉ̀răa	*trumpet*
frog	อบ ๆ	òp	*croak*
monkey	เจี๊ยก	jée·ak	*squeal*
rooster	เอ๊กอีเอ๊กเอ๊ก	ék-ee-êk-êk	*cock-a-doodle-doo*

I'm attending a ...	ผม/ดิฉัน	pŏm/dì-chăn gam-
	กำลงอยู่ใน ...	lang yòo nai ... m/f
conference	ที่ประชุม	têe bràa-chum
course	ที่อบรม	têe òp-rom
meeting	ที่ประชุม	têe bràa-chum
trade fair	งานแสดงสินค้า	ngahn sa-daang
		sĭn káh

I'm with ...	ผม/ดิฉัน อยู่กับ ...	pŏm/dì-chăn
		yòo gàp ... m/f
(Sahaviriya	(บริษัทสหวิริยา)	(bor-rí-sàt sà-hà-
Company)		wí-rí-yah)
my colleague(s)	เพื่อนงาน	pêu·an ngahn
(two) others	อีก (สอง) คน	èek (sŏrng) kon

I'm alone.
อยู่คนเดียว   yòo kon dee·o

I have an appointment with ...
ผม/ดิฉัน มีนัดกับ ...   pŏm/dì-chăn mee nát
                                           gàp ... m/f

I'm staying at ..., room ...
พักอยู่ที่ ... ที่ห้อง ...   pák yòo têe ... têe
                                           hôrng ...

I'm here for (two) days/weeks.
อยู่ที่นี้ (สอง) วัน/อาทิตย์   yòo têe née (sŏrng) wan/
                                           ah-tít

Here's my ...
นี่คือ ... ของงผม/ดิฉัน   nêe keu ... kŏrng
                                           pŏm/dì-chăn m/f

What's your ...?	... ของคุณคืออะไร	... kŏrng kun keu à-rai
address	ที่อยู่	têe yòo
email address	ที่อยู่อีเมล	têe yòo ee-mairn
fax number	เบอร์แฟกซ์	beu fàak
mobile number	เบอร์มือถือ	beu meu tĕu
pager number	เบอร์เครื่องเพจ	beu krêu·ang pét
work number	เบอร์ที่ทำงาน	beu têe tam ngahn

Where's the ...?	... อยู่ที่ไหน	... yòo têe năi
business centre	ศูนย์ธุรกิจ	sŏon tú-rá-gìt
conference	การประชุม	gahn bà-chum
meeting	การประชุม	gahn bà-chum

I need ...	ต้องการ ...	đôrng gahn ...
a computer	เครื่องคอมพิวเตอร์	krêu·ang korm-pew-đeu
an Internet connection	ที่ต่ออินเตอร์เนต	têe đòr in-đeu-nét
an interpreter	ล่าม	lâhm
more business cards	นามบัตรอีก	nahm bàt èek
to send a fax	ส่งแฟกซ์	sòng fàak

That went very well.
ก็ล่วงไปด้วยดีนะ
gôr lôo·ang bai dôo·ay dee ná

Thank you for your time.
ขอบคุณที่ให้เวลา
kòrp kun têe hâi wair-lah

Shall we go for a drink?
จะไปดื่มกันไหม
jà bai dèum gan măi

Shall we go for a meal?
จะไปทานอาหารกันไหม
jà bai tahn ah-hăhn gan măi

It's on me.
ผม/ดิฉันเลี้ยงนะ
pŏm/dì-chăn lée·ang ná m/f

senior & disabled travellers

คนเดินทางพิการและคนเดินทางสูงอายุ

Services for senior and disabled travellers are very limited in Thailand, but these phrases should help you with your needs.

Should you require special assistance make sure you get up-to-date information on facilities before you leave. The elderly are treated with great respect and older travellers will find that Thai people often go out of their way to accommodate their needs.

I have a disability.
ผม/ดิฉัน พิการ
pŏm/dì-chăn pí-gahn m/f

I need assistance.
ผม/ดิฉัน ต้องการความ
ช่วยเหลือ
pŏm/dì-chăn đôrng gahn
kwahm chôo·ay lĕu·a m/f

What services do you have for people with a disability?
มีบริการอะไรบ้างสำหรับ
คนพิการ
mee bor·rí-gahn à-rai bâhng
săm·ràp kon pí-gahn

Is there wheelchair access?
รถเข็นคนพิการเข้าได้ไหม
rót kĕn kon pí-gahn kôw
dâi măi

How wide is the entrance?
ทางเข้ากว้างเท่าไร
tahng kôw gwâhng tôw rai

I'm deaf.
ผม/ดิฉัน หูหนวก
pŏm/dì-chăn hŏo nòo·ak m/f

I have a hearing aid.
ผม/ดิฉัน ใช้หูเทียม
pŏm/dì-chăn chái hŏo
tee·am m/f

How many steps are there?
มีบันใดกี่ขั้น
mee ban-dai gèe kân

Is there a lift?
มีลิฟท์ไหม   mee líp măi

Are there rails in the bathroom?
ในห้องน้ำมีราวจับไหม   nai hôrng nám mee row
                                         jàp măi

Could you help me cross the street safely?
ช่วย ผม/ดิฉัน ข้าม   chôo·ay pŏm/dì-chăn
ถนนได้ไหม   kâhm tà-nŏn dâi măi m/f

Is there somewhere I can sit down?
มีที่ไหนที่จะนั่งได้ไหม   mee têe năi têe jà nâng
                                         dâi măi

person with a disability	คนพิการ	kon pí-gahn
older person	คนสูงอายุ	kon sŏong ah-yú
ramp	ทางลาด	tahng lâht
walking frame	กรอบเหล็กช่วยเดิน	gròrp lèk chôo·ay deun
walking stick	ไม้เท้า	mái tów
wheelchair	รถเข็น	rót kĕn

travelling with children

Is there a …?	มี … ไหม	mee … măi
baby change room	ห้องเปลี่ยนผ้าอ้อม	hôrng blèe·an pâh ôrm
child discount	ลดราคาสำหรับเด็ก	lót rah·kah săm·ràp dèk
child-minding service	บริการดูแลเด็ก	bor·rí·gahn doo laa dèk
child's portion	อาหารขนาดของเด็ก	ah·hăhn kà·nàht kŏrng dèk
crèche	ที่ฝากเลี้ยงเด็ก	têe fàhk lée·ang dèk

I need a/an …	ต้องการ …	đôrng gahn …
(English-speaking) babysitter	พี่เลี้ยงเด็ก (ที่พูดภาษาอังกฤษได้)	pêe lée·ang dèk (têe pôot pah·săh ang·grit dâi)
child car seat	เบาะนั่งสำหรับเด็ก	bò nâng săm·ràp dèk
cot	เปล	blair
highchair	เก้าอี้เด็ก	gôw·êe dèk
potty	กระโถน	grà·tŏhn
pram	รถเข็นเด็ก	rót kĕn dèk
sick bag	ถุงอ้วก	tŭng ôo·ak

Where's the nearest …?	… ที่ใกล้เคียงอยู่ที่ไหน	… têe glâi kee·ang yòo têe năi
playground	สนามเด็กเล่น	sà·năhm dèk lên
swimming pool	สระว่ายน้ำ	sà wâi nám
tap	ก๊อกน้ำ	górk nám
toyshop	ร้านขายของเล่น	ráhn kăi kŏrng lên

Do you sell ...?	ที่นี่ขาย ... ไหม	têe née kăi ... măi
baby painkillers	ยาแก้ปวด	yah gâa bòo·at
	สำหรับเด็ก	săm·ràp dèk
baby wipes	ผ้าเช็ดมือเปียก	pâh chét meu bèe·ak
disposable nappies	ผ้าอ้อมแบบ ใช้แล้วทิ้ง	pâh ôrm bàap chái láa·ou tíng
tissues	กระดาษทิชชู่	grà·dàht tít·chôo
Do you hire ...?	มี ... ให้เช่าไหม	mee ... hâi chôw măi
prams	รถเข็น	rót kĕn
strollers	รถเข็นแบบพับได้	rót kĕn bàap páp dâi

Is there space for a pram?
มีที่สำหรับรถเข็นไหม   mee têe săm·ràp rót kĕn măi

Could I have some paper and pencils, please?
ขอกระดาษเขียนเล่นและ   kŏr grà·dàht kĕe·an lên láa
ดินสอหน่อย   din·sŏr nòy

Are there any good places to take children around here?
แถวนี้มีที่ดีๆ สำหรับเด็กไหม   tăa·ou née mee têe dee
    dee săm·ràp dèk măi

Are children allowed?
เด็กเข้าได้ไหม   dèk kôw dâi măi

Where can I change a nappy?
เปลี่ยนผ้าอ้อมได้ที่ไหน   blèe·an pâh ôrm dâi têe năi

Do you mind if I breast-feed here?
ที่นี่ให้นมลูกได้ไหม   têe née hâi nom lôok dâi măi

Is this suitable for ... -year-old children?
อันนี้เหมาะสมสำหรับเด็ก   an née mò sŏm săm·ràp
อายุ ... ขวบไหม   dèk ah·yú ... kòo·ap măi

For ages see **numbers & amounts**, page 35.

Do you know a doctor who's good with children?
รู้จักหมอที่เก่งเรื่อง เด็กไหม   róo jàk mŏr têe gèng
    rêu·ang dèk măi

For health issues, see **health**, page 191.

talking about children

When's the baby due?
ก่ำหนดคลอดวันที่เท่าไร
gam-nòt klôrt wan têe tôw rai

Have you thought of a name for the baby yet?
หาชื่อให้เด็กได้หรือยัง
hăh chêu hâi dèk dâi rĕu yang

Is this your first child?
เป็นลูกคนแรกไหม
ɓen lôok kon râak măi

How many children do you have?
มีลูกกี่คน
mee lôok gèe kon

What a beautiful child!
เด็กน่ารักจริงๆ
dèk nâh rák jing jing

Is it a boy or a girl?
เป็นผู้หญิงหรือผู้ชาย
ɓen pôo yĭng rĕu pôo chai

How old is he/she?
อายุกี่ขวบ
ah-yú gèe kòo·ap

Does he/she go to school?
เข้าโรงเรียนหรือยัง
kôw rohng ree·an rĕu yang

What's his/her name?
เขาชื่ออะไร
kŏw chêu à-rai

Is he/she well-behaved?
เป็นเด็กดีหรือเปล่า
ɓen dèk dee rĕu ɓlòw

He/She ...	เขา ...	kŏw ...
has your eyes	มีตาเหมือนคุณ	mee ɗah mĕu·an kun
looks like you	หน้าเหมือนคุณ	nâh mĕu·an kun

talking with children

When is your birthday?
วันไหนวันเกิดของ หนู
wan năi wan gèut kŏrng nŏo

Do you go to school?
หนูไปโรง เรียนไหม
nŏo bai rohng ree·an măi

Do you go to kindergarten?
หนูไปอนุบาลไหม
nŏo bai à-nú-bahn măi

What grade are you in?
ที่โรง เรียนหนูอยู่ชั้นอะไร
têe rohng ree·an nŏo yòo chán à-rai

Do you like ...?   หนูชอบ ... ไหม   nŏo chôrp ... măi
    school   โรง เรียน   rohng ree·an
    sport   กีฬา   gee·lah
    your teacher   อาจารย์ของ หนู   ah-jahn kŏrng nŏo

Do you learn English?
เรียนภาษาอังกฤษไหม
ree·an pah-săh ang-grìt măi

I come from very far away.
ฉันมาจากที่ไกลมาก
chăn mah jàhk têe glai mâhk

rug rats

When speaking to children it's customary to use endearing forms of address that may change with the age and gender of the child. The informal second-person pronoun teu เธอ (you) may be used for children above thirteen years of age, but younger children are often addressed as nŏo หนู (lit: mouse). The best way to address a teenager is by their nickname. If in doubt, just ask:

What's your nickname?
ชื่อเล่นคืออะไร
chêu lên keu à-rai

basics

พื้นฐาน

Yes.	ใช่	châi
No.	ไม่	mâi
Please.	ขอ	kŏr
Thank you (very much).	ขอบคุณ (มาก ๆ)	kòrp kun (mâhk mâhk)
You're welcome.	ยินดี	yin dee
Excuse me. (to get attention)	ขอโทษ	kŏr tôht
Excuse me. (to get past)	ขออภัย	kŏr à-pai
Sorry.	ขอโทษ	kŏr tôht

greetings & goodbyes

การทักทายและการลา

In Thailand instead of asking 'What are you up to?', it's customary to ask 'Where are you going?', 'Where have you been?' and even 'Have you eaten?'. How you choose to answer is not so important – these greetings are really just a way of affirming a friendly connection.

Hello.	สวัสดี	sà-wàt-dee
Hi.	หวัสดี	wàt-dee
Where are you going?	ไปไหน	pai năi
Where have you been?	ไปไหนมา	pai năi mah
Have you eaten?	กินข้าวหรือยัง	gin kôw rĕu yang

Good day. (for morning, afternoon and evening)
สวัสดี
sà-wàt-dee

Good night.
ราตรีสวัสดิ์
rah-đree sà-wàt

How are you?
สบายดีไหม
sà-bai dee măi

Fine. And you?
สบายดี ครับ/ค่ะ แล้วคุณล่ะ
sà-bai dee kráp/kâ, láa·ou
kun lâ m/f

What's your name?
คุณชื่ออะไร
kun chêu à-rai

My name is …
ผม/ดิฉัน ชื่อ …
pŏm/dì-chăn chêu … m/f

I'd like to introduce you to …
นี่คือ …
nêe keu …

This is my …
นี่คือ … ของ ผม/ดิฉัน
nêe keu … kŏrng
pŏm/dì-chăn m/f

child	ลูก	lôok
colleague	เพื่อนงาน	pêu·an ngahn
friend	เพื่อน	pêu·an
husband	ผัว	pŏo·a
partner (intimate)	แฟน	faan
wife	เมีย	mee·a

For other family members, see **family**, page 107.

I'm pleased to meet you.
ยินดีที่ได้รู้จัก
yin-dee têe dâi róo jàk

See you later.
เดี๋ยวพบกันใหม่
dĕe·o póp gan mài

Goodbye.	ลาก่อน	lah gòrn
See you!	เจอกันนะ	jeu gan ná
Good night.	ราตรีสวัสดิ์	rah-đree sà-wàt
Bon voyage!	เดินทางด้วย	deun tahng dôo·ay
	สวัสดิภาพนะ	sà-wàt-dì-pâhp ná

addressing people

Thais will quickly establish your age when they first meet you which helps to establish the appropriate forms of address. An older person is addressed as pêe พี่ (elder) while a younger person will be addressed as nórng น้อง (younger) or more likely just by name. Kinship terms are used even for people who aren't related. So a woman may be called bâa ป้า or náa น้า (auntie), or even yai ยาย (grandma) and a man may be called lung ลุง (uncle) or bòo ปู่ (grandpa). The Thai language does have words that correspond to the English terms Mr/Ms/Mrs/Miss but these are only ever used in writing:

Mr	นาย	nai
Ms/Mrs	นาง	nahng
Miss	นางสาว	nahng sŏw

mind your language

When speaking of people of high social rank it's customary to use the appropriate pronoun (usually tâhn ท่าน). This applies especially to monks and royalty. Monks and the royal family are treated with high reverence, so if you want to be sure of not offending anyone, tread lightly when discussing them.

meeting people

making conversation

What a beautiful day!
อากาศดีนะ — ah-gàht dee ná

It's so hot today!
วันนี้ร้อนจัง — wan née rórn jang

It's very cold today!
วันนี้หนาวมาก — wan née nǒw mâhk

Do you live here?
คุณอยู่ที่นี่หรือเปล่า — kun yòo têe née rěu bplòw

Where do you come from?
คุณมาจากไหน — kun mah jàhk nǎi

Where are you going?
จะไปไหน — jà bai nǎi

What are you doing?
กำลังทำอะไรอยู่ — gam-lang tam à-rai yòo

Do you like it here?
ชอบที่นี่ไหม — chôrp têe née mǎi

I love it here.
ชอบที่นี่มาก — chôrp têe née mâhk

---

wâi me?

Although Western codes of behaviour are becoming more familiar in Thailand, the country still has its own proud traditions. One of these is the wâi ไหว้, the prayer-like gesture of hands held together in front of the chin, which is used in everyday interactions. The wâi is generally used in situations where Westerners would shake hands. Thus you would wâi when meeting a person for the first time, and also when meeting a person after an absence, or for the first time for that day. A wâi is always called for when meeting a person older than you or with a respected social position. Usually the younger person is expected to wâi first.

What's this called?
อันนี้เรียกว่าอะไร

an née rêe·ak wâh à-rai

Can I take a photo (of you)?
ถ่ายรูป (คุณ) ได้ไหม

tài rôop (kun) dâi măi

That's (beautiful), isn't it!
นั่น (สวย) นะ

nân (sŏo·ay) ná

Just joking.
พูดเล่นเฉย ๆ

pôot lên chĕu·i chĕu·i

Are you here on holiday?
คุณมาที่นี้พักผ่อนหรือเปล่า

kun mah têe née pák pòrn
rĕu blòw

I'm here ... ฉันมาที่นี้ มา…

chăn mah têe née
mah …

    for a holiday พักผ่อน

pák pòrn

    on business ทำธุระ

tam tú-rá

    to study ศึกษา

sèuk-săh

How long are you here for?
คุณจะมาพักที่นี้นานเท่าไร

kun jà mah pák têe née
nahn tôw-rai

I'm here for (four) days/weeks.
มาพักที่นี้ (สี่) วัน/อาทิตย์

mah pák têe née (sèe)
wan/ah-tít

nationalities

Where are you from?
คุณมาจากไหน

kun mah jàhk năi

I'm from ... ผม/ดิฉัน มาจาก

pŏm/dì-chăn mah
    ประเทศ … jàhk brà-têt … m/f

    Australia ออสเตรเลีย

or-sà-đrair-lee·a

    Canada แคนาดา

kaa-nah-dah

    Singapore สิงคโปร์

sĭng-ká-boh

age

How old ...?	... อายุเท่าไร	... ah-yú tôw-rai
are you	คุณ	kun
is your daughter	ลูกสาวของคุณ	lôok sŏw kŏrng kun
is your son	ลูกชายของคุณ	lôok chai kŏrng kun

I'm ... years old.
ฉันอายุ ... ปี   chăn ah-yú ... bee

He/She is ... years old.
เขาอายุ ... ปี   kŏw ah-yú ... bee

Too old!
อายุมากเกินไป   ah-yú mâhk geun bai

I'm younger than I look.
ฉันอายุน้อยกว่าที่คิด   chăn ah-yú nóy gwàh têe kít

For your age, see **numbers & amounts**, page 35.

occupations & studies

What's your occupation?
คุณมีอาชีพอะไร   kun mee ah-chêep à-rai

I'm a ...	ฉันเป็น ...	chăn ben ...
civil servant	ข้าราชการ	kâh râht-chá-gahn
farmer	ชาวไร่	chow râi
journalist	นักข่าว	nák kòw
teacher	ครู	kroo

I work in …	ฉันทำงานทางด้าน …	chăn tam ngahn tahng dâhn …
administration	บริหาร	bor-rí-hărn
health	สุขภาพ	sùk-kà-pâhp
sales & marketing	การค้าและตลาด	gahn káh láa đà-làht

I'm …	ฉัน …	chăn …
retired	ปลดเกษียณแล้ว	ɓlòt gà-sĕe·an láa·ou
self-employed	ทำธุรกิจส่วนตัว	tam tú-rá-gìt sòo·an đoo·a
unemployed	ว่างงาน	wâhng ngahn

What are you studying?
คุณกำลังเรียนอะไร · kun gam-lang ree·an à-rai yòo

I'm studying …	ผม/ดิฉัน กำลังเรียน …	pŏm/dì-chăn gam-lang ree·an … m/f
humanities	มนุษยศาสตร์	má-nút-sà-yá-sàht
science	วิทยาศาสตร์	wít-tá-yah-sàht
Thai	ภาษาไทย	pah-săh tai

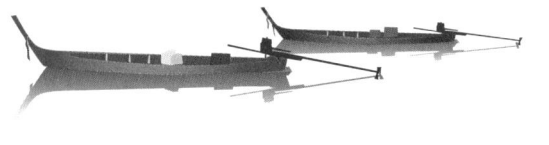

family

ครอบครัว

When talking about families in Thailand you can't just say 'I have three brothers and two sisters' as it isn't the gender that counts, but the age. So a Thai would say 'I have three youngers and two elders'. You'd have to enquire further to find out how many of those were sisters and how many brothers.

Do you have a ...?	มี ... ไหม	mee ... măi
I (don't) have a ...	(ไม่) มี ...	(mâi) mee ...
brother (older)	พี่ชาย	pêe chai
brother (younger)	น้องชาย	nórng chai
daughter	ลูกสาว	lôok sŏw
family	ครอบครัว	krôrp kroo·a
father (pol)	บิดา	bì-dah
father (inf)	พ่อ	pôr
husband (pol)	สามี	săh-mee
husband (inf)	ผัว	pŏo·a
mother (pol)	มารดา	mahn-dah
mother (inf)	แม่	mâa
partner (intimate)	แฟน	faan
sister (older)	พี่สาว	pêe sŏw
sister (younger)	น้องสาว	nórng sŏw
son	ลูกชาย	lôok chai
wife (pol)	ภรรยา	pan-rá-yah
wife (inf)	เมีย	mee·a

I'm ...	ผม/ดิฉัน ...	pŏm/dì-chăn ... m/f
married	แต่งงานแล้ว	đàang ngahn láa·ou
not married	ยังไม่แต่งงาน	yang mâi đàang ngahn
separated	หย่ากันแล้ว	yàh gan láa·ou
single	เป็นโสดอยู่	ɓen sòht yòo

I live with someone.
อยู่ร่วมกับคนอื่น
yòo rôo·am gàp kon èun

Are you married?
คุณแต่งงานหรือยัง
kun đàang ngahn rĕu yang

Do you have any children?
มีลูกหรือยัง
mee lôok rĕu yang

Not yet.
ยัง
yang

Speaking about your or somebody else's extended family is complicated in Thai as you need to specify which side of the family you're referring to, and sometimes even how old the person is relative to the mother or father. Use the table below to find out how to talk about aunts, uncles and grandparents:

uncle	(mother's older brother)	ลุง	lung
	(mother's younger brother)	น้า	náh
	(father's older brother)	ลุง	lung
	(father's younger brother)	อา	ah
aunt	(mother's older sister)	ป้า	bâh
	(mother's younger sister)	อา	ah
	(father's older sister)	ป้า	bâh
	(father's younger sister)	อา	ah
grandmother	(mother's side)	ยาย	yai
	(father's side)	ย่า	yâh
grandfather	(mother's side)	ตา	đah
	(father's side)	ปู่	boo

farewells

การลา

Tomorrow is my last day here.
พรุ่งนี้เป็นวันสุดท้ายที่นี่   prûng née ben wan sùt tái têe née

Here's my ...	นี่คือ ... ของผม/ดิฉัน	nêe keu ... kŏrng pŏm/dì-chăn m/f
What's your ...?	... ของคุณคืออะไร	... kŏrng kun keu à-rai
address	ที่อยู่	têe yòo
email address	ที่อยู่อีเมล	têe yòo ee-men
phone number	เบอร์โทรศัพท์	beu toh-rá-sàp

If you come to (Scotland) you can stay with me.

ถ้ามา (ประเทศสกอตแลนด์)
มาพักกับฉันได้

tâh mah ̀brà-têt (sà-kórt-
laan) mah pák gàp chăn dâi

Keep in touch!

ติดต่อมานะ

̀dìt ̀dòr mah ná

It's been great meeting you.

ดีใจมากที่ได้พบกับคุณ

dee jai mâhk têe dâi póp
gàp kun

---

local talk

Hey!	เฮ้ย	héu·i
Great!	ยอด	yôrt
Sure.	แน่นอน	nâa norn
Maybe.	บางที	bahng tee
No way!	ไม่มีทาง	mâi mee tahng
Just a minute.	เดี๋ยวก่อน	̌dĕe·o gòrn
It's OK.	ไม่เป็นไร	mâi ̀ben rai
No problem.	ไม่มีปัญหา	mâi mee ̀ban-hǎh
Oh, no!	ตายแล้ว	̀dai láa·ou
Oh my god!	คุณพระช่วย	kun prá chôo·ay

well wishing

การอวยพร

Bless you!	จงเจริญ	jong jà-reun
Bon voyage!	เดินทางโดย	deun tahng dôo·ay
	สวัสดิภาพนะ	sà-wàt-dì-pâhp
Congratulations!	ขอแสดงความ	kŏr sà-daang kwahm
	ยินดีด้วย	yin-dee dôo·ay
Good luck!	โชคดีนะ	chôhk dee ná
Happy birthday!	สุขสันต์วันเกิด	sùk-săn wan gèut
Merry Christmas!	สุขสันต์วันคริสต์มาส	sùk-săn wan krít-mâht
Happy New Year!	สวัสดีปีใหม่	sà-wàt-dee ̀bee mài

common interests

แหล่งความสนใจทั่วไป

Do you like ...?	ชอบ ... ไหม	chôrp ... măi
I (don't) like ...	ผม/ดิฉัน (ไม่)	pŏm/dì-chăn (mâi)
	ชอบ ...	chôrp ... m/f
cooking	ทำอาหาร	tam ah-hăhn
dancing	เต้นรำ	đên ram
drawing	เขียนภาพ	kĕe·an pâhp
music	ดนตรี	don-đree
painting	ระบายสี	rá-bai sĕe
photography	ถ่ายภาพ	tài pâhp
socialising	การสังคม	gahn săng-kom
surfing the Internet	เล่นอินเตอร์เนต	lên in-đeu-nét
travelling	การท่องเที่ยว	gahn tôrng têe·o
watching TV	ดูโทรทัศน์	doo toh-rá-tát
Where can	จะเข้า ... ได้ที่ไหน	jà kôw ... dâi tee năi
I enrol in ...?		
Can you	คุณแนะนำที่ ...	kun náa nam têe ...
recommend a ...?	ได้ไหม	dâi măi
Thai cookery	เรียนทำอาหาร	ree·an tam ah-
course	ไทย	hăhn tai
Thai language	เรียนภาษาไทย	ree·an pah-săh tai
course		
massage	เรียนนวดแผน	ree·an nôo·at
course	โบราณ	păan boh-rahn
meditation	เรียนวิธีทำสมาธิ	ree·an wí-tee tam
course		sà-mah-tí

What do you do in your spare time?

คุณทำอะไรเวลาว่าง   kun tam à-rai wair-lah
wâhng

For sporting activities, see **sport**, page 137.

music

Do you ...?	คุณ ... ไหม	kun ... mǎi
dance	เต้นรำ	đên ram
go to concerts	ไปดูการแสดง	bai doo gahn sà-daang
listen to music	ฟังดนตรี	fang don-đree
play an instrument	เล่นเครื่องดนตรี	lên krêu·ang don-đree

What ... do you like?	คุณชอบ ... อะไรบ้าง	kun chôrp ... à-rai bâhng
bands	วงดนตรี	wong don-đree
music	ดนตรี	don-đree
singers	นักร้อง	nák rórng

classical music	เพลงคลาสสิค	pleng klah-sìk
blues	เพลงบลูส์	pleng bloo
electronic music	เพลงเทคโน	pleng ték-noh
jazz	ดนตรีแจ๊ช	don-đree jáat
pop	เพลงป๊อบ	pleng bórp
rock	เพลงร๊อค	pleng rórk
world music	ดนตรีโลก	don-đree lôhk

Planning to go to a concert? See **tickets**, page 46 and **going out**, page 121.

cinema & theatre

หนังและละคร

What's showing at the cinema tonight?
มีอะไรฉายที่โรงหนังคืนนี้   mee à-rai chǎi têe rohng nǎng keun née

What's showing at the theatre tonight?
มีอะไรแสดงที่โรงละคร คืนนี้   mee à-rai sà-daang têe rohng lá-korn keun née

Is it in English?
เป็นภาษาอังกฤษไหม · ɓen pah-săh ang-grìt măi

Does it have (English) subtitles?
มีบรรยาย (ภาษาอังกฤษ) · mee ban-yai (pah-săh
ด้วยไหม · ang-grìt) dôo·ay măi

Who's in it?
ใครแสดง · krai sà-daang

Have you seen ...?
คุณเคยดู ... ไหม · kun keu·i doo ... măi

Is this seat taken?
ที่นั่งนี้มีใครเอาหรือยัง · têe nâng née mee krai
ow rĕu yang

I feel like going	ผม/ดิฉัน รู้สึก	pŏm/dì-chăn róo-sèuk
to a ...	อยากจะไปดู ...	yàhk jà ɓai doo... m/f
Did you like the ...?	คุณชอบ ... ไหม	kun chôrp ... măi
film	หนัง	năng
folk opera	ลิเก	lí-gair
Ramayana play	โขน	kŏhn
Thai dancing	รำไทย	ram tai
maw lam	หมอลำ	mŏr lam
temple fair	งานวัด	ngahn wát

I (don't) like ...	ผม/ดิฉัน (ไม่)	pŏm/dì-chăn (mâi)
	ชอบ ...	chôrp ... m/f
action movies	หนังบู๊	năng bóo
animated films	หนังการ์ตูน	năng gah-đoon
comedies	หนังตลก	năng đà-lòk
documentaries	สารคดี	săh-rá-ká-dee
erotic movies	หนังโป๊	năng ɓóh
Thai cinema	หนังไทย	năng tai
horror movies	หนังผี	năng pĕe
sci-fi movies	หนังวิทยาศาสตร์	năng wít-tá-yah-sàht
short films	หนังเรื่องสั้น	năng rêu·ang sân

I thought it was …	ผม/ดิฉัน คิดว่ามัน …	pŏm/dì-chăn kít wâh man … m/f
excellent	ยอด	yôrt
long	ยาว	yow
OK	ก็โอเค	gôr oh-kair

thai tunes

From Western-inspired house beats to flowing classical melodies, Thailand resounds with music. Listen out for some of these distinctively Thai styles:

traditional Thai music
เพลงไทยเดิม
pleng tai deum

Thai country music
เพลงลูกทุ่ง
pleng lôok tûng

country music of Lao and Northeastern Thailand (*maw lam*)
เพลงหมอลำ
pleng mŏr lam

Thai classical orchestra
ดนตรีปี่พาทย์
don-đree bèe pâht

bamboo xylophone music
ดนตรีระนาด
don-đree rá-nâat

Thai folk opera (*li-ke*)
เพลงลิเก
pleng lí-gair

feelings

ความรู้สึก

Key words in expressing emotions in Thai are jai ใจ (heart or mind) and occasionally ah-rom อารมณ์ (similar to the English 'mood'). The phrase ah-rom dee อารมณ์ดี means 'a good mood', while ah-rom mâi dee อารมณ์ไม่ดี means 'bad mood' or 'not a good mood'. The expression ah-rom sĕe·a อารมณ์เสีย refers to 'a mood turning sour'.

Are you …?	คุณ … ไหม	kun … măi
I'm (not) …	ผม/ดิฉัน	pŏm/dì-chăn
	(ไม่) …	(mâi) … m/f
annoyed	รำคาญ	ram-kahn
cold	หนาว	nŏw
disappointed	ผิดหวัง	pìt wăng
embarrassed	อับอาย	àp-ai
happy	ดีใจ	dee jai
hot	ร้อน	rórn
hungry	หิว	hĕw
in a hurry	รีบร้อน	rêep rórn
sad	เศร้า	sôw
surprised	ประหลาดใจ	b̀rà-làht jai
thirsty	หิวน้ำ	hĕw nám
tired	เหนื่อย	nèu·ay
worried	กังวล	gang-won

If feeling unwell, see **health**, page 191.

opinions

Did you like it?
คุณชอบไหม

kun chôrp măi

What do you think of it?
คุณว่าอย่างไร

kun wâh yàhng rai

I thought it	ผม/ดิฉัน	pŏm/dì-chăn
was …	คิดว่ามัน …	kít wâh man … m/f
It's …	มัน …	man …
awful	สุดแย่	sùt yâa
beautiful	น่าประทับใจ	nâh ̀brà-táp jai
boring	น่าเบื่อ	nâh bèu·a
great	เยี่ยม	yêe·am
interesting	น่าสนใจ	nâh sŏn-jai
OK	ก็โอเค	gôr oh-kair
strange	แปลก	̀blàak
too expensive	แพงเกินไป	paang geun ̀bai

mood swings

a little	นิดหน่อย	nít-nòy
I'm a little	ผม/ดิฉัน รู้สึกผิด	pŏm/dì-chăn róo-sèuk
disappointed.	หวังนิดหน่อย	pìt wăng nít-nòy m/f
extremely	อย่างยิ่ง	yàhng yîng
I'm extremely	ผม/ดิฉัน เสียใจ	pŏm/dì-chăn sĕe·a
sorry.	อย่างยิ่ง	jai yàhng yîng m/f
very	มาก	mâhk
I feel very lucky.	ผม/ดิฉัน รู้สึก	pŏm/dì-chăn róo-sèuk
	โชคดีมาก	chôhk dee mâhk m/f

politics & social issues

Who do you vote for?
คุณลงคะแนนเสียงให้ใคร　　kun long ká-naan sěe·ang
　　　　　　　　　　　　hâi krai

I support the … party.
ผม/ดิฉัน สนับสนุนพรรค …　pŏm/dì-chăn sà-nàp sà-nŭn
　　　　　　　　　　　　pák … m/f

I'm a member of　ผม/ดิฉัน เป็นสมาชิก　pŏm/dì-chăn ben sà-
the … party.　　พรรค …　　　　　mah-chik pák … m/f
　　communist　　คอมมิวนิสต์　　korm-mew-nít
　　conservative　หัวเก่า　　　　　hŏo·a gòw
　　democratic　　ประชาธิปไตย　　brà-chah-tí-bà-đai
　　green　　　　อนุรักษ์นิยม　　à-nú-rák ní-yom
　　liberal　　　เสรีนิยม　　　　săir-ree ní-yom
　　(progressive)
　　social　　　ประชาธิปไตย　　brà-chah-tí-bà-đai
　　democratic　สังคมนิยม　　　săng-kom ní-yom
　　socialist　　สังคมนิยม　　　săng-kom ní-yom

a matter of heart

The Thai word jai ใจ is used extensively in everyday conversation. It can mean both 'heart' (centre of the emotional
self) or 'mind'. When it's attached to the end of a word it
describes an emotional state, whereas at the beginning of
a word it describes a personality trait.

น้อยใจ	nóy jai	**to be peeved**
ใจน้อย	jai nóy	**to be petty**
ร้อนใจ	rórn jai	**to be agitated**
ใจร้อน	jai rórn	**to be impetuous**
ดีใจ	dee jai	**to be happy**
ใจดี	jai dee	**to be kind**

Did you hear about …?
ได้ยินเรื่อง … ไหม   dâi yin rêu·ang … măi

Do you agree with it?
เห็นด้วยไหม   hĕn dôo·ay măi

I (don't) agree with …
ผม/ดิฉัน (ไม่) เห็นด้วยกับ …   pŏm/dì-chăn (mâi) hĕn
                          dôo·ay gàp … m/f

How do people feel about …?
คนรู้สึกอย่างไรเรื่อง …   kon róo-sèuk yàhng rai
                          rêu·ang …

In my country we're concerned about …
ในประเทศของผม/ดิฉัน   nai brà-têt kŏrng pŏm/dì-chăn
เราสนใจเรื่อง …   row sŏn-jai rêu·ang … m/f

How can we protest against …?
เราจะประท้วงเรื่อง …   row jà brà-tóo·ang
ได้อย่างไร   rêu·ang … dâi yàhng rai

How can we support …?
เราจะสนับสนุนเรื่อง …   row jà sà-nàp sà-nŭn
ได้อย่างไร   rêu·ang … dâi yàhng rai

AIDS	โรคเอดส์	rôhk èt
animal rights	สิทธิของสัตว์	sìt-tí kŏrng sàt
	เดรัจฉาน	dair-rát-chăhn
corruption	ความทุจริต	kwahm tú-jà-rìt
crime	อัชญากรรม	àt-chá-yah-gam
discrimination	การกีดกัน	gahn gèet gan
drugs	ยาเสพติด	yah sèp đìt
the economy	เศรษฐกิจ	sèt-tà-gìt
education	การศึกษา	gahn sèuk-săh

the environment	สิ่งแวดล้อม	sìng wâat lórm
equal opportunity	การให้โอกาส เท่าเทียมกัน	gahn hâi oh-gàht tôw tee·am gan
globalisation	โลกาภิวัตน์	loh-gah-pí-wát
human rights	สิทธิมนุษยชน	sìt-tí má-nút-sà-yá- chon
immigration	การอพยพเข้าเมือง	gahn òp-pá-yóp kôw meu·ang
indigenous issues	เรื่องคนพื้นเมือง	rêu·ang kon péun meu·ang
indigenous rights	สิทธิของคนพื้นเมือง	sìt-tí kŏrng kon péun meu·ang
inequality	ความไม่เสมอภาค	kwahm mâi sà-měu pâhk
the monarchy	สถาบันมหากษัตริย์	sà-tăh-ban má-hăh gà-sàt
party politics	การเมืองระหว่าง พรรค	gahn meu·ang rá- wàhng pák
racism	การเหยียดผิว	gahn yèe·at pĕw
sex tourism	การเที่ยวทางเพศ	gahn têe·o tahng pêt
sexism	เพศนิยม	pêt ní-yom
social welfare	การประชา สงเคราะห์	gahn ̀brà-chah sŏng-kró
terrorism	การก่อการร้าย	gahn gòr gahn rái
unemployment	ความว่างงาน	kwahm wâhng ngahn
US foreign policy	นโยบายต่างประเทศ ของสหรัฐอเมริกา	ná-yoh-bai ̀dàhng ̀brà-têt kŏrng sà-hà- rát à-mair-rí-gah
the war in ...	สงครามใน ...	sŏng-krahm nai ...

the environment

Is there a ... problem here?
ที่นี่มีปัญหาเรื่อง ... ไหม têe née mee ban-hăh
rêu·ang ... măi

What should be done about ...?
ควรจะทำอย่างไรเรื่อง ... koo·an jà tam yàhng rai
rêu·ang ...

conservation	การอนุรักษ์สิ่งแวดล้อม	gahn à-nú-rák sìng wâat lórm
deforestation	การทำลายป่า	gahn tam lai bàh
drought	ภาวะขาดแคลนน้ำ	pah-wá kàht klaan nám
ecosystem	ระบบนิเวศ	rá-bòp ní-wêt
endangered species	สัตว์ที่ใกล้จะสูญพันธุ์	sàt têe glâi jà sŏon pan
hydroelectricity	พลังไฟฟ้าจากน้ำ	pá-lang fai fáh jàhk nám
irrigation	การทดน้ำ	gahn tót nám
pesticides	ยาฆ่าแมลง	yah kâh má-laang
pollution	มลภาวะ	mon-pah-wá
toxic waste	ขยะมีพิษ	kà-yà mee pít
water supply	แหล่งน้ำใช้	làng nám chái
Is this a protected ...?	อันนี้เป็น ... สงวนไหม	an née ben ... sà-ngŏo·an măi
jungle	ป่า	bàh
park	อุทยาน	ù-tá-yahn
species	สัตว์	sàt

where to go

ที่ไป

What's there to do in the evenings?
มีอะไรบ้างให้ทำตอนเย็น   mee à-rai bâhng hâi tam
đorn yen

Where shall we go?
จะไปไหนกันดี   jà ɓai nǎi gan dee

What's on …?	มีอะไรทำ …	mee à-rai tam …
locally	แถวๆ นี้	tǎa·ou tǎa·ou née
this weekend	เสาร์อาทิตย์นี้	sǒw ah-tít née
today	วันนี้	wan née
tonight	คืนนี้	keun née

Where can I find …?	จะหา … ได้ที่ไหน	jà hǎh … dâi têe nǎi
clubs	ไนท์คลับ	nai kláp
gay venues	สถานบันเทิง	sà-tǎhn ban-teung
	สำหรับคนเกย์	sǎm-ràp kon gair
places to eat	ที่ทานอาหาร	têe tahn ah-hǎhn
pubs	ผับ	pàp

Is there a	มีคู่มือ … สำหรับ	mee kôo meu … sǎm-
local … guide?	แถวนี้ไหม	ràp tǎa·ou née mǎi
entertainment	สถานบันเทิง	sà-tǎhn ban-teung
film	ภาพยนตร์	pâhp-pá-yon
gay	เกย์	gair
music	คนตรี	don-đree

I feel like going	ผม/ดิฉัน รู้สึก	pŏm/dì-chăn róo-sèuk
to a …	อยากจะไป …	yàhk jà bai … m/f
bar	บาร์	bah
café	ร้านกาแฟ	ráhn gah-faa
concert	ดูการแสดง	doo gahn sà-daang
film	ดูหนัง	doo năng
full moon	งานปาร์ตี้พระจันทร์	ngahn bah-đêe prá
party	เต็มดวง	jan đem doo·ang
karaoke bar	คาราโอเกะ	kah-rah-oh-gé
nightclub	ไนท์คลับ	nai kláp
party	งานปาร์ตี้	ngahn bah-đêe
performance	ดูงานแสดง	doo ngahn
		sà-daang
pub	ผับ	pàp
restaurant	ร้านอาหาร	ráhn ah-hăhn

For more on bars and drinks, see **eating out**, page 153.

invitations

การเชิญชวน

What are you	คุณทำอะไรอยู่ …	kun tam à-rai yòo …
doing …?		
now	เดี๋ยวนี้	dĕe·o née
this weekend	เสาร์อาทิตย์นี้	sŏw ah-tít née
tonight	คืนนี้	keun née

Would you like	อยากจะไป … ไหม	yàhk jà bai … măi
to go (for a) …?		
I feel like going	ฉันรู้สึกอยาก	chăn róo-sèuk
(for a) …	จะไป …	yàhk jà bai …
coffee	กินกาแฟ	gin gah-faa
dancing	เต้นรำ	đên ram
drink	ดื่ม	dèum
meal	ทานอาหาร	tahn ah-hăhn
out somewhere	เที่ยวข้างนอก	têe·o kâhng nôrk
walk	เดินเล่น	deun lên

My round.
ตาของฉันนะ
đah kŏrng chăn ná

Do you know a good restaurant?
รู้จักร้านอาหารดีๆไหม
róo jàk ráhn ah-hăhn dee dee măi

Do you want to come to the concert with me?
คุณอยากจะไปงานแสดง
กับฉันไหม
kun yàhk jà bai ngahn sà-daang gàp chăn măi

We're having a party.
เรากำลังจัดงานเลี้ยงอยู่
row gam-lang jàt ngahn lée·ang yòo

You should come.
คุณน่าจะมานะ
kun nâh jà mah ná

responding to invitations

Sure!
ได้เลย
dâi leu·i

Yes, I'd love to.
ไป ครับ/ค่ะ ดีใจมากเลย
bai kráp/kâ, dee jai mâhk leu·i m/f

That's very kind of you.
คุณใจดีนะ
kun jai dee ná

No, I'm afraid I can't.
ขอโทษนะไปไม่ได้
kŏr tôht ná, bai măi dâi

Sorry, I can't sing.
ขอโทษ ร้องเพลงไม่เป็น
kŏr tôht, rórng pleng mâi ben

Sorry, I can't dance.
ขอโทษ เต้นรำไม่เป็น
kŏr tôht, đên ram mâi ben

What about tomorrow?
พรุ่งนี้ได้ไหม
prûng née dâi măi

arranging to meet

What time will we meet?
จะพบกันกี่โมง   jà póp gan gèe mohng

Where will we meet?
จะพบกันที่ไหน   jà póp gan têe năi

Let's meet at …   พบกัน … ดีไหม   póp gan … dee măi
 (eight pm)   (สองทุ่ม)   (sŏrng tûm)
 the (entrance)   ที่ (ทางเข้า)   têe (tahng kôw)

'shitting' yourself

The word kêe ขี้ on its own means 'shit', but if you chat enough with the Thai people you'll hear this word used in a wealth of different ways. At its most colourful, kêe is used to describe the 'by-products' of someone's personality in negative character traits such as kêe gèe·at ขี้เกียจ (lazy), kêe gloo·a ขี้กลัว (timid), kêe klàht ขี้ขลาด (cowardly), kêe móh ขี้โม้ (boastful), and kêe moh-hŏh ขี้โมโห (hot-tempered). It's also used to describe all manner of real by-products such as kêe lêu·ay ขี้เลื่อย (saw dust), kêe lèk ขี้เหล็ก (iron filings), and kêe gleu·a ขี้เกลือ (salty residue).

At its most vulgar kêe denotes various secretions of the body – as in kêe đah ขี้ตา (eye excretion, ie 'sleep'), kêe hŏo ขี้หู (ear wax), kêe môok ขี้มูก (snot) and kêe klai ขี้ไคล (grime of the skin). The words you'll hear if you're giving too small a tip are kêe nĕe·o ขี้เหนียว (stingy), often creatively translated as 'sticky shit'.

I'll pick you up.
ฉันจะมารับคุณ   chăn jà mah ráp kun

Are you ready?
พร้อมหรือยัง   prórm rĕu yang

I'm ready.
พร้อมแล้ว   prórm láa·ou

I'll be coming later.
ฉันจะมาทีหลัง   chăn jà mah tee lăng

Where will you be?
คุณจะอยู่ที่ไหน   kun jà yòo têe năi

If I'm not there by (nine pm), don't wait for me.
ถ้าถึงเวลา (สามทุ่ม) ฉัน   tâh tĕung wair-lah (săhm
ไม่มา ไม่ต้องรอนะ   tûm) chăn mâi mah mâi
    đông ror ná

OK!
ตกลง   đòk long

I'll see you then.
เจอกันตอนนั้น   jeu gan đorn nán

See you later.
เดี๋ยวพบกันทีหลัง   dĕe·o póp gan têe lăng

See you tomorrow.
เดี๋ยวพบกันพรุ่งนี้   dĕe·o póp gan prûng née

I'm looking forward to it.
ตื่นเต้นจัง   đèun đên jang

Sorry I'm late.
ขอโทษที่มาช้า   kŏr tôht têe mah cháh

Never mind.
ไม่เป็นไร   mâi ben rai

drugs

I don't take drugs.
ฉันไม่เสพยา   chăn mâi sèp yah

I take ... occasionally.
ฉัน เอา ... เป็นบางครั้ง   chăn ow ... ฿en bahng kráng

Do you want to have a smoke?
จะสูบไหม   jà sòop măi

Do you have a light?
มีไฟไหม   mee fai măi

asking someone out

การขอไปเที่ยวกัน

Would you like to do something (tomorrow)?
คุณอยากจะไปทำอะไรสัก
อย่าง (พรุ่งนี้) ไหม

kun yàhk jà bai tam à-rai sàk
yàhng (prûng née) măi

Where would you like to go (tonight)?
คุณอยากจะไปไหน (คืนนี้)

kun yàhk jà bai năi (keun
née)

Yes, I'd love to.
ไปครับ/ค่ะ ดีใจมาก

bai kráp/kâ, dee jai mâhk m/f

I'm busy.
ฉันติดธุระ

chăn đìt tú-rá

What a babe!
น่ารักจัง

nâh rák jang

He/She gets around.
เขา/เธอเที่ยวเก่งนะ

kŏw/teu têe·o gèng ná

pick-up lines

Would you like a drink?
จะดื่มอะไรไหม — jà dèum à-rai măi

You look like someone I know.
คุณนี้หน้าคุ้นๆ — kun née nâh kún kún

You're a fantastic dancer.
คุณเต้นรำเก่งมากเลย — kun đên ram gèng mâhk leu·i

Can I ...? ... ได้ไหม — ... dâi măi
  dance with you เต้นกับคุณ đên gàp kun
  sit here นั่งที่นี่ nâng têe née
  take you home พาคุณกลับบ้าน pah kun glàp bâhn

rejections

I'm here with my boyfriend/girlfriend.
ฉันอยู่กับแฟน — chăn yòo gàp faan

Excuse me, I have to go now.
ขอโทษนะ ต้องไปแล้ว — kŏr tôht ná, đôrng bai láa·ou

I'd rather not.
คิดว่าไม่นะ — kít wâh mâi ná

No, thank you.
ไม่นะ ครับ/ค่ะ ขอบคุณ — mâi ná kráp/kâ, kòrp kun m/f

the hard word

Leave me alone! อย่ายุ่งกับฉัน yàh yûng gàp chăn

getting closer

I like you very much.
ฉันชอบคุณมากๆ chăn chôrp kun mâhk mâhk

Can I kiss you?
จูบคุณได้ไหม jòop kun dâi măi

Do you want to come inside for a while?
จะเข้ามาข้างในหน่อยไหม jà kòw mah kâhng nai nòy măi

Do you want a massage?
อยากให้นวดไหม yàhk hâi nôo·at măi

safe sex

Do you have a condom?
มีถุงยางไหม mee tŭng yahng măi

Let's use a condom.
ใช้ถุงยางกันเถิด chái tŭng yahng gan tèut

I won't do it without protection.
ฉันจะไม่ทำถ้าไม่มี chăn jà mâi tam tâh mâi mee
อะไรป้องกัน à-rai bòrng gan

sex

I want to make love to you.
ฉันอยากจะร่วมรักกับเธอ chăn yàhk jà rôo·am rák gàp teu

romance

129

Kiss me.	จูบฉันเถิด	jòop chăn tèut
I want you.	ต้องการเธอแล้ว	đôrng gahn teu láa·ou
Let's go to bed.	ไปที่นอนนะ	ɓai têe norn ná
Touch me here.	แตะฉันตรงนี้	đàa chăn đrong née
Do you like this?	แบบนี้ชอบไหม	ɓàap née chôrp măi
I (don't) like that.	(ไม่) ชอบ	(mâi) chôrp
I think we should stop now.	คิดว่าหยุดดีกว่า	kít wâh yùt dee gwàh
Oh yeah!	ใช่เลย	châi leu·i
Oh my god!	คุณพระช่วย	kun prá chôo·ay
That's great.	ยอดเลย	yôrt leu·i
Easy tiger!	ใจเย็นๆนะ	jai yen yen ná

It helps to have a sense of humour.

ต้องมีอารมณ์ขันหน่อย đôrng mee ah-rom kăn nòy

afterwards

ช่วงหลัง

That was …	นั่นก็ …	nân gôr …
amazing	น่าอัศจรรย์	nâh àt-sà-jan
weird	แปลก	ɓlàak
wild	รุนแรง	run raang
Can I …?	… ได้ไหม	… dâi măi
call you	โทรคุณ	toh kun
meet you tomorrow	พบกับคุณพรุ่งนี้	póp gàp kun prûng née
stay over	ค้างที่นี่	káhng têe née

love

I love you.
ฉันรักเธอ   chǎn rák teu

You're great.
คุณนี่ยอดเลย   kun nêe yôrt leu·i

I think we're good together.
ฉันคิดว่าเราสอง คนเข้ากันได้ดี   chǎn kít wâh row sǒrng
                                       kon kôw gan dâi dee

Will you ...?   เธอจะ ... ไหม   teu jà ... mǎi
  go out with me   ไปเที่ยวกับฉัน   bai têe·o gàp chǎn
  live with me   มาอยู่กับฉัน   mah yòo gàp chǎn
  marry me   แต่ งงานกับฉัน   đàang ngahn gàp
                                                   chǎn

---

sweet nothings

  Darling   สุดที่รัก   sùt têe rák
  Honey   ยอดรัก   yôrt rák
  My love   ที่รัก   têe rák
  Sweetheart   หวานใจ   wǎhn jai

---

problems

Are you seeing someone else?
เธอกำลังพบกับคนอื่นไหม   teu gam-lang póp gàp kon
                                       èun mǎi

He/She is just a friend.
เขาแค่เพื่อนเฉยๆ   kǒw kâa pêu·an chěu·i chěu·i

I never want to see you again.
ฉันไม่อยากจะเห็นหน้าเธอ   chǎn mâi yàhk jà hěn nâh
อีกแล้ว   teu èek láa·ou

I don't think it's working out.
ฉันรู้สึกว่ามันกำลังเป็น
ไปไม่ได้

chăn róo-sèuk wâh man
gam-lang ben bai mâi dâi

We'll work it out.
เราจะหาทางแก้ไข

row jà hăh tahng gâa kăi

leaving

I have to leave tomorrow.
ฉันต้องไปพรุ่งนี้

chăn đôrng bai prûng née

I'll …	ฉันจะ …	chăn jà …
come and visit you	มาเยี่ยมคุณ	mah yêe·am kun
keep in touch	ติดต่อนะ	đìt đòr ná
miss you	คิดถึงคุณ	kít tĕung kun

beliefs & cultural differences
ความเชื่อถือและความแตกต่างทางวัฒนธรรม

religion

ศาสนา

What's your religion?
คุณนับถือศาสนาอะไร

kun náp-tĕu sàht-sà-năh à-rai

I'm not religious.
ฉันไม่สนใจเรื่องศาสนา

chăn mâi sŏn-jai rêu·ang
sàht-sà-năh

Buddhist	ชาวพุทธ	chow pút
Catholic	คริสตัง	krít-sà-đang
Christian	คริสเตียน	krít-sà-đee·an
Hindu	ชาวฮินดู	chow hin-doo
Jewish	ชาวยิว	chow yew
Muslim	ชาวอิสลาม	chow ìt-sà-lahm
I (don't) believe	ผม/ดิฉัน (ไม่)	pŏm/dì-chăn (mâi)
in ...	เชื่อเรื่อง ...	chêu·a rêu·ang ... m/f
astrology	โหราศาสตร์	hŏh-rah-sàht
fate	ชะตากรรม	chá-đah gam
God	พระเจ้า	prá jôw
Can I ... here?	... ที่นี่ได้ไหม	... têe née dâi măi
Where can I ...?	จะ ... ได้ที่ไหน	jà ... dâi têe năi
attend a service	ร่วมพิธี	rôo·am pí-tee
practise meditation	ฝึกสมาธิ	fèuk sà-mah-tí
pray	สวดมนต์	sòo·at mon

Is there a meditation teacher here?
ที่นี่มีอาจารย์สอนสมาธิไหม

têe née mee ah-jahn sŏrn
sà-mah-tí măi

chanting	การสวดมนต์	gahn sòo·at mon
meditation	การทำสมาธิ	gahn tam sà·mah·tí
monastery	วัด	wát
novice monk	เณร	nen
nun	แม่ชี	mâa chee
ordained monk	พระ	prá
shrine	แท่นพระ	tâan prá
stupa	พระสฺตูป	prá sà·tòop
temple	วัด	wát

cultural differences

ความแตกต่างทางวัฒนธรรม

Is this a local or national custom?
นี่เป็นประเภณีประจำ
ชาติหรือเฉพาะท้องถิ่น
nêe ben bprà·pair·nee bprà·jam
châht rĕu chá·pó tórng tìn

I don't want to offend you.
ผม/ดิฉัน ไม่อยากจะทำ
ผิดประเพณีของคุณ
pŏm/dì·chăn mâi yàhk jà
tam pìt bprà·pair·nee kŏrng
kun m/f

I'm not used to this.
ผม/ดิฉัน ไม่คุ้นเคยกับ
การทำอย่างนี้
pŏm/dì·chăn mâi kún keu·i
gàp gahn tam yàhng née m/f

I'd rather not join in.
ผม/ดิฉัน คิดว่าไม่ร่วมดีกว่า
pŏm/dì·chăn kít wâh mâi
rôo·am dee gwàh m/f

I didn't mean to do anything wrong.
ผม/ดิฉันไม่ได้เจตนาทำ
อะไรผิด
pŏm/dì·chăn mâi dâi
jèt·đà·nah tam à·rai pìt m/f

I'm sorry, it's against my ...	ขอโทษนะ มันขัด กับ ... ของ ผม/ดิฉัน	kŏr tôht ná man kàt gàp ... kŏrng pŏm/ dì·chăn m/f
beliefs	ความเชื่อถือ	kwahm chêu·a tĕu
religion	ศาสนา	sàht·sà·năh

When's the gallery open?
หอแสดงเปิดกี่โมง · hŏr sà-daang bèut gèe mohng

When's the museum open?
พิพิธพันธ์ เปิดกี่โมง · pí-pít-tá-pan bèut gèe mohng

What kind of art are you interested in?
คุณสนใจศิลปะแบบไหน · kun sŏn-jai sĭn-lá-bà bàap năi

What's in the collection?
มีอะไรบ้างในชุดนี้ · mee à-rai bâhng nai chút née

What do you think of ...?
คุณคิดอย่างไรเรื่อง ... · kun kít yàhng rai rêu·ang ...

I'm interested in ...
ผม/ดิฉัน สนใจ ... · pŏm/dì-chăn sŏn-jai ... m/f

I like the works of ...
ผม/ดิฉัน ชอบงานของ ... · pŏm/dì-chăn chôrp ngahn kŏrng ... m/f

It reminds me of ...
ทำให้นึกถึง ... · tam hâi néuk tĕung ...

... art	ศิลปะ ...	sĭn-lá-bà ...
graphic	การเขียน	gahn kĕe·an
modern	สมัยใหม่	sà-măi mài
performance	การแสดง	gahn sà-daang

past glories

Sukhothai period (13th–15th centuries AD)
ยุคสุโขทัย · yúk sù-kŏh-tai

Ayuthaya period (14th–18th centuries AD)
ยุคอยุธยา · yuk à-yút-tá-yah

Srivijaya period (7th–13th centuries AD)
ยุคศรีวิชัย · yúk sĕe-wí-chai

artwork	งานศิลปะ	ngahn sĭn-lá-Ƀà
curator	ผู้ดูแล	pôo doo laa
design	การออกแบบ	gahn òrk bàap
etching	ภาพแกะพิมพ์	pâhp gàa pim
exhibit	งานแสดง	ngahn sà-daang
exhibition hall	หอนิทรรศการ	hŏr ní-tát-sà-gahn
installation	งานติดตั้ง	ngahn đìt đâng
opening	งานเปิด	ngahn Ƀèut
painter	ช่างเขียน	châhng kĕe·an
painting	ภาพระบาย	pâhp rá-bai
period	ยุค	yúk
print	ภาพพิมพ์	pâhp pim
sculptor	ช่างปั้น	châhng Ƀân
sculpture (cut)	รูปสลัก	rôop sà-làk
sculpture (moulded)	รูปปั้น	rôop Ƀân
statue	รูปหล่อ	rôop lòr
studio	ห้องทำงาน	hôrng tam ngahn
style	แบบ	bàap
technique	เทคนิค	ték-ník

sporting interests

ความสนใจเกี่ยวกับกีฬา

What sport	คุณ ...	kun ...
do you ...?	กีฬาอะไร	gee-lah à-rai
play	เล่น	lên
follow	ติดตาม	đìt đahm

I play (do) ...	ผม/ดิฉัน เล่น ...	pŏm/dì-chăn lên ... m/f
I follow ...	ผม/ดิฉัน ติดตาม ...	pŏm/dì-chăn đìt đahm ... m/f
athletics	กรีฑา	gree-tah
badminton	แบดมินตัน	bàat-min-đan
basketball	บาสเกตบอล	bah-sà-gèt born
boxing	มวยสากล	moo·ay săh-gon
football (soccer)	ฟุตบอล	fút-born
karate	คาราเต้	kah-rah-tê
muay Thai	มวยไทย	moo·ay tai
table tennis	ปิงปอง	bing-borng
takraw	เซปักตะกร้อ	sair bàk đà-grôr
tennis	เทนนิส	ten-nít
scuba diving	การดำน้ำใช้ถังออกซิเยน	gahn dam nám chái tăng òok-sí-yen
volleyball	วอลเลย์บอล	worn-lair-born
I ...	ผม/ดิฉัน ...	pŏm/dì-chăn ... m/f
cycle	ขี่จักรยาน	kèe jàk-gà-yahn
run	วิ่ง	wîng
walk	เดิน	deun

Do you like (soccer)?
คุณชอบ (ฟุตบอล) ไหม kun chôrp (fút-born) măi

Yes, very much.
ชอบมาก chôrp mâhk

Not really.
ไม่เท่าไร mâi tôw-rai

I like watching it.
ชอบดู chôrp doo

Who's your	ใครเป็น ...	krai ben ... têe
favourite ...?	ที่คุณชอบที่สุด	kun chôrp têe-sùt
sportsperson	นักกีฬา	nák gee-lah
team	ทีมกีฬา	teem gee-lah

going to a game

การไปดูเกม

Would you like to go to a game?
คุณอยากจะไปดูเกมไหม kun yàhk jà bai doo gem măi

Who are you supporting?
คุณเชียร์ใคร kun chee-a krai

Who's ...?	ใครกำลัง ... อยู่	krai gam-lang ... yòo
playing	เล่น	lên
winning	ชนะ	chá-ná

sports talk

What a ...!	... ยอดเลย	... yôrt leu·i
goal	ประตู	brà-doo
hit	ต่อย	đòy
kick	เตะ	đè
pass	ส่งลูก	sòng lôok
performance	เล่น	lên

Thai boxing, or *muay Thai* is a national sport of international popularity. Keep ahead of the action with these boxing terms:

boxing ring	เวทีมวย	wair-tee moo·ay
elbow	ศอก	sòrk
kick	เตะ	đè
knee	เข่า	kòw
knockout	ชนะน็อค	chá-na nórk
points decision	ชนะคะแนน	chá-ná ká-naan
punch	ชก	chók
referee	กรรมการ	gam-má-gahn
round	ยก	yók

That was a ... game!	นั่นเป็นเกม ...	nân ben gem ...
bad	ห่วย	hoo·ay
boring	น่าเบื่อ	nâh bèu·a
great	เยี่ยม	yêe·am

playing sport

การเล่นกีฬา

Do you want to play?
คุณอยากจะเล่นไหม
kun yàhk jà lên mǎi

Can I join in?
ฉันร่วมด้วยได้ไหม
chǎn rôo·am dôo·ay dâi mǎi

That would be great.
นั่นก็เยี่ยม
nân gôr yêe·am

I can't.
ไม่ได้
mâi dâi

I have an injury.
ฉันบาดเจ็บ
chǎn bàht jèp

Where's a good place to ...?	ที่ไหนมีที่ที่ ... ดี	tée năi mee têe têe ... dee
fish	หาปลา	hăh blah
go horse riding	ขี่ม้า	kèe máh
run	วิ่ง	wîng
snorkel	ดำน้ำใช้ท่อหายใจ	dam nám chái tôr hăi jai
surf	เล่นโต้คลื่น	lên đôh klêun
Where's the nearest ...?	ที่ไหน ... ที่ใกล้เคียง	têe năi ... têe glâi kee·ang
golf course	สนามกอล์ฟ	sà-năhm gòrp
gym	ห้องออกกำลังกาย	hôrng òrk gam-lang gai
swimming pool	สระว่ายน้ำ	sà wâi nám
tennis court	สนามเทนนิส	sà-năhm ten-nít

Do I have to be a member to attend?
ต้องเป็นสมาชิกจึงจะไปได้ไหม   đôrng ben sà-mah-chík jeung jà bai dâi măi

Is there a women-only session?

มีเวลาสำหรับเฉพาะผู้หญิงไหม   mee wair-lah săm-ràp
chà-pó pôo yĭng măi

Where are the changing rooms?

ห้องเปลี่ยนผ้าอยู่ที่ไหน   hôrng blèe·an pâh yòo
têe năi

What's the charge per ...?	คิดค่า ... ละเท่าไร	kít kâh ... lá tôw-rai
day	วัน	wan
game	เกม	gem
hour	ชั่วโมง	chôo·a mohng
visit	ครั้ง	kráng

Can I hire a ...?	เช่า ... ได้ไหม	chôw ... dâi măi
ball	ลูกบอล	lôok born
bicycle	จักรยาน	jàk-gà-yahn
court	สนาม	sà-năhm
racquet	ไม้ตี	mái đee

diving

การดำน้ำ

Where's a good diving site?

ที่ไหนมีที่ดำน้ำที่ดี   têe năi mee têe dam nám
têe dee

Is the visibility good?

การมองเห็นชัดไหม   gahn morng hĕn chát măi

How deep is the dive?

ดำได้ลึกเท่าไร   dam dâi léuk tôw-rai

I need an air fill.

ต้องเติมออกซิเยน   dôrng đeum òok-sí-yen

Are there ...?	มี ... ไหม	mee ... măi
currents	กระแสน้ำแรง	grà-săe nám raang
sharks	ปลาฉลาม	blah chà-lăhm
whales	ปลาวาฬ	blah-wahn

I want to hire (a) ...	อยากจะเช่า ...	yàhk jà chôw ...
buoyancy vest	เสื้อชูชีพ	sêu·a choo chêep
diving equipment	อุปกรณ์ดำน้ำ	ùp·bà·gorn dam nám
flippers	ตีนกบ	đeen gòp
mask	หน้ากากดำน้ำ	nâh gàhk dam nám
regulator	เครื่องปรับลม	krêu·ang bràp lom
snorkel	ท่อหายใจ	tôr hǎi jai
tank	ถังออกซิเยน	tǎng òrk·sí·yen
weight belt	เข็มขัดถ่วงน้ำหนัก	kěm·kàt tòo·ang nám·nàk
wetsuit	ชุดหนัง	chút nǎng
I'd like to ...	ฉันอยากจะ ...	chǎn yàhk jà ...
explore caves	ไปสำรวจถ้ำ	bai sǎm·ròo·at tâm
explore wrecks	ไปสำรวจซาก เรือเก่า	bai sǎm·ròo·at sâhk reu·a gòw
go night diving	ไปดำน้ำกลางคืน	bai dam nám glahng keun
go scuba diving	ไปดำน้ำใช้ถัง ออกซิเยน	bai dam nám chái tǎng òrk·sí·yen
go snorkelling	ไปดำน้ำใช้ท่อ หายใจ	bai dam nám chái tôr hǎi jai
join a diving tour	ไปเข้าคณะดำน้ำ	bai kôw ká·ná dam nám
learn to dive	เรียนวิธีดำน้ำ	ree·an wí·tee dam nám

buddy	เพื่อน	pêu·an
cave	ถ้ำ	tâm
diving boat	เรือสำหรับการ ไปดำน้ำ	reu·a sǎm·ràp gahn bai dam nám
diving course	หลักสูตรดำน้ำ	làk sòot dam nám
night dive	ดำน้ำกลางคืน	dam nám glahng keun
wreck	ซากเรือเก่า	sâhk reu·a gòw

soccer

Who plays for (Thai Farmers Bank)?
ใครเล่นให้ทีม (ธนาคาร
กสิกรไทย)

krai lên hâi teem (tá-nah-kahn gà-sì-gorn tai)

He's a great player.
เขาเป็นนักเล่นที่เก่ง

kǒw ben nák lên têe gèng

He played brilliantly in the match against (Cambodia).
เขาเล่นเก่งมากตอนที่เล่น
แข่งกับ (เขมร)

kǒw lên gèng mâhk đorn têe lên kàang gàp (kà-měn)

Which team is at the top of the league?
ทีมไหนอยู่ที่หนึ่งในการแข่งขัน

teem nǎi yòo têe nèung nai gahn kàang kǎn

What a great/terrible team!
ทีมนี้ยอด/ฮวยเลย

teem née yôrt/hoo-ay leu-i

ball	ลูกบอล	lôok born
coach	โค้ช	kóht
corner	เตะมุม	đè mum
expulsion	ไล่ออก	lâi òrk
fan	แฟนบอล	faan born
foul	ฟาวล์	fow
free kick	เตะกินเปล่า	đè gin blòw
goal	ประตู	brà-đoo
goalkeeper	ผู้รักษาประตู	pôo rák-sah brà-đoo
manager	ผู้จัดการทีม	pôo-jàt-gahn teem
offside	ล้ำหน้า	lám nâh
penalty	เตะลูกโทษ	đè lôok tôht
player	นักเล่น	nák lên
red card	ใบแดง	bai daang
referee	กรรมการผู้ตัดสิน	gam-má-gahn pôo đàt sǐn
striker	ตัวยิง	đoo-a ying
throw in	ทุ่มเข้า	tûm kôw
yellow card	ใบเหลือง	bai lěu-ang

tennis

I'd like to play tennis.
อยากจะเล่นเทนนิส
yàhk jà lên ten-nít

Can we play at night?
เล่นกลางคืนได้ไหม
lên glahng keun dâi măi

I need my racquet restrung.
ต้องตึงเอ็นไม้เทนนิสใหม่
đôrng đeung en mái
ten-nít mài

ace	เสิร์ฟลูกม่า	sèup lôok kâh
advantage	ได้เปรียบ	dâi brèe·ap
fault	ฟอลท์	forn
game, set, match	จบการแข่งขัน	jòp gahn kàang kăn
grass	หญ้า	yâh
hard court	สนามแข็ง	sà-năhm kăang
net	เนต	nét
play doubles	เล่นคู่	lên kôo
racquet	ไม้ตี	mái đee
serve	เสิร์ฟ	sèup
set	เซท	sét
tennis ball	ลูกบอล	lôok born

scoring

What's the score?	ได้คะแนนเท่าไร	dâi ká-naan tôw-rai
draw/even	เสมอกัน	sà-měr gan
love (zero)	ศูนย์	sŏon
match-point	แต้มชนะการแข่งขัน	đâam chá-ná gahn kàang kăn
nil (zero)	สูญ	sŏon

water sports

Can I book a lesson?
จองบทเรียนได้ไหม
jorng bòt ree·an dâi măi

Can I hire (a) ...   เช่า ... ได้ไหม   chôw ... dâi măi
- **boat**   เรือ   reu·a
- **canoe**   เรือคนู   reu·a ká-noo
- **kayak**   เรือใคยัก   reu·a kai-yák
- **life jacket**   เสื้อชูชีพ   sêu·a choo chêep
- **snorkelling**   อุปกรณ์ดำน้ำใช้   ùp-bà-gorn dam
- **gear**   ท่อหายใจ   nám chái tôr hǎi jai
- **water-skis**   สกีน้ำ   sà-gee nám
- **wetsuit**   ชุดหนัง   chút năng

Are there any ...?   มี ... ไหม   mee ... măi
- **reefs**   หินโสโครก   hǐn sǒh-krôhk
- **rips**   กระแสใต้น้ำ   grà-sǎe đâi nám
- **water hazards**   อันตรายในน้ำ   an-đà-rai nai nám

guide	ไกด์	gai
motorboat	เรือติดเครื่อง	reu·a đìt krêu·ang
oars	ไม้พาย	mái pai
sailing boat	เรือใบ	reu·a bai
surfboard	กระดานโต้คลื่น	grà-dahn đôh klêun
surfing	การเล่นกระดานโต้คลื่น	gahn lên grà-dahn đôh klêun
wave	คลื่น	klêun
windsurfing	การเล่นกระดานโต้ลม	gahn lên grà-dahn đôh lom

golf

How much …?	… เท่าไร	… tôw-rai
for a round	เล่นรอบหนึ่ง	lên rôrp nèung
to play 9/18	เล่นเก้า/สิบแปด	lên gôw/sìp-bàat
holes	หลุม	lŭm

Can I hire golf clubs?
เช่าไม้ตีได้ไหม   chôw mái đee dâi măi

What's the dress code?
ต้องแต่งตัวอย่างไร   đôrng đàang đoo·a yàhng rai

Do I need golf shoes?
ต้องใช้รองเท้ากอล์ฟหรือเปล่า   đôrng chái rorng tów gòrp
                                        rĕu Ъlòw

Soft or hard spikes?
ปุ่มแข็งหรือปุ่มนุ่ม   Ъùm kăang rĕu Ъùm nûm

---

put a smile on your dial

Thailand has been called the Land of Smiles, and not without reason. It's cool to smile, and Thai people seem to smile and laugh at the oddest times (such as if you trip over something or make a mistake). It's important to realise that they're not laughing at you, but with you: it's a way of releasing the tension of embarrassment and saying it's OK.

Thais feel negative emotions just as much as anyone else, but the culture does not encourage the outward expression of them. It's considered bad form to blow up in anger in public, and trying to intimidate someone into doing what you want with a loud voice and red face will only make you look bad.

hiking

การเดินป่า

Where can I ...?	จะ ... ได้ที่ไหน	jà ... dâi têe năi
buy supplies	ซื้อเสบียง	séu sà-bee-ang
find someone who knows this area	หาคนที่รู้จักพื้น ที่แถวๆ นี้	hăh kon têe róo jàk péun têe tăe·ou tăe·ou née
get a map	หาแผนที่	hăh păan têe
hire hiking gear	เช่าอุปกรณ์เดินป่า	chôw ùp·bà·gorn deun bàh

How ...?	... เท่าไร	... tôw-rai
high is the climb	การปีนสูง	gahn been sŏong
long is the trail	ทางไกล	tahng glai

Do we need a guide?
ต้องมีไกด์ไหม
đôrng mee gai măi

Are there guided treks?
มีการนำทางเดินป่าไหม
mee gahn nam tahng deun bàh măi

Can you recommend a trekking company?
คุณแนะนำบริษัทนำ
เที่ยวตามป่าได้ไหม
kun náe-nam bor-rí-sàt nam têe·o đahm bàh dâi măi

How many people will be on the trek?
จะเดินป่ากี่คน
jà deun bàh gèe kon

Do you provide transport?
บริการรถถึงที่ด้วยไหม
bor-rí-gahn rót tĕung têe dôo·ay măi

Exactly when does the trek begin and end?
การเดินเริ่มต้นและจบลง
ที่ไหนกันแน่
gahn deun rêum đôn láa jòp long têe năi gan nâe

Will there be other tourists in the area at the same time?

จะมีนักท่องเที่ยวคนอื่นอยู่แถว
นั้นในเวลาเดียวกันไหม

jà mee nák tông têe·o kon
èun yòo tăa·ou nán nai
wair-lah dee·o gan măi

Can the guide speak the local languages?

ไกด์พูดภาษาท้องถิ่นได้ไหม

gai pôot pah-săh tórng tìn
dâi măi

Is it safe?

ปลอดภัยไหม

bòrt pai măi

Are there land mines in the area?

มีทุ่นระเบิดฝังอยู่แถวนี้ไหม

mee tûn rá-bèut făng yòo
tăa·ou née măi

Is it safe to leave the trail?

ถ้าออกจากทางจะปลอดภัยไหม

tâh òrk jàhk tahng jà bòrt
pai măi

When does it get dark?

ตกค่ำกี่โมง

đòk kâm gèe mohng

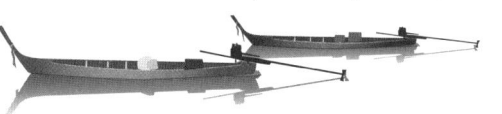

Do we need
to take ...?

จะต้องเอา ... ไป
ด้วยไหม

jà đôrng ow ... bai
dôo·ay măi

  bedding

เครื่องนอน

krêu·ang norn

  food

อาหาร

ah-hăhn

  water

น้ำ

nám

Is the track ...?

ทาง ... ไหม

tahng ... măi

  (well-)marked

หมายไว้ (ชัด)

măi wái (chát)

  open

เปิด

bèut

  scenic

มีทิวทัศน์สวย

mee tew-tát sŏo·ay

Which is
the ... route?

ทางไหน .... ที่สุด

tahng năi ... têe sùt

  easiest

ง่าย

ngâi

  most interesting

น่าสนใจ

nâh sŏn-jai

  shortest

ใกล้

glâi

Where can I find the …?	จะหา ... ได้ที่ไหน	jà hăh … dâi têe năi
camping ground	ค่ายพัก	kâi pák
nearest village	หมู่บ้านใกล้ที่สุด	mòo bâhn glâi têe sùt
showers	ห้องน้ำฝักบัว	hôrng nám fàk boo·a
toilets	ห้องส้วม	hôrng sôo·am

Where have you come from?
คุณเดินทางมาจากไหน
kun deun tahng mah jàhk năi

How long did it take?
ใช้เวลานานเท่าไร
chái wair-lah nahn tôw-rai

Does this path go to …?
ทางนี้ไป ... ไหม
tahng née bai … măi

Can I go through here?
ไปทางนี้ได้ไหม
bai tahng née dâi măi

Is the water OK to drink?
น้ำกินได้ไหม
nám gin dâi măi

I'm lost.
ฉันหลงทาง
chăn lŏng tahng

Where can I buy …?	จะซื้อ ... ได้ที่ไหน	jà séu … dâi têe năi
bottled water	น้ำดื่มขวด	nám dèum kòo·at
iodine	ไอโอดีน	ai-oh-deen
mosquito repellent	ยากันยุง	yah gan yung
water purification tablets	ยาเม็ดทำให้น้ำบริสุทธิ์	yah mét tam hâi nám bor-rí-sùt

beach

Where's the … beach?	ชายหาด ... อยู่ที่ไหน	chai hàht … yòo têe năi
best	ที่ดีที่สุด	têe dee têe sùt
nearest	ที่ใกล้ที่สุด	têe glâi têe sùt
public	สาธารณะ	săh-tah-rá-ná

ห้ามกระโดดน้ำ
hâhm grà-dòht nám **No Diving.**

ห้ามว่ายน้ำ
hâhm wâi nám **No Swimming.**

Is it safe to dive here?
ที่นี่กระโดดน้ำปลอดภัยไหม tée née grà-dòht nám blòrt
pai măi

Is it safe to swim here?
ที่นี่ว่ายน้ำปลอดภัยไหม tée née wâi nám blòrt
pai măi

What time is high/low tide?
น้ำ ขึ้น/ลง กี่โมง nám kêun/long gèe mohng

Do we have to pay?
จะต้องเสียเงินไหม jà đôrng sĕe·a ngeun măi

**Where can I
hire a …?** จะเช่า … ได้ที่ไหน jà chôw … dâi tée năi

  sea canoe เรือคนูทะเล reu·a ká-noo tá-lair
  windsurfer กระดานโต้ลม grà-dahn đôh lom

**How much for
a/an …?** … เท่าไร … tôw-rai

  chair เก้าอี้ gôw-êe
  umbrella ร่ม rôm

rá-wang grà-săa đâi nám
ระวังกระแสใต้น้ำ **Be careful of the undertow!**

an-đà-rai
อันตราย **It's dangerous!**

weather

What's the weather like?
อากาศเป็นอย่างไร   ah-gàht ben yàhng rai

What will the weather be like tomorrow?
พรุ่งนี้อากาศจะเป็นอย่างไร   prûng-née ah-gàht jà ben
yàhng rai

It's ...	มัน ...	man ...
cloudy	ฟ้าคลุ้ม	fáh klúm
cold	หนาว	nŏw
fine	แจ่มใส	jàam săi
flooding	กำลังน้ำท่วม	gam-lang nám tôo·am
hot	ร้อน	rórn
raining	มีฝน	mee fŏn
sunny	แดดจ้า	dàat jâh
warm	อุ่น	ùn
windy	มีลม	mee lom
Where can I buy ...?	จะซื้อ ... ได้ที่ไหน	jà séu .... dâi têe năi
a rain jacket	เสื้อกันฝน	sêu·a gan fŏn
an umbrella	ร่ม	rôm

For words and phrases related to seasons, see **time & dates**, page 37.

flora & fauna

What ... is that?	นั่น ... อะไร	nân ... à-rai
animal	สัตว์	sàt
flower	ดอกไม้	dòrk mái
plant	ต้น	đôn
tree	ต้นไม้	đôn mái

outdoors

151

What's it used for?
ใช้ประโยชน์อะไร

chái bprà-yòht à-rai

Can you eat the fruit?
ผลมันกินได้ไหม

pŏn man gin dâi măi

Is it …?	มัน … ไหม	man … măi
common	หาง่าย	hăh ngâi
dangerous	อันตราย	an-dà-rai
endangered	ใกล้จะสูญพันธุ์	glâi jà sŏon pan
protected	เป็นของสงวน	bpen kŏrng sà-ngŏo·an
rare	หายาก	hăh yâhk

bamboo	ไม้ไผ่	mái pài
cobra	งูเห่า	ngoo hòw
elephant	ช้าง	cháhng
king cobra	งูจงอาง	ngoo jong-ahng
monkey	ลิง	ling
orchid	กล้วยไม้	glôo·ay mái
tiger	เสือโคร่ง	sĕu·a krôhng

The cultural importance of food in Thailand can hardly be underestimated. In fact, a common Thai pleasantary is gin kŏw rĕu yang กินข้าวหรือยัง which means 'Have you eaten yet?'. If your answer is yang ยัง (lit: not yet) this chapter will help you put food on your plate.

key language

ศัพท์สำคัญ

breakfast	อาหารเช้า	ah-hăhn chów
lunch	อาหารกลางวัน	ah-hăhn glahng wan
dinner	อาหารเย็น	ah-hăhn yen
snack	อาหารว่าง	ah-hăhn wâhng

I'd like ...
ผม/ดิฉัน ต้องการ ... pŏm/dì-chăn đôrng gahn ... m/f

Please.	ขอ	kŏr
Thank you.	ขอบคุณ	kòrp kun
I'm starving!	หิวจะตาย	hĕw jà đai

finding a place to eat

การหาที่จะทานอาหาร

Where would you go for ...?	ถ้าคุณจะ ... คุณจะ ไปไหน	tâh kun jà ... kun jà bai năi
a cheap meal	ไปหาอาหา รราคาถูกๆ	bai hăh ah-hăhn rah-kah tòok tòok
local specialities	ไปหาอาหารรส เด็ดๆของแถวนี้	bai hăh ah-hăhn rót dèt dèt kŏrng tăa·ou née

Can you recommend a ...	แนะนำ ... ได้ ไหม	náa-nam ... dâi măi
bar	บาร์	bah
café	ร้านกาแฟ	ráhn gah-faa
Hainan chicken shop	ร้านข้าวมันไก่	ráhn kôw man gài
noodle shop	ร้านก๋วยเตี๋ยว	ráhn gŏo·ay đĕe·o
rice and curry shop	ร้านข้าวราดแกง	ráhn kôw râht gaang
rice and red pork shop	ร้านข้าวหมูแดง	ráhn kôw mŏo daang
rice gruel shop	ร้านโจ๊ก	ráhn jóhk
rice soup shop	ร้านข้าวต้ม	ráhn kôw đôm
restaurant	ร้านอาหาร	ráhn ah-hăhn

I'd like to reserve a table for ...	ผม/ดิฉัน อยากจะ จองโต๊ะสำหรับ ...	pŏm/dì-chăn yàhk jà jorng đó săm-ràp ... m/f
(two) people	(สอง) คน	(sŏrng) kon
(eight pm)	เวลา (สองทุ่ม)	wair-lah (sŏrng tûm)

I'd like ..., please.	ขอ ... หน่อย	kŏr ... nòy
a menu in English	รายการอาหาร เป็นภาษาอังกฤษ	rai gahn ah-hăhn ben pah-săh ang-grìt
a table for (five)	โต๊ะสำหรับ (ห้า) คน	đó săm-ràp (hâh) kon
nonsmoking	ที่เขตห้ามสูบบุหรี่	têe kèt hâhm sòop bù-rèe
smoking	ที่เขตสูบบุหรี่ได้	têe kèt sòop bù-rèe dâi
the drink list	รายการเครื่องดื่ม	rai gahn krêu·ang dèum
the menu	รายการอาหาร	rai gahn ah-hăhn

Are you still serving food?
ยังบริการอาหารไหม   yang bor-rí-gahn ah-hăhn măi

How long is the wait?
ต้องรอนานเท่าไร   đôrng ror nahn tôw-rai

at the restaurant

What would you recommend?
คุณแนะนำอะไรบ้าง — kun náa-nam à-rai bâhng

What's in that dish?
จานนั้นมีอะไร — jahn nán mee à-rai

I'll have that.
เอาอันนั้นนะ — ow an nán ná

Is service included in the bill?
ค่าบริการรวมในบิลล์ด้วยไหม — kâh bor-rí-gahn roo·am nai bin dôo·ay mǎi

Are these complimentary?
ของเหล่านี้แถมไหม — kǒrng lòw née tǎam mǎi

I'd like ...	อยากจะทาน ...	yàhk jà tahn ...
the chicken	ไก่	gài
a local speciality	อาหารพิเศษของถิ่นนี้สักอย่างหนึ่ง	ah-hǎhn pí-sèt kǒrng tìn née sàk yàhng nèung
a meal fit for a king	อาหารอย่างดี	ah-hǎhn yàhng dee

I'd like it with ...	ต้องการแบบมี ...	đôrng gahn bàap mee ...
I'd like it without ...	ต้องการแบบไม่มี ...	đôrng gahn bàap mâi mee ...
chilli	พริก	prík
garlic	กระเทียม	grà-tee·am
nuts	ถั่ว	tòo·a
oil	น้ำมัน	nám man

For other specific meal requests, see **vegetarian & special meals**, page 169.

listen for ...

kun chôrp ... măi
คุณชอบ ... ไหม **Do you like ...?**

jà hâi jàt tam yàhng rai
จะให้จัดท่าอย่างไร **How would you like that cooked?**

pŏm/dì-chăn kŏr náa-nam ... m/f
ผม/ดิฉัน ขอแนะนำ ... **I suggest the ...**

For more words you might see on a menu, see the **menu decoder**, page 171.

at the table

ที่โต๊ะอาหาร

Please bring ...	ขอ ... หน่อย	kŏr ... nòy
the bill	บิลล์	bin
a cloth	ผ้า	pâh
a serviette	ผ้าเช็ดปาก	pâh chét bàhk
a (wine)glass	แก้ว(ไวน์)	gâa·ou (wai)

FOOD

อาหารเรียกน้ำย่อย	ah-hǎhn rêe·ak nám yôy	**Appetisers**
น้ำซุป	nám súp	**Soups**
อาหารว่าง	ah-hǎhn wâhng	**Entrées**
ผักสด	pàk sòt	**Salads**
อาหารจานหลัก	ah-hǎhn jahn làk	**Main Courses**
ของหวาน	kǒrng wǎhn	**Desserts**
เหล้าให้เจริญอาหาร	lôw hâi jà-reun ah-hǎhn	**Aperitifs**
น้ำอัดลม	nám àt lom	**Soft Drinks**
สุรา	sù-rah	**Spirits**
เบียร์	bee·a	**Beer**
ไวน์ขาว	wai kǒw	**White Wine**
ไวน์แดง	wai daang	**Red Wine**

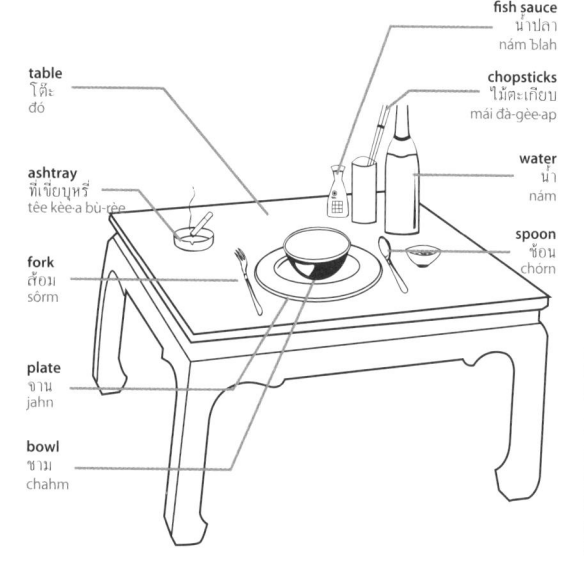

fish sauce
น้ำปลา
nám blah

chopsticks
ไม้ตะเกียบ
mái đà-gèe·ap

water
น้ำ
nám

spoon
ช้อน
chórn

table
โต๊ะ
đó

ashtray
ที่เขี่ยบุหรี่
têe kèe·a bù-rèe

fork
ส้อม
sôrm

plate
จาน
jahn

bowl
ชาม
chahm

talking food

I love this dish.
อาหารนี้ชอบจัง
ah-hǎhn née chôrp jang

I love the local cuisine.
ชอบอาหารท้องถิ่นมาก
chôrp ah-hǎhn tórng tìn mâhk

That was delicious!
อร่อยมาก
à-ròy mâhk

My compliments to the chef.
ขอฝากคำชมให้พ่อครัวด้วย
kǒr fàhk kam chom hâi pôr kroo·a dôo·ay

I'm full.
อิ่มแล้ว
ìm láa·ou

This is ...	อันนี้ ...	an née ...
(too) cold	เย็น (เกินไป)	yen (geun bai)
spicy	เผ็ด	pèt
superb	อร่อยมาก	à-ròy mâhk

breakfast

What's a typical breakfast?
ปกติอาหารเช้าทานอะไร
bò-gà-đì ah-hǎhn chów tahn à-rai

bacon	หมูเบค่อน	mǒo bair-kôrn
bread	ขนมปัง	kà-nǒm bang
butter	เนย	neu·i
cereal	ซีเรียล	see-ree·an

… egg(s)	ไข่ …	kài …
boiled	ต้ม	đôm
fried	ดาว	dow
hard-boiled	ต้มแข็ง	đôm kǎeng
poached	ทอดน้ำ	tôrt nám
scrambled	กวน	goo·an

milk	นม	nom
muesli	มิวส์ลี่	mew-lêe
omelette	ไข่เจียว	kài jee·o
rice gruel	โจ๊ก	jóhk
rice gruel with egg	โจ๊กใส่ไข่	jóhk sài kài
rice soup	ข้าวต้ม	kôw đôm
toast	ขนมปังปิ้ง	kà-nǒm bang bîng

For other breakfast items, see **self-catering**, page 165, and the **menu decoder**, page 171.

street food

What's that called?
อันนั้นเรียกว่าอะไร   an nán rêe·ak wâh à-rai

baked custard sweet	ขนมหม้อแกง	kà-nǒm môr gaang
coconut roasties	ขนมครก	kà-nǒm krók
deep-fried dough	ปาท่องโก๋	bah-tôrng-gǒh
mixed nuts	ไก่สามอย่าง	gài sǎhm yàhng
rice noodles	ก๋วยเตี๋ยว	gǒo·ay děe·o
roast chicken and sticky rice	ข้าวเหนียวไก่ย่าง	kôw něe·o gài yâhng
roast fish/meat balls	ลูกชิ้นปลา/เนื้อปิ้ง	lôok chín blah/ néu·a bîng
steamed buns	ซาลาเปา	sah-lah-bow
sweet sticky rice in bamboo	ข้าวหลาม	kôw lǎhm

condiments

Do you have ...?	มี ... ไหม	mee ... măi
chilli sauce	น้ำพริก	nám prík
dipping sauces	น้ำจิ้ม	nám jîm
fish sauce	น้ำปลา	nám ɓlah
ground peanuts	ถั่วลิสงป่น	tòo·a lí·sŏng ɓòn
ground red pepper	พริกป่น	prík ɓòn
ketchup/tomato sauce	ซอสมะเขือเทศ	sórt má·kĕu·a têt
pepper	พริกไทย	prík tai
salt	เกลือ	gleu·a
sliced hot chillies in fish sauce	พริกน้ำปลา	prík nám ɓlah
sliced chillies in vinegar	พริกน้ำส้ม	prík nám sôm

For additional items, see the **menu decoder**, page 171.

methods of preparation

I'd like it ...	ต้องการ ...	đôrng gahn ...
I don't want it ...	ไม่ต้องการ ...	mâi đôrng gahn ...
boiled	ต้ม	đôm
deep-fried	ทอด	tôrt
fried	ผัด	pàt
grilled	ย่าง	yâhng
medium	ปานกลาง	ɓahn glahng
rare	ไม่สุกมาก	mâi sùk mâhk
re-heated	อุ่นใหม่	ùn mài
spicy	เผ็ด	pèt
steamed	นึ่ง	nêung
well-done	สุกมากหน่อย	sùk mâhk nòy
without ...	ไม่มี ...	mâi mee ...

in the bar

Excuse me!
ขออภัย
kŏr à-pai

I'm next.
ฉันต่อไป
chăn đòr ɓai

I'll have …
จะเอา …
jà ow …

Same again, please.
ขออีกครั้งหนึ่ง
kŏr èek kráng nèung

No ice, thanks.
ไม่ใส่น้ำแข็ง ขอบคุณ
mâi sài nám kăang kòrp kun

I'll buy you a drink.
ฉันจะซื้อของดื่มให้คุณ
chăn jà séu kŏrng dèum
hâi kun

What would you like?
จะรับอะไร
jà ráp à-rai

It's my round.
ตาของฉันนะ
đah kŏrng chăn ná

How much is that?
เท่าไร
tôw-rai

Do you serve meals here?
ที่นี่บริการอาหารด้วยไหม
têe née bor-rí-gahn ah-hăhn
dôo·ay măi

---

listen for …

kít wâh kun dèum mâhk por láa·ou ná
คิดว่าคุณดื่มมากพอแล้วนะ **I think you've had enough.**

kun jà ráp à-rai
คุณจะรับอะไร **What are you having?**

sàng kráng sùt tái ná kráp/kâ m/f
สั่งครั้งสุดท้ายนะ ครับ/ค่ะ **Last orders.**

161

nonalcoholic drinks

... mineral water	น้ำแร่ ...	nám râa ...
sparkling	อัดลม	àt lom
still	ธรรมดา	tam-má-dah
... water	น้ำ ...	nám ...
boiled	ต้ม	đôm
purified	บริสุทธิ์	bor-rí-sùt
Chinese tea	น้ำชาจีน	nám chah jeen
iced coffee	กาแฟเย็น	gah-faa yen
iced lime juice	น้ำมะนาวใส่น้ำตาล	nám má-now sài
with sugar		nám-đahn
iced tea	น้ำชาเย็น	nám chah yen
orange juice	น้ำส้มคั้น	nám sôm kán
soft drink	น้ำอัดลม	nám àt lom
(hot) water	น้ำ (ร้อน)	nám (rórn)
(cup of) coffee	กาแฟ (ถ้วยหนึ่ง)	gah-faa (tôo·ay nèung)
(cup of) tea	ชา (ถ้วยหนึ่ง)	chah (tôo·ay nèung)
... with milk	... ใส่นม	... sài nom
... without	... ไม่ใส่	... mâi sài
sugar	น้ำตาล	nám-đahn
tea leaves	ใบชา	bai chah

coffee

black coffee	กาแฟดำ	gah-faa dam
decaffeinated	กาแฟไม่มีกาเฟอีน	gah-faa mâi
coffee		mee ga-fair-een
iced coffee	กาแฟเย็น	gah-faa yen
strong coffee	กาแฟแก่	gah-faa gàa
Thai filtered coffee	กาแฟถุง	gah-faa tǔng
weak coffee	กาแฟอ่อน	gah-faa òrn
white coffee	ใส่นม	sài nom

FOOD

162

alcoholic drinks

a shot of ...	... ช็อตหนึ่ง	... chórt nèung
distilled spirits	เหล้า	lôw
gin	จิน	jin
herbal liquor	เหล้ายาดอง	lôw yah dorng
jungle liquor	เหล้าเถื่อน	lôw tèu·an
Mekong whisky	วิสกีแม่โขง	wít·sà·gee mâa köhng
rum	เหล้ารัม	lôw ram
vodka	เหล้าวอดก้า	lôw vôrt·gâh
whisky	วิสกี้	wít·sà·gêe
white liquor	เหล้าขาว	lôw köw
a glass/bottle of ... wine	ไวน์ ... แก้วหนึ่ง/ ขวดหนึ่ง	wai ... gâa·ou nèung/ kòo·at nèung
red	แดง	daang
white	ขาว	köw
a ... of beer	เบียร์ ... หนึ่ง	bee·a ... nèung
glass	แก้ว	gâa·ou
jug	เหยือก	yèu·ak
large bottle	ขวดใหญ่ขวด	kòo·at yài kòo·at
pint	ไพนต์	pai
small bottle	ขวดเล็กขวด	kòo·at lék kòo·at

garçon!

When calling for the attention of a waiter or waitress, make sure you use the correct form of address. A waiter is called bŏy บ๋อย which is easy enough to remember – just think of the English word 'boy' and raise the tone as if you are asking a question.

A waitress is referred to as nórng น้อง (lit: younger) but this may also be used for both sexes.

drinking up

Cheers!
ไชโย — chai-yoh

This is hitting the spot.
เข้าท่า — kôw tâh

I feel fantastic!
รู้สึกดีมาก — róo-sèuk dee mâhk

I think I've had one too many.
สงสัยฉันดื่มมากไปสัก
แก้วหนึ่งกระมัง — sŏng-săi chăn dèum mâhk bai
sàk gâa·ou nèung grà-mang

I'm feeling drunk.
เมาแล้ว — mow láa·ou

I feel ill.
รู้สึกไม่สบาย — róo-sèuk mâi sà-bai

I think I'm going to throw up.
สงสัยจะอ้วก — sŏng-săi jà ôo·ak

Where's the toilet?
ห้องส้วมอยู่ไหน — hôrng sôo·am yòo năi

I'm tired, I'd better go home.
เหนื่อยแล้ว กลับบ้านดีกว่า — nèu·ay láa·ou, glàp bâhn dee
gwàh

Can you call a taxi for me?
เรียกแท็กซี่ให้หน่อยได้ไหม — rêe·ak táak-sêe hâi nòy dâi măi

I don't think you should drive.
คิดว่าคุณไม่ขับรถดีกว่า — kít wâh kun mâi kàp rót dee
gwàh

buying food

What's the local speciality?
อาหารรสเด็ดๆ ของแถว
นี้คืออะไร
ah-hǎhn rót dèt dèt kǒng
tǎe·ou née keu à-rai

What's that?
นั่นคืออะไร
nân keu à-rai

Can I taste it?
ชิมได้ไหม
chím dâi mǎi

Can I have a bag, please?
ขอถุงใบหนึ่ง
kǒr tǔng bai nèung

How much is (a kilo of mangoes)?
(มะม่วงกิโลหนึ่ง) เท่าไร
(má-môo·ang gì-loh nèung)
tôw-rai

How much?
เท่าไร
tôw-rai

Less.	น้อยลง	nóy long
A bit more.	มากขึ้นหน่อย	mâhk kêun nòy
Enough!	พอแล้ว	por láa·ou

listen for ...

mee à-rai jà hâi chôo·ay mǎi
มีอะไรจะให้ช่วยไหม **Can I help you?**

jà ow à-rai kráp/ká **m/f**
จะเอาอะไรครับ/คะ **What would you like?**

jà ow à-rai èek mǎi
จะเอาอะไรอีกไหม **Would you like anything else?**

(hâh) bàht
(ห้า) บาท **That's (five) baht.**

I'd like ...	ต้องการ ...	đôrng gahn ...
(200) grams	(สองร้อย) กรัม	(sŏrng róy) gram
half a dozen	ครึ่งโหล	krêung lŏh
a dozen	โหลหนึ่ง	lŏh nèung
half a kilo	ครึ่งกิโล	krêung gì-loh
a kilo	กิโลหนึ่ง	gì-loh nèung
(two) kilos	(สอง) กิโล	(sŏrng) gì-loh
a bottle	ขวดหนึ่ง	kòo·at nèung
a jar	กระปุกหนึ่ง	grà-bùk nèung
a packet	ห่อหนึ่ง	hòr nèung
a piece	ชิ้นหนึ่ง	chín nèung
(three) pieces	(สาม) ชิ้น	(săhm) chín
a slice	ชิ้นหนึ่ง	chín nèung
(six) slices	(หก) ชิ้น	(hòk) chín
a tin	กระป๋องหนึ่ง	grà-bŏrng nèung
(just) a little	(แต่) นิดหน่อย	(đàa) nít-nòy
more	อีก	èek
that one	อันนั้น	an nán
this one	อันนี้	an née

Do you have ...?	มี ... ไหม	mee ... măi
anything cheaper	ถูกกว่า	tòok gwàh
other kinds	ชนิดอื่น	chá-nít èun

cooked	สุก	sùk
cured	บ่ม	bòm
dried	ตากแห้ง	đàhk hâang
fresh	สด	sòt
frozen	แช่แข็ง	châa kăang
smoked	อบควัน	òp kwan
raw	ดิบ	dip
pickled	ดอง	dorng

Where can I find the ... section?	จะหาแผนก ... ได้ที่ไหน	jà hăh pà-nàak ... dâi têe năi
dairy	อาหารจำพวกนม	ah-hăhn jam-pôo·ak nom
fish	ปลา	blah
frozen goods	อาหารแช่แข็ง	ah-hăhn châa kăng
fruit and vegetable	ผักผลไม้	pàk pŏn-lá-mái
meat	เนื้อ	néu·a
poultry	เนื้อไก่	néu·a gài

fruity farangs

One of the first words that many people learn in Thailand is fà-ràng ฝรั่ง which means a foreigner of Western descent. There are several theories as to the origin of the word. One of the most popular is that fà-ràng is an abbrevation of fà-ràng seht (French person).

More accurately, the word relates to the Germanic Franks who participated in the crusades. The name gave rise to the arabic word *faranji* meaning European Christian (hence 'foreigner' in the Middle East) and reached Thailand via Persian trade routes.

Neighbouring countries have very similar words for foreigner. In Cambodia, Westerners are called *barang*, and in Vietnam they are called *pha-rang* or *pha-lang-xa*. In Thailand fà-ràng also means 'guava' (possibly because guavas are not native to Thailand), so Westerners seen eating guavas may find themselves the butt of silly puns.

cooking utensils

Could I please borrow a/an …?	ขอยืม … หน่อย	kŏr yeum … nòy
I need a/an …	ต้องการ …	đôrng gahn …
bottle opener	เครื่องเปิดขวด	krêu·ang bèut kòo·at
bowl	ชาม	chahm
can opener	เครื่องเปิดกระป๋อง	krêu·ang bèut grà·bŏrng
chopping board	เขียง	kěe·ang
chopsticks	ตะเกียบ	đà·gèe·ap
corkscrew	เหล็กไขจุกขวด	lèk kǎi jùk kòo·at
cup	ถ้วย	tôo·ay
fork	ส้อม	sôrm
fridge	ตู้เย็น	đôo yen
frying pan	กระทะ	grà·tá
glass	แก้ว	gâa·ou
knife	มีด	mêet
meat cleaver	มีดสับ	mêet sàp
microwave	ตู้ไมโครเวฟ	đôo mai-kroh-wêp
oven	เตาอบ	đow òp
plate	จาน	jahn
rice cooker	หม้อหุงข้าว	môr hǔng kôw
saucepan	หม้อ	môr
spoon	ช้อน	chórn
wok	กระทะ	grà·tá

vegetarian & special meals

ordering food

การสั่งอาหาร

I eat only vegetarian food.
ผม/ดิฉัน ทานแต่อาหารเจ
pŏm/dì-chăn tahn đàa ah-hăhn jair m/f

Is there a … restaurant near here?
มีร้านอาหาร … อยู่แถวๆ นี้ไหม
mee ráhn ah-hăhn … yòo tăa·ou tăa·ou née măi

Do you have … food?	มีอาหาร … ไหม	mee ah-hăhn … măi
halal	อาหารที่จัดทำตาม หลักศาสนาอิสลาม	ah-hăhn têe jàt tam đahm làk sàht- sà-năh ìt-sà-lahm
kosher	อาหารที่จัดทำตาม หลักศาสนายิว	ah-hăhn têe jàt tam đahm làk sàht- sà-năh yew
vegetarian	เจ	jair

I don't eat …
ผม/ดิฉัน ไม่ทาน …
pŏm/dì-chăn mâi tahn … m/f

Is it cooked in/ with …?
อันนี้ทำกับ … ไหม
an née tam gàp … măi

Could you prepare a meal without …?	ทำอาหารไม่ ใส่ … ได้ไหม	tam ah-hăhn mâi sài … dâi măi
butter	เนย	neu·i
eggs	ไข่	kài
fish	ปลา	ฺblah
meat stock	ซุปก้อนเนื้อ	súp gôrn néu·a
MSG	ชูรส	choo-rót
pork	เนื้อหมู	néu·a mŏo
poultry	เนื้อไก่	néu·a gài
red meat	เนื้อแดง	néu·a daang

169

special diets & allergies

I'm (a) …	ผม/ดิฉัน …	pŏm/dì-chăn … m/f
vegan	ไม่ทานอาหารที่	mâi tahn ah-hăhn
	มาจากสัตว์	têe mah jàhk sàt
vegetarian	ทานอาหารเจ	tahn ah-hăhn jair

I'm on a special diet.
ผม/ดิฉัน ทานอาหารพิเศษ pŏm/dì-chăn tahn ah-hăhn
pí-sèt m/f

I'm allergic to …	ผม/ดิฉัน แพ้ …	pŏm/dì-chăn páa …
chilli	พริก	prík
dairy produce	อาหารจำพวกนม	ah-hăhn jam-pôo·ak nom
eggs	ไข่	kài
gelatine	วุ้น	wún
gluten	แป้ง	bâang
honey	น้ำผึ้ง	nám pêung
MSG	ชูรส	choo-rót
nuts	ถั่ว	tòo·a
seafood	อาหารทะเล	ah-hăhn tá-lair
shellfish	หอย	hŏy

go nuts

Note that in Thai the generic word for nuts (tòo·a ถั่ว) also includes beans. So you need to specify precisely which variety of nuts you are allergic to. Refer to the dictionary for individual nut varieties.

menu decoder
พจนานุกรมอาหาร

These Thai dishes and ingredients are listed alphabetically, by pronunciation, so you can easily understand what's on offer and ask for what takes your fancy.

Can you recommend a local speciality?

แนะนำ อาหารรสเด็ดๆของ   náa-nam ah-hǎhn rót dèt
แถวนี้ได้ไหม   dèt kõrng tǎa-ou née dâi mǎi

Do you serve …?

มี … ไหม   mee … mǎi

b

bai đeu-i ใบเตย *pandanus leaves – used primarily to add a vanilla-like flavour to Thai sweets*

bai đorng ใบตอง *banana leaves*

bai gà-prow ใบกะเพรา *'holy basil' – so-called due to its sacred status in India*

bai hõh-rá-pah ใบโหระพา *'sweet basil' – a hardy, large-leafed plant used in certain* gaang *(curries), seafood dishes & especially* pàt pèt *(hot stir-fries)*

bai maang-lák ใบแมงลัก *known variously as Thai basil, lemon basil or mint basil – popular in soups & as a condiment for* kà-nôm jeen nám yah & láhp

bai mà-gròot ใบมะกรูด *kaffir lime leaves*

bai sà-rá-naa ใบสะระแหน่ *native spearmint leaves used in* yam & láhp *& eaten raw in North-Eastern Thailand*

bà-mèe บะหมี่ *yellowish noodles made from wheat flour & sometimes egg*

bà-mèe gée-o boo บะหมี่เกี๊ยวปู *soup containing* bà-mèe, *won ton & crab meat*

bà-mèe hâang บะหมี่แห้ง *bà-mèe served in a bowl with a little garlic oil, meat, seafood or vegetables*

bà-mèe nám บะหมี่น้ำ *bà-mèe with broth, meat, seafood or vegetables*

boo-a loy บัวลอย *'floating lotus' – boiled sticky rice dumplings in a white syrup of sweetened & lightly salted coconut milk*

bòo-ap บวบ *gourd*

bòo-ap lèe-am บวบเหลี่ยม *sponge gourd*

bòo-ap ngoo บวบงู *snake gourd*

ъ

ъah-tôrng-gòh ปาท่องโก๋ *fried wheat pastry similar to an unsweetened doughnut*

bèt เป็ด *duck*

bèt đũn เป็ดตุ๋น *steamed duck soup generally featuring a broth darkened by soy sauce & spices such as cinnamon, star anise or Chinese five-spice*

bèt yâhng เป็ดย่าง *roast duck*

ъlah ปลา *fish*

ъlah bèuk ปลาบึก *giant Mekong catfish*

171

blah chôm ปลาช่อน serpent-headed fish – a freshwater variety

blah daak dee-o-o ปลาแดกเดียว see blah-rah

blah daat dèe-o ปลาตากเดียว 'half-day dried fish' – fried & served with a spicy mango salad

blah duk ปลาดุก catfish

blah ga-dàk ปลากะตัก type of anchovy used in nám blah (fish sauce)

blah ga-pong ปลากะพง ocean perch • seabass

blah gŏw ปลาเก๋า grouper • reef cod

blah gòp-bòrk ปลากระบอก mullet

blah kem ปลาเค็ม preserved salted fish

blah klúk ka-min ปลาคลุกขมิ้น fresh fish rubbed with a paste of turmeric, garlic & salt before grilling or frying

blah lài ปลาไหล freshwater eel

blah lòt ปลาหลด saltwater eel

blah mèuk gloo-ay ปลาหมึกกล้วย squid • calamari

blah mèuk grà-dorng ปลาหมึกกระดอง cuttlefish

blah mèuk pàt pong ga-rèe ปลาหมึกผัดผงกะหรี่ squid stir-fried in curry powder

blah mèuk bîng ปลาหมึกปิ้ง dried, roasted squid flattened into a sheet via a hand-cranked press then toasted over hot coals – a favourite night-time street snack

blah nèung bóoay ปลานึ่งบ๊วย freshwater fish steamed with Thai lemon basil, lemon-grass & any other vegetables (North-East Thailand)

blah nin ปลานิล tilapia (variety of Thailand)

blah pòw ปลาเผา fish wrapped in banana leaves or foil & roasted over (or covered in) hot coals

blah sah-deen ปลาซาร์ดีน sardine

blah săm-lee ปลาสำลี cottonfish

blah săm-lee dàat dèe-o ปลาสำลีตากเดียว 'half-day-dried cottonfish' – whole cottonfish sliced lengthways & left to dry in the sun for half a day, then fried quickly in a wok

blah săm-lee pòw ปลาสำลีเผา 'fire-roasted cottonfish' – cottonfish roasted over coals

blah too ปลาทู mackerel

blah-rah ปลาร้า 'rotten fish' – unpasteurised version of nám blah sold in earthenware jars (North-East Thailand)

bòr daak ปอแตก 'broken fish trap soup' – mòm yam with the addition of either sweet or holy basil & a melange of seafood, usually including squid, crab, fish, mussels & shrimp

boo ปู crab

boo nah ปูนา field crabs

boo òp wún-sên ปูอบวุ้นเส้น bean thread noodles baked in a lidded, clay pot with crab & seasonings

boo pàt pong ga-rèe ปูผัดผงกะหรี่ crab in the shell stir-fried in curry powder & eggs

boo ta-lair ปูทะเล sea crab

bor-bée-a tôrt เปาะเปี๊ยะทอด egg rolls

bor-bée-a sòt เปาะเปี๊ยะสด fresh spring rolls

bor-bée-a tôrt เปาะเปี๊ยะทอด fried spring rolls

c

cha-om ชะอม bitter acacia leaf

chom-pôo ชมพู่ rose apple

d

daang moh แตงโม watermelon

da-gôh ตะโก้ popular steamed sweet made from tapioca flour & coconut milk over a layer of sweetened seaweed gelatine

da-krai ตะไคร้ lemongrass – used in curry pastes, tôm yam, yam & certain kinds of lahp

đam màhk hùng ตำหมากหุ่ง *see* sôm đam

đam sôm ตำส้ม *see* sôm đam

đam-ráp gàp kòw ตำรับกับข้าว *basic
handed-down recipes*

đôm ต้ม *Isaan soup similar to* đôm yam
*made with lemongrass, galangal, spring
onions, kaffir lime leaves & fresh whole
prik kêe nŏo, seasoned before serving
with lime juice & fish sauce (also known
as* đôm sàap)

đôm brêe-o ต้มเปรี้ยว *'boiled sour' –* đôm
yam *soup with added tamarind*

đôm fàk ต้มฟัก *Isaan* đôm *made with
green squash, often eaten with duck
salad*

đôm gài sài bai má-kǎhm òrn ต้มไก่ใส่ใบ
มะขามอ่อน *Isaan* đôm *made with
chicken & tamarind leaves*

đôm kàh gài ต้มข่าไก่ *'boiled galangal
chicken' – includes lime, chilli & coconut
milk (Central Thailand)*

đôm sàap ต้มแซบ *see* đôm

đôm woo-a ต้มวัว *Isaan* đôm *made with
beef tripe & liver*

đôm yam ต้มยำ *popular soup made with
chilli, lemongrass, lime & usually
seafood*

đôm yam gûng ต้มยำกุ้ง *shrimp yam*

đôm yam hâang ต้มยำแห้ง *a dry version of*
đôm yam gûng

đôm yam bò đàak ต้มยำโป๊ะแตก đôm yam
with mixed seafood

đôn glôo-ay ต้นกล้วย *cross-section of the
heart of the banana stalk*

đôn hôrm ต้นหอม *'fragrant plant' – spring
onion or scallions*

đôw hôo เต้าหู้ *tofu (soybean curd)*

đôw jèe-o เต้าเจี้ยว *paste of salted, fermented soybeans, either yellow or black*

đôw jèe-o dam เต้าเจี้ยวดำ *black-bean
sauce*

f

fák ฟัก *gourd • squash*

fák kěe-o ฟักเขียว *wax gourd*

fák ngoo ฟักงู *snake or winter melon*

fák torng ฟักทอง *golden squash or Thai
pumpkin*

fà-ràng ฝรั่ง *guava (the word also refers to
a Westerner of European descent)*

fěu เฝือ *another name for* gŏo-ay-děe-o
(rice noodles)

fŏy torng ฝอยทอง *'golden threads' – small
bundle of sweetened egg-yolk threads in
Thai desserts*

g

gaang แกง *classic chilli-based curries for
which Thai cuisine is famous, as well as
any dish with a lot of liquid (thus it can
refer to soups)*

gaang bàh แกงป่า *'forest curry' – spicy
curry which uses no coconut milk*

gaang đai blah แกงไตปลา *curry made with
fish stomach, green beans, pickled bamboo
shoots & potatoes (South Thailand)*

gaang gah-yŏo แกงกะหยู *curry made
with fresh cashews – popular in Phuket
& Ranong*

gaang gà-rèe gài แกงกะหรี่ไก่ *curry similar
to an Indian curry, containing potatoes
& chicken*

gaang hang-lair แกงฮังเล *rich Burmese-
style curry with no coconut milk*

gaang hó แกงโฮะ *spicy soup featuring
pickled bamboo shoots (North Thailand)*

gaang jèut แกงจืด *'bland soup' – plain
Cantonese-influenced soup in which
cubes of soft tofu, green squash, Chinese radish, bitter gourd, ground pork
& mung bean noodles are common
ingredients*

menu decoder

gaang jèut wún sên un — bean noodle soup, *gaang jèut* mung bean

gaang kàa un — soup made with saw-tooth coriander & bitter eggplant (North Thailand)

gaang ka-nŭn un — jackfruit curry – favoured in Northern Thailand but found elsewhere as well

gaang kĕe-o wăhn un — green curry

gaang kôo-a sàp-ba-rót un — a pan-roasted pineapple curry

gaang lee-ang un — spicy soup of green or black peppercorns, sponge gourd, baby corn, cauliflower & various greens, substantiated with pieces of chicken, shrimp or ground pork – probably one of the oldest recipes in Thailand

gaang lĕu-ang un — 'yellow curry' – spicy dish of fish cooked with green squash, pineapple, green beans & green papaya (South Thailand)

gaang mát-sà-màn un — Indian-influenced Muslim curry featuring a cumin, cinnamon & cardamom spice mix

gaang mèt ma-môo-ang him-ma-pahn un — cashew curry made with fresh cashews

gaang mòm un — Mon curry

gaang pàk hŏo-an un — soup containing tamarind juice (North Thailand)

gaang pàk wahn un — soup with 'sweet greens' (North Thailand)

gaang pà-naang un — similar to a regular red curry but thicker, milder & without vegetables

gaang pèt un — red curry

gaang pèt bèt yâang un — duck roasted Chinese-style in five-spice seasoning & mixed into Thai red curry

gaang sôm un — sour curry made with dried chillies, shallots, garlic & Chinese key (gra-chai)

gaang yôo-ak un — Kŏw rice over rice soupy, sweet

gah-làh — torch ginger – thinly-sliced flower buds from a wild ginger plant, sometimes used in the Southern Thai rice salad Kòw yam

gài — chicken

gài bair-dong — Betong dish of steamed chicken, chopped & seasoned with locally made soy sauce then stir-fried with vegetables

gài bîng — chicken grilled in the North-Eastern (Isaan) style (see *gài yâang*)

gài dun — steamed chicken soup generally featuring a broth darkened by soy sauce & spices such as cinnamon, star anise or Chinese five-spice mixture

gài hòr bai deu-i — chicken marinated in soy sauce & wrapped in pandanus leaves along with sesame oil, garlic & coriander root, then fried or grilled & served with a dipping sauce similar to the marinade

gài pat king — chicken stir-fried with ginger, garlic & chillies, seasoned with fish sauce

gài pàt mét ma-môo-ang him-ma-pahn — stir-fried sliced chicken in dried chillies & cashews

gài sahm yàhng — 'three kinds of chicken' – chicken, chopped ginger, peanuts, chilli peppers & lime pieces to be mixed together & eaten by hand

gài tôrt — fried chicken

gài yâhng ไก่ย่าง Isaan-style grilled chicken (gài bîng or gài bîng in Isaan dialect) marinated in garlic, coriander root, black pepper & salt or fish sauce & cooked slowly over hot coals

ga-bì น้ำพริก shrimp paste

gàp glâam กับแกล้ม 'drinking food' – dishes specifically meant to be eaten while drinking alcoholic beverages

ga-rèe แกง Thai equivalent of the Anglo-Indian term 'curry'

gà-tí น้ำกะทิ coconut milk

gíaw ต้ม won ton – triangle of dough wrapped around ground pork or fish

glûay กล้วย banana

glûay bòo-at chee กล้วยบวชชี 'ordaining bananas' – banana chunks floating in a white syrup of sweetened & lightly salted coconut milk

glûay hŏrm กล้วยหอม fragrant banana

glûay kài กล้วยไข่ 'egg banana' – native to Kamphaeng Phet

glûay lép meu nahng กล้วยเล็บมือนาง 'princess fingernail banana' – native to Chumphon Province in Southern Thailand

glûay náam wáh กล้วยน้ำว้า thick-bodied, medium-length banana

glûay tôrt กล้วยทอด batter-fried banana

gòh-bee กาแฟ Thai Hokkien dialect for coffee, used especially in Trang province

gòh-bee dam กาแฟดำ sweetened black coffee (Trang province)

gòh-bee dam mâi sài nám-dahn กาแฟดำไม่ใส่น้ำตาล unsweetened black coffee (Trang province)

gòo-ay ก๋วยเตี๋ยว rice noodles made from pure rice flour mixed with water to form a paste which is then steamed to form wide, flat sheets

gŏo-ay dĕe-o ก๋วยเตี๋ยวแห้ง dry rice noodles

gŏo-ay dĕe-o hâhng su-kŏh-tai ก๋วยเตี๋ยวแห้งสุโขทัย 'Sukhothai dry rice noodles' – thin rice noodles served in a bowl with peanuts, barbecued pork, ground dried chilli, green beans & bean sprouts

gŏo-ay dĕe-o jan-ta-bù-ree ก๋วยเตี๋ยวจันทบุรี (Chanthaburi) dried rice noodles

gŏo-ay dĕe-o lôok chín blah ก๋วยเตี๋ยวลูกชิ้นปลา rice noodles with fish balls

gŏo-ay dĕe-o náam ก๋วยเตี๋ยวน้ำ rice noodles served in a bowl of plain chicken or beef stock with bits of meat, pickled cabbage & a coriander-leaf garnish

gŏo-ay dĕe-o pàt ก๋วยเตี๋ยวผัด fried rice noodles with sliced meat, Chinese kale, soy sauce & various seasonings – a favourite crowd-pleaser at temple festivals all over the country

gŏo-ay dĕe-o pàt kêe mow ก๋วยเตี๋ยวผัดขี้เมา 'drunkard's fried noodles' – wide rice noodles, fresh basil leaves, chicken or pork, seasonings & fresh sliced chillies

gŏo-ay dĕe-o pàt tai ก๋วยเตี๋ยวผัดไทย a plate of thin rice noodles stir-fried with dried or fresh shrimp, beansprouts, fried tofu, egg & seasonings (pàt tai for short)

gŏo-ay dĕe-o râht nâh ก๋วยเตี๋ยวราดหน้า noodles braised in a light gravy made with cornstarch-thickened stock, then combined with either pork or chicken, Chinese broccoli or Chinese kale & oyster sauce

gŏo-ay dĕe-o râht nâh ta-lair ก๋วยเตี๋ยวราดหน้าทะเล with seafood

gŏo-ay dĕe-o reu-a ก๋วยเตี๋ยวเรือ 'boat noodles' – concoction of dark beef broth & rice noodles originally sold only on boats that frequented the canals of Rangsit

góo-ay jáp น้ำ thick broth of sliced Chinese mushrooms & bits of chicken or pork

gòp กบ frog – used as food in Northern & North-Eastern Thailand

góy หมู raw spicy minced-meat salad

gôy woo-a เนื้อ raw spicy minced-meat salad of beef

grà-chai กระชาย Chinese key – root in the ginger family used as a traditional remedy for a number of gastrointestinal ailments

grà-yah-sàh-rot กระยาสารท sweet, popular at certain Buddhist festivals

gung น้ำ refers to a variety of different shrimps, prawns & lobsters

gung gù-lah-dam กุ้งกุลาดำ tiger prawn

gung mang-gorn กุ้งมังกร dragon prawn' – refers to lobster

gung pàt king กุ้งผัดขิง prawns stir-fried in ginger

gung pàt sà-dor กุ้งผัดสะตอ beans stir-fried with chillies, shrimp & shrimp paste (South Thailand)

gung súp bpáang tôrt กุ้งชุบแป้งทอด batter-fried shrimp

h

hâng gà-ti น้ำกะทิ coconut milk

het hörm เห็ดหอม shiitake mushrooms

hom daang หอมแดง shallots • scallions

hǒo-a blee kà-tón หัวปลี banana flower – a purplish, oval-shaped bud that has a tart & astringent mouth feel when eaten raw as an accompaniment to lâhp in the North-East

hǒo-a gà-ti น้ำกะทิ coconut cream

hǒo-a blee kà-ti หัว Chinese radish

hǒo-a pàk gàht หัวผักกาด giant white radish

hòr mok ห่อหมก hòr mòk soufflé-like dish made by steaming a mixture of red curry paste, beaten eggs, coconut milk & fish in a banana-leaf cup (Central Thailand)

hòr mok ta-lair ห่อหมกทะเล hòr mòk made by steaming a mixture of red curry paste, beaten eggs, coconut milk & mixed seafood in a banana-leaf cup (Central Thailand)

hòr mok Koy ma-laang พอ green mussel shells – hòr mòk cooked inside green mussel shells

hoy หอย clams & oysters (generic)

hoy kraang หอยแครง cockle

hoy ma-laang pôo หอยแมลงภู่ green mussel

hoy nahng rom หอยนางรม oyster

hoy pat หอยพัด scallop

hoy tort หอยทอด fresh oysters quickly fried with beaten eggs, mung bean sprouts & sliced spring onions (Central Thailand)

j

jáo-ou nám เจา see nám jáo-ou

jáo-ou hom น้ำเจา North-Eastern version of Central Thailand's popular Thai sukiyaki (su-gêe-yah-gêe) but includes beef entrails, egg, water spinach, cabbage & cherry tomatoes

jóhk gài ไก่ thick rice soup with chicken

jóhk mŏo หมู thick rice soup with pork – meatballs

k

kàh ข่า galangal (also known as Thai ginger)

kài fu ไข่ฟู egg

kài ไข่ egg

kài blah mòk ไข่ปลาหมก eggs in their shells skewered on a sharp piece of bamboo & grilled over hot coals

kài blah mòk ไข่ปลาหมก egg, fish & red curry paste steamed in a banana-leaf cup & topped with strips of kaffir lime leaves (South Thailand)

kai jee-o ไข่เจียว Thai omelette – offered as a side dish or filler for a multidish meal

kai look keu-i ไข่ลูกเขย 'son-in-law eggs' – eggs that are boiled then fried and served with a sweet sauce

kai mot daang ไข่มดแดง a red ant larvae used in soups (North-East Thailand)

kài pàk bûng ไข่ผักบุ้ง small green plant that grows on the surface of ponds, bogs & other still waters (North-East Thailand)

kai pat het hoo noo ไข่ผัดเห็ดหูหนู stir-fried with mouse-ear mushrooms

kai sai ไข่ไส้ omelette wrapped around a filling of fried ground pork, tomatoes, onions & chillies

kà-min ขมิ้น turmeric – popular in South-ern Thai cooking

ka-nom beu-ang ขนมเบื้อง Vietnamese vegetable crepe prepared in a wok

ka-nom bow-lang ขนมบ้าหลัง a mix of black sticky rice, shrimp, coconut, black pepper & chilli steamed in a banana-leaf packet – favoured by Thai Muslims in Ao Phang-Nga

ka-nom jeen ขนมจีน 'Chinese Pastry' – rice noodles produced by pushing rice-flour paste through a sieve into boiling water – served on a plate & mixed with various curries

ka-nom jeen chow nam ขนมจีนหน้าน้ำ noodle dish featuring a mixture of pineapple, coconut, dried shrimp, ginger & garlic served with ka-nom jeen

ka-nom jeen nam ngèe-o ขนมจีนน้ำเงี้ยว sweet & spicy Yunnanese noodle dish with pork rib meat, tomatoes & black-bean sauce fried with a curry paste of chillies, coriander root, lemongrass, galangal, turmeric, shallots, garlic & shrimp paste

ka-nom jeen nam yah ขนมจีนน้ำยา thin Chinese rice noodles doused in a Malay-style ground fish curry sauce served with fresh cucumbers, steamed long green beans, parboiled mung bean sprouts, grated papaya, pickled cabbage & fresh pineapple chunks (South Thailand)

ka-nom jeen tôrt man ขนมจีนทอดมัน thin rice noodles with fried fish cake from Phetchaburi

ka-nom jèep ขนมจีบ Chinese dumplings filled with shrimp or pork

ka-nom krôk ขนมครก lightly salted & sweetened mixture of coconut milk & rice flour poured into half-round moulds in a large, round iron grill

ka-nom mor gaang ขนมหม้อแกง double-layered baked custard from Phetchaburi, made with puréed mung beans, eggs, coconut milk & sugar

ka-nom tee-an ขนมเทียน 'candle pastry' – mixture of rice or corn flour, sweetened coconut milk & sesame seeds, steamed in a tall slender banana-leaf packet

ka-nom tôo-ay ขนมถ้วย sweet made from tapioca flour & coconut milk steamed in tiny porcelain cups

ka-nun ขนุน jackfruit (also known as mahk mèe in Isaan dialect)

keun-chài ขึ้นฉ่าย Chinese celery

king ขิง ginger

kôrng cham ของชำ refers to sundries like vegetable oil, fish sauce, sugar, soy sauce, salt, coffee, dried noodles, canned food, rice, curry paste, eggs, liquor & cigarettes

kôrng wahn ของหวาน sweets

kôw ข้าว rice

kôw blow ข้าวเปล่า plain rice

kôw bao ข้าวเบา 'light rice' – early season rice

kow bra-dap din ข้าวประดับดิน 'earth-adorn-ing rice' – small lumps of rice left as offerings at the base of temple stupas or beneath banyan trees during Buddhist festivals kǒw bǔn ข้าวปุ้น *Lao/Isaan term for ka-nŏm jeen*

kǒw châa ข้าวแช่ *soupy rice eaten with small bowls of assorted foods*

kǒw châa pét-bù-ree ข้าวแช่เพชรบุรี *moist chilled rice served with sweetmeats – a hot season Mon speciality*

kǒw đôm ข้าวต้ม *boiled rice soup, a popular late-night meal*

kǒw đôm gà-tí ข้าวต้มกะทิ *Thai sweets made of sticky rice, coconut milk & grated coconut wrapped in a banana leaf*

kǒw đôm mát ข้าวต้มมัด *Thai sweets made of sticky rice & coconut milk, black-beans or banana pieces wrapped in a banana leaf*

kǒw đôn reu-doo ข้าวต้นฤดู *'early season' rice*

kǒw gaang ข้าวแกง *curry over rice*

kǒw glahng ข้าวกลาง *'middle rice' – rice that matures mid-season*

kǒw glàm ข้าวกล่ำ *type of sticky rice with a deep purple, almost black hue, for use in desserts and, in Northern Thailand, to produce a mild home-made rice wine of the same name*

kǒw glôrng ข้าวกล้อง *brown rice*

kǒw grée-ap gúng ข้าวเกรียบกุ้ง *shrimp chips*

kǒw hǒrm má-lí ข้าวหอมมะลิ *jasmine rice*

kǒw jôw ข้าวเจ้า *white rice*

kǒw kôo-a bòn ข้าวคั่วป่น *uncooked rice dry-roasted in a pan till it begins to brown, then pulverised with a mortar & pestle – one of the most important ingredients in* lâhp

kǒw lǎhm ข้าวหลาม *sticky rice & coconut steamed in a bamboo joint, a Nakhon Pathom speciality*

kǒw man gài ข้าวมันไก่ *Hainanese dish of sliced steamed chicken over rice cooked in chicken broth & garlic*

kǒw môk gài ข้าวหมกไก่ *Southern version of chicken biryani – rice & chicken cooked together with cloves, cinnamon & turmeric, traditionally served with a bowl of plain chicken broth, a roasted chilli sauce & sliced cucumbers, sugar & red chillies*

kǒw mǒo daang ข้าวหมูแดง *red pork over rice*

kǒw nah bee ข้าวนาปี *'one-field-per-year' rice*

kǒw nah brang ข้าวนาปรัง *'off-season' rice*

kǒw nàk ข้าวหนัก *'heavy rice' – late season rice*

kǒw něe-o ข้าวเหนียว *sticky rice that is popular in Northern & North-Eastern Thailand*

kǒw něe-o má-môo-ang ข้าวเหนียวมะม่วง *sliced fresh ripe mangoes served with sticky rice and sweetened with coconut milk*

kǒw pàt ข้าวผัด *fried rice*

kǒw pàt bai gà-prow ข้าวผัดใบกะเพรา *chicken or pork stir-fry served over rice with basil*

kǒw pàt mǒo kài dow ข้าวผัดหมูไข่ดาว *fried rice with pork and a fried egg*

kǒw pàt nâam ข้าวผัดแหนม *fried rice with* nâam

kǒw pôht ข้าวโพด *corn*

kǒw pôht òrn ข้าวโพดอ่อน *baby corn*

kǒw râht gaang ข้าวราดแกง *curry over rice*

kǒw râi ข้าวไร่ *plantation rice or mountain rice*

kǒw sǎhn ข้าวสาร *unmilled rice*

kǒw sǒo-ay ข้าวสวย *cooked rice*

kǒw soy ข้าวซอย *a Shan or Yunnanese egg-noodle dish with chicken or beef curry, served with shallot wedges, sweet-spicy pickled cabbage, lime & a thick red chilli sauce* kôw yam ข้าวยำ traditional breakfast of cooked dry rice, grated toasted coconut, bean sprouts, kaffir lime leaves, lemon-grass & dried shrimp, with powdered chilli & lime (South Thailand)

krêu-ang gaang เครื่องแกง a curry paste created by mashing, pounding & grinding an array of ingredients with a stone mortar & pestle to form an aromatic, thick & very pungent-tasting paste (also known as nám prík gaang)

krêu-ang gaang pèt เครื่องแกงเผ็ด red krêu-ang gaang made with dried red chillies

l

lahng sàht ลางสาด oval-shaped fruit with white fragrant flesh, grown in Utaradit Province

lâhp ลาบ spicy minced meat salad made by tossing minced meat, poultry or fresh-water fish with lime juice, fish sauce, chillies, fresh mint leaves, chopped spring onion & pulverised rice (North-Eastern Thailand)

lâhp bèt ลาบเป็ด duck lâhp, an Ubon Ratchathani speciality

lâhp bèt daang ลาบเป็ดแดง a red duck lâhp which uses duck blood as part of the sauce

lâhp bèt kŏw ลาบเป็ดขาว white duck lâhp

lam yai ลำไย longan fruit (also known as 'dragon's eyes')

la-mut ละมุด sapodilla fruit

lôok chin plah ลูกชิ้นปลา fish balls

lôok gra-wahn ลูกกระวาน cardamom

lôok sùp paddì ลูกชุบ 'dipped fruit' – sweets made of soybean paste, sugar & coconut milk that are boiled, coloured & fashioned to look exactly like miniature fruits & vegetables

m

maang dah nah แมงดานา a water beetle found in rice fields & used in certain kinds of nám prík (chilli & shrimp paste)

ma-da-ba มะตะบะ roti (unleavened bread) stuffed with chopped chicken or beef with onions & spices

ma-fai มะไฟ rambeh fruit

ma-gòrk มะกอก astringent-flavoured fruit resembling a small mango (also known in English as amberella, Thai olive or Otaheite apple)

ma-gròot มะกรูด kaffir lime – small citrus fruit with a bumpy & wrinkled skin

ma-kâhm มะขาม tamarind

ma-kâhm bee-ak มะขามเปียก the flesh & seeds of the husked tamarind fruit pressed into red-brown clumps

ma-kěu-a มะเขือ eggplant • aubergine

ma-kěu-a bro มะเขือเปราะ 'Thai eggplant' – popular curry ingredient

ma-kěu-a poo-ang มะเขือพวง 'pea egg-plant' – popular curry ingredient, espe-cially for gaang kěe-o-wǎhn

ma-kěu-a têt มะเขือเทศ tomatoes

ma-kěu-a yow มะเขือยาว 'long eggplant' – also called Japanese eggplant or Oriental eggplant in English

ma-lá-gor sòok มะละกอสุก paw paw • papaya

ma-môo-ang มะม่วง mango

man fa-ràng tôrt มันฝรั่งทอด fried potatoes

man fa-ràng มันฝรั่ง potato

man gâ-ou มันแกว yam root • *jícama*

ma-now มะนาว lime

ma-prow òrn มะพร้าวอ่อน young green coconut

ma-prow มะพร้าว coconut

mee pan น้ำพัน spicy mix of thin rice noo-dles, bean sprouts & coriander leaf rolled in rice paper – a specialty of Laplae district in Uttaradit Province

mée-ang kam เมี่ยงคำ do-it-yourself appetiser in which chunks of ginger, shallot, peanuts, coconut flakes, lime & dried shrimp are wrapped in wild tea leaves or lettuce

mét má-môo-ang hǐm-má-pahn tórt เม็ดมะม่วงหิมพานต์ทอด fried cashew nuts

moo òp หมูอบ roasted pork

moo daang หมูแดง strips of bright red barbecued pork

moo sǎhm chán หมูสามชั้น 'three level pork' – cuts that include meat, fat & skin

moo yâhng หมูย่าง grilled strips of pork eaten with spicy dipping sauces

mǒo yor หมูยอ sausage resembling a large German frankfurter

น

naam mǒo หนามหมู pickled pork

naam หนาม 'pot sausage' – sausage made of ground pork, pork rind & cooked sticky rice & fermented in a clay pot with salt, garlic & chilli (North Thailand)

nòr mái หน่อไม้ bamboo shoots

nòr mái bree-o หน่อไม้เปรี้ยว pickled bamboo shoots

nám blah น้ำปลา fish sauce – thin, clear, amber sauce made from fermented anchovies & used to season Thai dishes

nám boo น้ำปู condiment made by pounding small field crabs into a paste & then cooking the paste in water until it becomes a slightly sticky black liquid (North Thailand)

nám dòw น้ำเต้า bottle gourd

nám jâa-ou น้ำแจ่ว Isaan dipping sauce for chicken, made by pounding dried red chilli flakes with shallots, shrimp paste & a little tamarind juice to make a thick jam-like sauce (also known as jà-ou)

nám jîm น้ำจิ้ม seafood dipping sauce, prík nám blah with the addition of minced garlic, lime juice & sugar

nám jîm gài น้ำจิ้มไก่ chicken dipping sauce – a mixture of dried red chilli flakes, honey (or sugar) & rice vinegar

nám kǎang got น้ำแข็งก้อน frozen sweets made with ice, sugar, & a little fruit juice

nám kǎang sǎi น้ำแข็งใส desserts with ice sugar, raw cane sugar, shrimp paste, fish sauce, salt, black pepper, shallots, galangal, kaffir lime leaves & lemon-grass (South Thailand)

nám mée-ang น้ำเมี่ยง ginger, shallot, shrimp paste, fish sauce & honey dip eaten with mee-ang with kâm

nám kǎo น้ำข้าว sweet & spicy topping for ka-nom jeen (North Thailand)

nám òy น้ำอ้อย raw, lumpy cane sugar • sugar cane juice

nám prík น้ำพริก thick chilli- & shrimp-paste dip usually eaten with fresh raw or steamed vegetables • a spicy-sweet peanut sauce used as a topping for ka-nom jeen (rice noodles)

nám prík chée fáh น้ำพริกชี้ฟ้า dipping sauce featuring dried chilli, garlic oil, salt & sugar – often cooked briefly to blend all the flavours & darken the chilli (North-East Thailand)

nám prík dàh daang น้ำพริกตาแดง 'red eye chilli dip' – very dry & hot

nám prík gaang น้ำพริกแกง see krêu-ang gaang

nám prík gà-bì น้ำพริกกะปิ nám prík *made with shrimp paste & fresh* prík kêe nöo *('mouse-dropping' chilli), usually eaten with mackerel that has been steamed & fried, or with fried serpent-headed fish (Central Thailand)*

nám prík kàh น้ำพริกข่า chilli dip made with galangal – often served with steamed or roasted fresh mushrooms (North Thailand)

nám prík maang dah น้ำพริกแมงดา water beetle chilli paste

nám prík nám bòo น้ำพริกน้ำปู chilli paste made with nám bòo, shallots, garlic & dried chillies (North Thailand)

nám prík nùm น้ำพริกหนุ่ม young chilli-paste dip made of fresh green chillies & roasted eggplant (North Thailand)

nám prík òrng น้ำพริกอ่อง chilli paste made by pounding dried red chillies, ground pork, tomatoes, lemongrass & various herbs, then cooking them till the pork is done (North Thailand)

nám prík pöw น้ำพริกเผา thick paste made with dried chillies roasted together with gà-bì & then mortar-blended with fish sauce & a little sugar or honey (often eaten with gài yâhng)

nám prík sêe-rah-chah น้ำพริกศรีราชา thick, orange, salty-sweet-sour-spicy bottled chilli sauce from Si Racha (south-east of Bangkok on the Gulf of Thailand)

nám see-éw น้ำซีอิ๊ว soy sauce

nám sôm prík น้ำส้มพริก sliced green chillies in vinegar

nám yah น้ำยา standard curry topping for kà-nöm jeen, made of Chinese key (grà-chai) & ground or pounded fish

nám-dahn béep น้ำตาลปีบ soft, light palm sugar paste – the most raw form of palm sugar

néu-a เนื้อ beef

néu-a dûn เนื้อตุ๋น steamed beef soup generally featuring a broth darkened by soy sauce & spices such as cinnamon, star anise or Chinese five-spice

néu-a nám dòk เนื้อน้ำตก 'waterfall beef' – sliced barbecued beef in a savoury dressing of lime juice, ground chilli & other seasonings

néu-a pàt nám-man höy เนื้อผัดน้ำมันหอย beef stir-fried in oyster sauce

nóy-nàh น้อยหน่า custard apple

p

pàt tai ผัดไทย abbreviation of göo-ay dée-o pàt tai

prík bòn พริกป่น dried red chilli (usually nám prík chée fáh), flaked or ground to a near powder

prík chée-fáh พริกชี้ฟ้า 'sky-pointing chilli' – also known as spur chilli, Thai Chilli and Japanese chilli

prík kêe nöo พริกขี้หนู 'mouse-dropping chilli' – the hottest chilli in Thailand (also known as bird's-eye chilli)

prík nám blah พริกน้ำปลา standard condiment of sliced fresh red & green prík kêe nöo (chilli) floating in fish sauce

prík nám sôm พริกน้ำส้ม young prík yòo-ak pickled in vinegar – a condiment popular with noodle dishes & Chinese food

prík tai พริกไทย black pepper (also known in English as Thai pepper)

prík wähn พริกหวาน 'sweet pepper' – green bell pepper

prík yòo-ak พริกหยวก banana-stalk chilli – a large chilli usually cooked or pickled

menu decoder

181

r

raht náa ราดหน้า shortened name for any gŏo-ay-dĕe-o ráht náa dish, frequently used when ordering

rahk prík รากพริก chillies smothered in garlic, chillies & onions – usually accompanies freshwater fish

roh-dee โรตี flat wheat bread, round & flat descended from the Indian paratha

roh-dee gaang โรตีแกง roti dipped in the sauce from a chicken, beef or crab curry

roh-dee glôo-ay โรตีกล้วย roti stuffed with fresh banana chunks or banana paste & sprinkled with sugar & condensed milk

roh-dee kài โรตีไข่ roti cooked with egg

s

sah-lah-bow ซาลาเปา steamed buns filled with stewed pork or sweet bean paste

see-ew dam ซีอิ๊วดำ black soy, – heavy, dark soy sauce

see-ew kŏw ซีอิ๊วขาว white soy, – light soy sauce

Kôy sauce

sow mǎm น้ำพริก sauce of pineapple, dried shrimp, coconut, ginger & garlic used as a topping for ka-nŏm jeen

sup ka-nún ซุปขนุน jackfruit soup with lime juice & chilli

sup ma-keu-a ซุปมะเขือ eggplant soup with Kôo-a bon, lime juice & chilli (North-East Thailand)

sup nor mái ซุปหน่อไม้ bamboo shoot soup – boiled or pickled bamboo shoots with Kôo-a bon, lime juice & chilli (North-East Thailand)

sa-dé néu-a satáy – short skewers of barbecued beef, pork or chicken that are served with a spicy peanut sauce

sa-dé moo สะเต๊ะหมู satáy pork

sa-dé néu-a สะเต๊ะเนื้อ satáy beef

sa-dor สะตอ a large, flat bean with a bitter taste (South Thailand)

sài òo-a ไส้อั่ว sausage made from a curry paste of dried chillies, garlic, shallots, lemongrass & kaffir lime peel, blended with ground pork, stuffed into pork intestines & then fried to produce a spicy red sausage (North Thailand)

sâng-ka-yah สังขยา custard

sâng-ka-yah fák torng สังขยาฟักทอง custard-filled pumpkin

sàp-pá-rót สับปะรด pineapple

sên-ràa-nâa เส้นราดหน้า mini

sên lék เส้นเล็ก thick rice noodles

sên mèe เส้นหมี่ thin rice noodles

sên yài เส้นใหญ่ medium-thick rice noodles

sôm dam ส้มตำ tart & spicy salad usually made with green paw paw (also known as dam som or dam mâhk hung)

sôm kĕe-o wǎhn ส้มเขียวหวาน mandarin orange

sôm oh ส้มโอ pomelo – popular in Northern Thailand

su-gêe ซูกี้ common abbreviation of su-gêe-yah-gêe (see below)

su-gêe-yah-gêe ซูกี้ยากี้ "hotpot" – peculiar Thai-Japanese hybrid involving a large stationary pot sitting on a gas burner to which diners add raw ingredients such as mung bean noodles, egg, water spinach & cabbage (Central Thailand)

t

tòo-a bon ถั่วป่น ground peanuts

tòo-a fák yow ถั่วฝักยาว long bean, yard bean, green bean, or cow pea

tòo-a lan-dow ถั่วลันเตา snow peas

tòo-a leu-ang ถั่วเหลือง soya bean

tòo-a ngôrk ถั่วงอก mung bean sprouts

tôa-a poo ถั่วพู angle bean – long green, bean-like vegetable which when cut into cross sections produces a four-pointed star

tòo-a tôrt ถั่วทอด fried peanuts

tàp-tim gròp ทับทิมกรอบ 'crisp rubies' – red-dyed chunks of fresh water chestnut in a white syrup of sweetened & slightly salted coconut milk

tòrt man blah ทอดมันปลา fried fish cake

tòrt man gûng ทอดมันกุ้ง fried shrimp cake

W

wún-sên วุ้นเส้น jellylike noodles made from mung bean & water to produce an almost clear noodle (sometimes called cellophane noodles, 'glass noodles' or bean thread noodles) in English

Y

yam dì ยำ hot & tangy salad containing a blast of lime, chilli, fresh herbs & a choice of seafood, roast vegetables, noodles or meats

yam blah dùk foo ยำปลาดุกฟู hot & tangy salad with fried shredded catfish, chillies, peanuts & a mango dressing

yam blah mèuk ยำปลาหมึก hot & tangy salad with squid

yam gài ยำไก่ hot & tangy salad with chicken & mint

yam het hǒrm ยำเห็ดหอม hot & tangy salad made with fresh shiitake mush-rooms

yam kài dow ยำไข่ดาว hot & tangy salad with fried eggs

yam ma-kěu-a yow ยำมะเขือยาว hot & tangy salad created by tossing a fresh-roasted or grilled long eggplant with shrimp, lime juice, ground pork, corian-der leaf, chillies, garlic & fish sauce

yam ma-môo-ang ยำมะม่วง hot & tangy salad with mango

yam met ma-môo-ang him-ma-pahn dì ยำเม็ดมะม่วงหิมพานต์ spicy cashew nut salad

yam néu-a ยำเนื้อ hot & tangy salad with grilled beef

yam prìk chée fáh ยำพริกชี้ฟ้า hot & tangy salad featuring พริกชี้ฟ้า nám prìk chée fáh fish bladder & cashew nuts mixed with nám blah, sugar, lime juice & chilli

yam sôm oh ยำส้มโอ hot & tangy salad made with pomelo (Chiang Mai)

yam tòa-a poo ยำถั่วพู hot & tangy salad with angle beans

yam wún-sên ยำวุ้นเส้น spicy salad made with warm mung bean noodles tossed with lime juice, fresh sliced prik kêe nǒo, mushrooms, dried or fresh shrimp, ground pork, coriander leaf, lime juice & fresh sliced chillies

yée-rah ยี่หร่า cumin

Mátsàman kaeng kâew taa
hăwm yîiràa rót ráwn raeng
chaai dai dâi kleun kaeng
raeng yàak hâi fài fān hăa

'Mátsàman, curried by the jewel of my eye,
fragrant with cumin, hot strong taste
Any man who has tasted her curry,
cannot help but dream of her.'

King Rama II composed this verse during his 1809-24 reign and virtually every Thai child memorises it in school. The poem reinforces a traditional Thai claim that a woman who prepares a good curry is *sanèh plaai ja-wàk* (the charm at the end of the ladle). The fact that a Buddhist king wrote an ode associated with a dish that translates as 'Muslim curry' shows how Indian style curries have long been accepted into the cosmopolitan culture of Thai cuisine. Here's how you can make it yourself:

Khrêuang kaeng mátsàman (Muslim curry paste)
- 5 peeled shallots
- 4 green peppercorns
- 2 whole heads of garlic, peeled
- 2 cloves
- 1 teaspoon minced fresh galangal
- 1 teaspoon salt
- 1 tablespoon coriander seeds
- 1 teaspoon cumin seeds
- 1 teaspoon shrimp paste
- 1 tablespoon sliced fresh lemongrass
- 4 dried red prík chée-fáh (sky-pointing chillies)

Slice open the dried chillies, shake out and discard the seeds and soak the chillies in warm water until they are soft and flexible.

Roast all other ingredients, one at a time, in a dry skillet or wok until aromatic and only slightly browned. Grind and mash all ingredients together in a mortar until a thick red-brown paste is formed. Adds lyrical relish to chicken, beef or vegetable dishes.

สิ่งจำเป็น

Help!	ช่วยด้วย	chôo·ay dôo·ay
Stop!	หยุด	yùt
Go away!	ไปให้พ้น	ɓai hâi pón
Thief!	ขโมย	kà·moy
Fire!	ไฟไหม้	fai mâi
Watch out!	ระวัง	rá·wang

It's an emergency.
เป็นเหตุฉุกเฉิน
ɓen hèt chùk·chĕun

Call a doctor!
ตามหมอหน่อย
đahm mŏr nòy

Call an ambulance!
ตามรถพยาบาล
đahm rót pá·yah·bahn

I'm ill.
ผม/ดิฉัน ป่วย
pŏm/dì·chăn ɓòo·ay m/f

My friend is ill.
เพื่อนของ ผม/ดิฉัน ป่วย
pêu·an kŏrng pŏm/dì·chăn ɓòo·ay m/f

My child is ill.
ลูกของ ผม/ดิฉัน ป่วย
lôok kŏrng pŏm/dì·chăn ɓòo·ay m/f

My friend has had an overdose.
เพื่อนของ ฉันเสพยาเกินขนาด
pêu·an kŏrng chăn sèp yah geun kà·nàht

He/She is having a/an …	เขากำลัง …	kŏw gam·lang …
allergic reaction	เกิดอาการแพ้	gèut ah·gahn páa
asthma attack	เป็นโรคหืด	ɓen rôhk hèut
baby	คลอดลูก	klôrt lôok
epileptic fit	เป็นลมบ้าหมู	ɓen lom bâh mŏo
heart attack	หัวใจวาย	hŏo·a jai wai

signs

แผนกฉุกเฉิน pà-nàak chùk-chĕun	**Emergency Department**
โรงพยาบาล rohng pá-yah-bahn	**Hospital**
ตำรวจ đam-ròo·at	**Police**
สถานีตำรวจ sà-tăh-nee đam-ròo·at	**Police Station**

Could you please help?
ช่วยได้ไหม — chôo·ay dâi măi

Can I use your phone?
ใช้โทรศัพท์ของคุณได้ไหม — chái toh-rá-sàp kŏrng kun dâi măi

I'm lost.
ผม/ดิฉัน หลงทาง — pŏm/dì-chăn lŏng tahng m/f

Where are the toilets?
ห้องน้ำอยู่ที่ไหน — hôrng nám yòo têe năi

police

ตำรวจ

Where's the police station?
สถานีตำรวจอยู่ที่ไหน — sà-tăh-nee đam-ròo·at yòo têe năi

Please telephone the Tourist Police.
ขอโทรตามตำรวจ
นักท่องเที่ยว — kŏr toh đahm đam-ròo·at nák tôrng têe·o

I want to report an offence.

ผม/ดิฉัน อยากจะแจ้งความ   pŏm/dì-chăn yàhk jà jâang kwahm m/f

I've been …   ผม/ดิฉัน โดน …   pŏm/dì-chăn dohn … m/f

He/She has been …   เขาโดน …   kŏw dohn …
   assaulted   ทำร้ายร่างกาย   tam rái râhng gai
   drugged   วางยา   wahng yah
   raped   ข่มขืน   kòm kĕun
   robbed   ขโมย   kà-moy

It was him/her.

เป็นคนนั้น   ben kon nán

My … was stolen.   … ของ ผม/ดิฉัน   … kŏrng pŏm dì-chăn
   ถูกขโมย   tòok kà-moy m/f
   backpack   เป้   bâir
   handbag   กระเป๋าหิ้ว   grà-bŏw hêw
   jewellery   เพชรพลอย   pét ploy
   money   เงิน   ngeun
   wallet   กระเป๋าเงิน   grà-bŏw ngeun

I've lost my …   ผม/ดิฉัน ทำ …   pŏm/dì-chăn tam …
   หายแล้ว   hăi láa-ou m/f
   bags   กระเป๋า   grà-bŏw
   credit card   บัตรเครดิต   bàt krair-dìt
   papers   เอกสาร   èk-gà-săhn
   passport   หนังสือเดินทาง   năng-sĕu deun tahng
   travellers cheques   เช็คเดินทาง   chék deun tahng

I have insurance.

ผม/ดิฉัน มีประกันอยู่   pŏm/dì-chăn mee brà-gan yòo m/f

You're charged with ...	คุณโดนจับ ข้อหา ...	kun dohn jàp kôr hăh ...
He/She is charged with ...	เขาโดนจับ ข้อหา ...	kŏw dohn jàp kôr hăh ...
assault	ทำร้ายร่างกาย	tam rái râhng gai
disturbing the peace	ก่อกวนความสงบ	gòr goo·an kwahm sà·ngòp
drug trafficking	การค้ายาเสพติด	gahn káh yah sèp đìt
littering	การทิ้งขยะ ไม่เป็นที่	gahn tíng kà·yà mâi ben têe
not having a visa	การไม่มีวีซ่า	gahn mâi mee wee·sâh
overstaying your visa	การอยู่เกินกำหนด ของวีซ่า	gahn yòo geun gam·nòt kŏrng wee·sâh
possession (of illegal substances)	การมีของผิด กฎหมายในความ ครอบครอง	gahn mee kŏrng pìt gòt·măi nai kwahm krôrp krorng
rape	การข่มขืน	gahn kòm kĕun
shoplifting	การขโมยของ ในร้าน	gahn kà·moy kŏrng nai ráhn
theft	การขโมย	gahn kà·moy

It's a ... fine.	เป็นการหมาย ปรับโทษ ...	ben gahn măi bràp tôht ...
littering	การทิ้งขยะ ไม่เป็นที่	gahn tíng kà·yà mâi ben têe
parking	การจอดรถผิด กฎหมาย	gahn jòrt rót pìt gòt·măi
speeding	การขับรถเร็ว เกินกำหนด	gahn kàp rót re·ou geun gam·nòt

What am I accused of?
ผม/ดิฉัน ถูกปรับข้อหาอะไร
pŏm/dì-chăn tòok bràp kôr
hăh à-rai m/f

I'm sorry.
ขอโทษ
kŏr tôht

I (don't) understand.
(ไม่) เข้าใจ
(mâi) kôw jai

I didn't realise I was doing anything wrong.
ผม/ดิฉัน ไม่รู้เลยว่าทำ
อะไรผิด
pŏm/dì-chăn mâi róo leu·i
wâh tam à-rai pìt m/f

I didn't do it.
ผม/ดิฉัน ไม่ได้ทำ
pŏm/dì-chăn mâi dâi tam m/f

Can I pay an on-the-spot fine?
เสียค่าปรับที่นี่ได้ไหม
sĕe·a kâh bràp têe née dâi măi

I want to contact my embassy.
ผม/ดิฉัน อยากจะติดต่อสถานทูต
pŏm/dì-chăn yàhk jà dìt
dòr sà-tăhn tôot m/f

I want to contact my consulate.
ผม/ดิฉัน อยากจะติดต่อกงศุล
pŏm/dì-chăn yàhk jà dìt
dòr gong-sŭn m/f

Can I make a phone call?
โทรได้ไหม
toh dâi măi

Can I have a lawyer who speaks English?
ขอทนายความที่พูดภาษา
อังกฤษได้ไหม
kŏr tá-nai kwahm têe pôot
pah-săh ang-grìt dâi măi

I didn't know that was in there.
ผม/ดิฉัน ไม่รู้ก่อนเลยว่ามีสิ่ง
นั้นอยู่ข้างในนั้น
pŏm/dì-chăn mâi róo gòrn
leu·i wâh mee sìng nán yòo
kâhng nai nán m/f

That's not mine.
นั่นไม่ใช่ของ ผม/ดิฉัน
nân mâi châi kŏrng pŏm/
dì-chăn m/f

This drug is for personal use.
ยานี้สำหรับการใช้ส่วนตัว
yah née săm-ràp gahn chái
sòo·an đoo·a

I have a prescription for this drug.

ผม/ดิฉัน มีใบสั่งจาก
แพทย์สำหรับยานี้

pŏm/dì-chăn mee bai sàng
jàhk pâat săm-ràp yah née m/f

What's the penalty for possession of …?	กำหนดโทษเท่าไร สำหรับการมี … ในค วามครอบครอง	gam-nòt tôht tôw-rai săm-ràp gahn mee … nai kwahm krôrp krorng
amphetamines	ยาบ้า	yah bâh
heroin	เฮโรอีน	hair-roh-een
marijuana	กัญชา	gan-chah
opium	ยาฝิ่น	yah fìn
psilocybin mushrooms	เห็ดขี้ควาย	hèt kêe kwai

Where's the nearest …?	… ที่ใกล้เคียง อยู่ที่ไหน	… têe glâi kee·ang yòo têe nǎi
(night) chemist	ร้านขายยา (กลางคืน)	ráhn kǎi yah (glahng keun)
dentist	หมอฟัน	mǒr fan
doctor	หมอ	mǒr
emergency department	แผนกฉุกเฉิน	pà-nàak chùk-chĕun
health centre (in rural areas)	สถานีอนามัย	sà-tǎh-nee à-nah-mai
hospital	โรงพยาบาล	rohng pá-yah-bahn
medical centre	คลินิก	klí-ník
optometrist	หมอตรวจสายตา	mǒr đròo·at sǎi đah

I need a doctor (who speaks English).

ผม/ดิฉัน ต้องการหมอ
(ที่พูดภาษาอังกฤษได้)

pǒm/dì-chǎn đôrng gahn mǒr (têe pôot pah-sǎh ang-grìt dâi) **m/f**

Could I see a female doctor?

พบกับคุณหมอผู้หญิงได้ไหม

póp gàp kun mǒr pôo yǐng dâi mǎi

Could the doctor come here?

หมอมาที่นี่ได้ไหม

mǒr mah têe née dâi mǎi

Is there an after-hours emergency number?

มีเบอร์โทรสำหรับเหตุฉุก
เฉินนอกเวลาทำงานไหม

mee beu toh sǎm-ràp hèt chùk-chĕun nôrk wair-lah tam ngahn mǎi

I've run out of my medication.

ยาของ ผม/ดิฉัน หมดแล้ว

yah kǒrng pǒm/dì-chǎn mòt láa·ou **m/f**

What's the problem?
เป็นอะไร ครับ/ค่ะ m/f   ɓen à-rai kráp/kâ **m/f**

Where does it hurt?
เจ็บตรงไหน   jèp đrong năi

Do you have a temperature?
มีไข้ไหม   mee kâi măi

How long have you been like this?
เป็นอย่างนี้มานานเท่าไร   ɓen yàhng née mah nahn tôw-rai

Have you had this before?
เคยเป็นไหม   keu·i ɓen măi

Have you had unprotected sex?
ได้มีเพศสัมพันธ์โดยขาด   dâi mee pêt săm-pan doy kàht
การป้องกันหรือเปล่า   gahn ɓông gan rĕu ɓlòw

Are you using contraception?
คุณใช้การคุมกำเนิด   kun chái gahn kum gam-
ไหม   nèut măi

Have you drunk unpurified water?
ได้ดื่มน้ำที่ไม่สะอาดไหม   dâi dèum nám têe mâi sà-àht măi

Are you allergic to anything?
คุณแพ้อะไรไหม   kun páa à-rai măi

Are you on medication?
คุณกำลังใช้ยาอยู่ไหม   kun gam-lang chái yah yòo măi

How long are you travelling for?
คุณจะเดินทางนานเท่าไร   kun jà deun tahng nahn tôw-rai

You need to be admitted to hospital.
คุณจะต้องเข้าโรง   kun jà đông kôw rohng
พยาบาล   pá-yah-bahn

You should have it checked when you go home.
เมื่อกลับถึงบ้านควรจะ   mêu·a glàp tĕung bâhn koo·an
ไปตรวจ   jà ɓai đròo·at

You should return home for treatment.
คุณควรจะกลับบ้าน   kun koo·an jà glap bâhn
เพื่อรักษา   pêu·a rák-săh

You're a hypochondriac.
คุณอุปาทาน   kun ùp-ɓah-tahn

This is my usual medicine.
นี่คือยาที่ ใช้ประจำ née keu yah têe chái bra-jam

I don't want a blood transfusion.
ไม่ต้องการถ่ายโลหิต mâi dôrng gahn tài loh-hìt

Please use a new syringe.
ขอใช้เข็มใหม่ kŏr chái kĕm mài

I have my own syringe.
ฉันมีเข็มของตัวเอง chăn mee kĕm kŏrng đoo·a eng

Can I have a receipt for my insurance?
ขอใบเสร็จด้วยสำหรับ kŏr bai sèt dôo·ay săm-ràp
บริษัทประกัน bor-rí-sàt bra-gan

I've been	ผม/ดิฉันได้ฉีดป้อง	pŏm/dì-chăn dâi
vaccinated	กันโรค ... แล้ว	chèet bŏrng gan
against ...		rôhk ... láa·ou m/f
He/She has been	เขาฉีดป้อง	kŏw chèet bŏrng
vaccinated	กันโรค ... แล้ว	gan rôhk ... láa·ou
against ...		
Japanese B	ไข้สมองอักเสบ	kâi sà-mŏrng
encephalitis		àk-sèp
rabies	พิษสุนัขบ้า	pít sù-nák bâh
tetanus	บาดทะยัก	bàht tá-yák
typhoid	ไข้รากสาดน้อย	kâi râhk sàht nóy
hepatitis A/B/C	ตับอักเสบ เอ/บี/ซี	đàp àk-sèp air/ bee/see

symptoms & conditions

อาการป่วย

I'm sick.
ผม/ดิฉัน ป่วย pŏm/dì-chăn bòo·ay m/f

My friend/child is sick.
เพื่อน/ลูกของ ผม/ pêu·an/lôok kŏrng pŏm/
ดิฉัน ป่วย dì-chăn bòo·ay m/f

It hurts here.
เจ็บตรงนี้ jèp đrong née

I've been ...	ผม/ดิฉัน ...	pŏm/dì-chăn ... m/f
He/She has been ...	เขา ...	kŏw ...
injured	บาดเจ็บ	bàht jèp
vomiting	อาเจียน	ah-jee-an

I feel ...	ผม/ดิฉันรู้สึก ...	pŏm/dì-chăn róo-sèuk ... m/f
anxious	กังวลใจ	gang-won jai
better	ดีขึ้น	dee kêun
depressed	กลุ้มใจ	glûm jai
dizzy	เวียนหัว	wee·an hŏo·a
hot and cold	หนาว ๆ ร้อน ๆ	nŏw nŏw rórn rórn
nauseous	คลื่นไส้	klêun sâi
shivery	ตัวสั่น	đoo·a sàn
strange	แปลกๆ	blàak blàak
weak	อ่อนเพลีย	òrn plee·a
worse	ทรุดลง	sút long

I have (a/an) ...	ผม/ดิฉัน ...	pŏm/dì-chăn ... m/f
He/She has (a/an) ...	เขา ...	kŏw ...
asthma	เป็นโรคหืด	ben rôhk hèut
constipation	เป็นท้องผูก	ben tórng pòok
cough	เป็นไอ	ben ai
dengue fever	เป็นไข้เลือดออก	ben kâi lêu·at òrk
depression	เป็นโรคกลุ้มใจ	ben rôhk glûm jai
diarrhoea	เป็นท้องร่วง	ben tórng rôo·ang
fever	เป็นไข้	ben kâi
fungal infection	ติดเชื้อรา	đìt chéu·a rah
heat exhaustion	แพ้แดด	páa dàat
heatstroke	แพ้แดด	páa dàat
intestinal worms	เป็นพยาธิ	ben pá-yâht
liver fluke	เป็นพยาธิใบไม้	ben pá-yâht bai mái
malaria	เป็นไข้มาเลเรีย	ben kâi mah-lair-ree·a
nausea	คลื่นไส้	klêun sâi
pain	ปวด	bòo·at
prickly heat	เป็นผด	ben pòt
sore throat	เจ็บคอ	jèp kor

I'm dehydrated.
ผม/ดิฉัน ขาดน้ำ

pŏm/dì-chăn kàht nám **m/f**

I can't sleep.
นอนไม่หลับ

norn mâi làp

I think it's the medication I'm on.
คิดว่าเป็นเพราะยาที่
กำลังใช้อยู่

kít wâh ben pró yah têe
gam-lang chái yòo

women's health

สุขภาพผู้หญิง

(I think) I'm pregnant.
(ดิฉันคิดว่า) ตั้งท้องแล้ว

(dì-chăn kít wâh) đâng
tórng láa·ou

I'm on the Pill.
ดิฉันกินยาคุมกำเนิดอยู่

dì-chăn gin yah kum gam-
nèut yòo

the doctor may say ...

Are you using contraception?
คุณใช้การคุมกำเนิดไหม

kun chái gahn kum gam-
nèut măi

Are you menstruating?
คุณเป็นระดูไหม

kun ben rá-doo măi

Are you pregnant?
คุณตั้งครรภ์หรือเปล่า

kun đâng kan rĕu blòw

When did you last have your period?
คุณมีระดูครั้งที่แล้วเมื่อไร

kun mee rá-doo kráng tee
láa·ou mêu·a rai

You're pregnant.
คุณตั้งครรภ์แล้ว

kun đâng kan láa·ou

I haven't had my period for (six) weeks.

ดิฉันไม่ได้เป็นระดูมา
(หก) อาทิตย์แล้ว

dì-chǎn mâi dâi ฿en rá-doo
mah (hòk) ah-tít láa·ou

I've noticed a lump here.

สังเกตว่ามีก้อนเนื้ออยู่ตรงนี้

sǎng-gèt wâh mee gôrn
néu·a yòo ɗrong née

I need ...	ดิฉันต้องการ ...	dì-chǎn ɗông gahn ...
a pregnancy test	ตรวจการตั้งท้อง	ɗròo·at gahn ɗâng tórng
contraception	การคุมกำเนิด	gahn kum gam-nèut
the morning-after pill	ยาคุมกำเนิดชนิดใช้วันหลัง	yah kum gam-nèut chá-nít chái wan lǎng

allergies

โรคภูมิแพ้

I'm allergic to ...	ผม/ดิฉัน แพ้ ...	pǒm/dì-chǎn páa ... **m/f**
He/She is allergic to ...	เขาแพ้ ...	kǒw páa ...
antibiotics	ยาปฏิชีวนะ	yah ฿à-ɗi-chee-wá-ná
anti-inflammatories	ยาแก้อักเสบ	yah gâa àk-sèp
aspirin	ยาแอสไพริน	yah àat-sà-pai-rin
bees	ตัวผึ้ง	ɗoo·a pêung
penicillin	ยาเพนนิซิลลิน	yah pen-ní-sin-lin
pollen	เกสรดอกไม้	gair-sǒrn dòrk mái
sulphur-based drugs	ยาที่ประกอบด้วยซัลเฟอร์	yah têe ฿rà-gòrp dôo·ay san-feu

For food-related allergies, see **vegetarian & special meals**, page 169.

parts of the body

My ... hurts.	... ของ ผม/ดิฉัน เจ็บ	... kŏrng pŏm/ dì-chăn jèp **m/f**
I can't move my ...	ขยับ ... ไม่ได้	kà-yàp ... mâi dâi
I have a cramp in my ...	เป็นตะคริวที่ ...	ben đà-krew têe ...
My ... is swollen.	... ของ ผม/ดิฉัน บวม	... kŏrng pŏm/ dì-chăn boo·am **m/f**

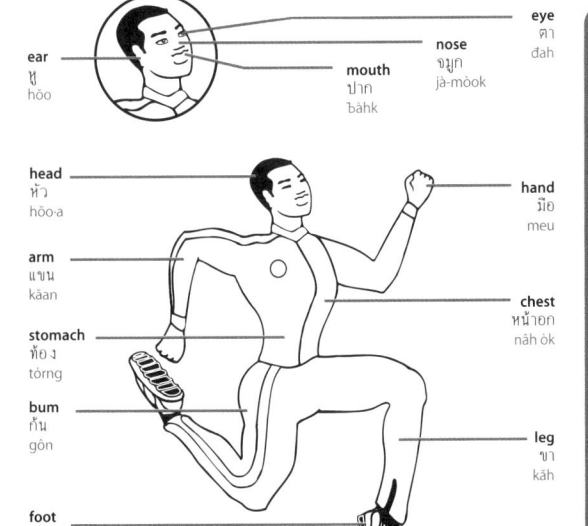

ear หู hŏo

eye ตา đah

nose จมูก jà-mòok

mouth ปาก bàhk

head หัว hŏo·a

hand มือ meu

arm แขน kăan

chest หน้าอก náh òk

stomach ท้อง tórng

bum ก้น gôn

leg ขา kăh

foot เท้า tów

alternative treatments

I don't use (Western medicine).
ผม/ดิฉินไม่ใช้ (ยาตะวันตก) pŏm/dì-chăn mâi chái (yah đà-wan đòk) **m/f**

I prefer ... ผม/ดิฉินนิยม ... pŏm/dì-chăn ní-yom ... **m/f**

Can I see someone who practices ...? พบกับหมอที่ชำนาญ ทาง ... ได้ไหม póp gàp mŏr têe cham-nahn tahng ... dâi măi

acupuncture	ฝังเข็ม	făng kĕm
herbal medicine	ยาสมุนไพร	yah sà-mŭn-prai
inner healing	การรักษาแบบใช้พลังภายใน	gahn rák-săh bàap chái pá-lang pai nai
Thai massage	การนวดแผนโบราณ	gahn nôo·at păan boh-rahn
traditional Thai medicine	ยาพื้นเมืองของประเทศไทย	yah péun meu·ang kŏrng brà-têt tai
naturopathy	การรักษาแบบบิธรรมชาต	gahn rák-săh bàap tam-má-châht
reflexology	การนวดเส้น	gahn nôo·at sên

chemist

I need something for ...
ต้องการยาสำหรับ ... đôrng gahn yah săm-ràp ...

Do I need a prescription for ...?
ต้องมีใบสั่งยาสำหรับ ... ไหม đôrng mee bai sàng yah săm-ràp ... măi

How many times a day?
วันละกี่ครั้ง wan lá gèe kráng

Will it make me drowsy?
จะทำให้ง่วงนอนไหม jà tam hâi ngôo·ang norn măi

Twice a day ...	วันละสองครั้ง ...	wan lá sŏrng kráng ...
after meals	หลังอาหาร	lăng ah-hăhn
before meals	ก่อนอาหาร	gòrn ah-hăhn
with food	พร้อมอาหาร	prórm ah-hăhn

Have you taken this before?
เคยใช้ยาแบบนี้มาก่อนไหม   keu·i chái yah bàap née mah gòrn măi

You must complete the course.
ต้องใช้ยาจนหมด   ôrng chái yah jon mòt

antifungal cream	ยาฆ่าเชื้อรา	yah kâh chéu·a rah
antimalarial medication	ยาป้องกันมาเลเรีย	yah ôrng gan mah-lair-ree·a
antiseptic	ยาฆ่าเชื้อ	yah kâh chéu·a
contraceptives	ยาคุมกำเนิด	yah kum gam-nèut
delousing preparation	ยาฆ่าเหา	yah kâh hŏw
diahorrea medicine	ยาระงับอาการท้องร่วง	yah rá-ngáp ah-gahn tórng rôo·ang
painkillers	ยาแก้ปวด	yah gâa ôo·at
thermometer	ปรอท	ôà-ròrt
rehydration salts	เกลือแร่	gleu·a râa
water filter	กรองน้ำ	grorng nám

dentist

I have a ...	ผม/ดิฉัน ...	pŏm/dì-chăn ... **m/f**
broken tooth	ฟันหัก	fan hàk
cavity	ฟันผุ	fan pù
toothache	ปวดฟัน	ôòo·at fan

I need (a/an) ...	ต้องการ ...	ôrng gahn ...
anaesthetic	ยาชา	yah chah
filling	อุดฟัน	ùt fan

I've lost a filling.
ที่อุดฟันหลุดไป — tée ùt fan lùt bai

My gums hurt.
เจ็บที่เหงือก — jèp têe ngèu·ak

I don't want it extracted.
ไม่อยากจะถอน — mâi yàhk jà tŏrn

Ouch!
เอ้า — ôw

---

the dentist may say ...

Open wide.
อ้าปากให้กว้าง — âh bàhk hâi gwâhng

This won't hurt a bit.
ไม่เจ็บหรอก — mâi jèp ròrk

Bite down on this.
กัดอันนี้ไว้ — gàt an née wái

Don't move.
อย่าขยับ — yàh kà·yàp

Rinse!
บ้วนปาก — bôo·an bàhk

Come back, I haven't finished.
กลับมานะ ยังไม่เสร็จ — glàp mah ná, yang mâi sèt

SUSTAINABLE TRAVEL

As the climate change debate heats up, the matter of sustainability becomes an important part of the travel vernacular. In practical terms, this means assessing our impact on the environment and local cultures and economies – and acting to make that impact as positive as possible. Here are some basic phrases to get you on your way …

communication & cultural differences

I'd like to learn some of your local dialects.

ผม/ดิฉันอยากจะเรียน   pŏm/dì-chăn yàhk jà ree·an
ภาษาพื้นเมืองของ   pah-săh péun meu·ang kŏrng
คุณบ้าง   kun bâhng m/f

Would you like me to teach you some English?

คุณอยากจะให้ผม/ดิฉัน   kun yàhk jà hâi pŏm/dì-chăn
สอนภาษาอังกฤษให้ไหม   sŏrn pah-săh ang-grìt hâi măi m/f

Is this a local or national custom?

อันนี้เป็นประเพณีระดับ   an née ben brà-pair-nee rá-dàp
ชาติหรือระดับท้องถิ่น   châht rěu rá-dàp tórng tìn

I respect your customs.

ผม/ดิฉันนับถือ   pŏm/dì-chăn náp-těu
ประเพณีของคุณ   brà-pair-nee kŏrng kun m/f

community benefit & involvement

What sorts of issues is this community facing?

ชุมชนนี้มี   chum chon née mee
ปัญหาอะไรบ้าง   ban-hăh à-rai bâhng

bribery	การติดสินบน	gahn dìt sĭn bon
corruption	ปัญหาความ	ban-hăh kwahm
	ทุจริต	tú-jà-rìt

freedom of the press	เสรีภาพของ สื่อมวลชน	sair-ree-pâhp kŏrng sèu moo·an chon
natural disasters	ภัยธรรมชาติ	pai tam-ma-châht·
poverty	ปัญหาความ ยากจน	฿an-hăh kwahm yâhk jon

I'd like to volunteer my skills.

ผม/ดิฉันอยากจะสมัคร รับใช้ความสามารถ ช่วยเหลือ	pŏm/dì-chăn yàhk jà sà-màk ráp chái kwahm săh-mâht chôo·ay lĕu·a m/f

Are there any volunteer programs available in this area?

โครงการอาสาสมัครมี บ้างไหมในท้องถิ่นนี้	krohng gahn ah-săh sà-màk mee bâhng măi nai tórng tìn née

environment

Where can I recycle this?

จะทิ้งอันนี้ได้ที่ไหน	jà tíng an née dâi têe năi

transport

Can we get there by public transport?

จะไปทางรถโดย สารได้ไหม	jà ฿ai tahng rót doy săhn dâi măi

Can we get there by bicycle?

จะไปทางรถ จักรยานได้ไหม	jà ฿ai tahng rót jàk-kà-yahn dâi măi

I'd prefer to walk there.

ขอเดินไปดีกว่า	kŏr deun ฿ai dee gwàh

accommodation

I'd like to stay at a locally run hotel.

ผม/ดิฉันอยากจะพักที่
โรงแรมที่มีคน
ท้อ งถิ่นบริหาร

pŏm/dì-chăn yàhk jà pák têe
rohng raam têe mee kon
tórng tìn bo-rí-hăhn m/f

Can I turn the air conditioning off and open the window?

ปิดแอร์เปิดหน้าต่าง
ได้ไหม

bìt air bèut nâh đàhng
dâi măi

Are there any ecolodges here?

มีสถานที่พักแบบ
ธรรมชาติแถวนี้ไหม

mee sà-tăhn têe pák bàap
tam-má-châht tăa·ou née măi

shopping

Where can I buy locally produced goods?

จะซื้อผลิตภัณฑ์ท้อ ง
ถิ่นได้ที่ไหน

jà séu pà-lìt-tá-pan tórng
tìn dâi têe năi

Where can I buy locally produced souvenirs?

จะซื้อที่ระลึกที่ทำใน
ท้อ งถิ่นได้ที่ไหน

jà séu têe rá-léuk têe tam nai
tórng tìn dâi têe năi

Is this made	อันนี้ทำมา	an née tam mah
from ...?	จาก...ไหม	jàhk ... măi
animal skin	หนังสัตว์	năng sàt
elephant tusks	งาช้าง	ngah cháhng
horn	เขาสัตว์	kŏw sàt
wildlife	สัตว์ป่า	sàt bàh

food

Do you sell ...?	คุณขาย...ไหม	kun kăi ... măi
locally produced	อาหารผลิต	ah-hăhn pà-lìt
food	จากท้อ งถิ่น	jàhk tórng tìn
organic	อาหารปลอด	ah-hăhn blòrt
produce	สารเคมี	săhn keh-mee

Can you tell me what traditional foods I should try?

คุณแนะนำอาหารพื้น   kun naa-nam ah-hăhn péun
เมืองได้ไหม   meu·ang dâi măi

sightseeing

Does your	บริษัทของคุณ	bò-rí-sàt kŏrng kun
company ...?	... ไหม	... măi
donate money	บริจาคเงิน	bò-rí-jàhk ngeun
to charity	เป็นการกุศล	ben gahn gù-sŏn
hire local	จ้างคนนำ	jâhng kon nam
guides	ทางของ	tahng kŏrng
	ท้องถิ่น	tórng tìn
visit local	เยี่ยมเยือน	yêe·am yeu·an
businesses	ทุรกิจท้องถิ่น	tú-rá-gìt tórng tìn

Does the guide	คนนำทางพูด	kon nam tahng pôot
speak ...?	ภาษา...ไหม	pah-săh ... măi
Isan	อีสาน	èe-săhn
Karen	กะเหรี่ยง	gà-rèe·ang
Lü	ลื้อ	léu
Northern Thai	ไทยเหนือ	tai nĕu·a
Nyaw	ญ้อ	yór
Phuan	พวน	poo·an
Phu Thai	ผู้ไท	pôo tai
Shan	ไทใหญ่	tai yài
Southern Thai	ไทยปักษ์ใต้	tai bàk đâi
Thai Dam	ไทยดำ	tai dam

Are cultural tours available?

มีบริการท่องเที่ยวดู   mee bò-rí-gahn tôrng têe·o doo
วัฒนธรรมไหม   wát-tá-ná-tam măi

DICTIONARY > english-thai

พจนานุกรม อังกฤษ-ไทย

The symbols ⓝ, ⓐ and ⓥ (indicating noun, adjective and verb) have been added for clarity where an English term could be either. Basic food terms have been included – for a more extensive list of ingredients and dishes, see the menu decoder.

A

abortion การทำแท้ง gahn tam táang
about เรื่อง t เรื่อง rêu-ang
above ข้างบน kâhng bon
abroad ต่างประเทศ dtàhng bpra-tét
accident อุบัติเหตุ u-bat-di-het
accommodation ที่พัก têe pák
account บัญชี ban-chee
across ข้ามฟาก kâhm fâhk
activist นักเคลื่อนไหว nák bra-too-ang
actor นักแสดง nák sa-daang
acupuncture การฝังเข็ม gahn fǎng kěm
adaptor หม้อแปลง mór blaang
addiction การติดยา gahn dit
address ที่อยู่ têe yòo
administration การบริหาร gahn bor-rí-hǎhn
admission (price) ค่าเข้าชม kâh kôw
admit (let in) ให้เข้าไป hâi kôw
adult ผู้ใหญ่ pôo yài
advertisement การโฆษณา gahn
advice คำแนะนำ kam náa-nam
aerobics การเต้นแอโรบิค gahn dén aa-roh-bik
aeroplane เครื่องบิน krêu-ang bin
Africa ทวีปแอฟริกา tá-wêep aa-fri-gah
after หลัง lǎng
afternoon ตอนบ่าย dorn bài
afternoon (this) บ่าย (นี้) bài (née)

aftershave ครีมโกนหนวด kreem tah lǎng gohn nòo-at
again อีก èek
age อายุ ah-yu
ago (three days) (สามวัน) ... ก่อน (sǎhm wan) ... gòn
agree (with an opinion) เห็นด้วย hěn dôo-ay
agree (to do something) ตกลง dtòk long
agriculture การเกษตรกรรม gà-sèt-dà-gam
ahead ข้างหน้า kâhng nâh
AIDS โรคเอดส์ rôhk èd
air อากาศ ah-gàht
air-conditioned vehicle รถปรับอากาศ rót bràp ah-gàht
air-conditioning ปรับอากาศ bràp ah-gàht
airline สายการบิน săi gahn bin
airmail ไปรษณีย์อากาศ brai-sa-nee ah-gàht
airplane เครื่องบิน krêu-ang bin
airport สนามบิน sa-nǎhm bin
airport tax ภาษีสนามบิน pah-sěe
aisle (on plane) ทางเดิน tahng deun
alarm clock นาฬิกาปลุก nah-li-gah blùk
alcohol เหล้า lôw
all ทั้งหมด táng mòt
allergy การแพ้ gahn páa
alley ตรอก dtròk
almond อัลมอนด์ ah-man

B

almost เกือบ gèu·ap
alone เดียว dèe·o
already แล้ว láa·ou
also ด้วย dôo·ay
altar แท่นพระ tâan prá
altitude ระยะสูง rá·yá sŏong
always ตลอดไป ɖà·lòrt pai
ambassador ทูต tôot
ambulance รถพยาบาล rót pá·yah·bahn
American football ฟุตบอลอเมริกัน
    fút·born à·mair·rí·gan
anaemia โรคโลหิตจาง rôhk loh·hìt jahng
ancient โบราณ boh·rahn
and และ láa
angry โกรธ gròht
animal สัตว์ sàt
ankle ข้อเท้า kôr tów
another อีก (อัน) หนึ่ง èek (an) nèung
answer ⓝ คำตอบ kam ɖòrp
ant มด mót
antibiotics ยาปฏิชีวนะ yah pà·ɖì·chee·
    wá·ná
antinuclear ต่อต้านพลังงานนิวเคลียร์ ɖòr
    ɖâhn pá·lang ngahn new·klee·a
antique วัตถุโบราณ wát·tù boh·rahn
antiseptic ยาฆ่าเชื้อ yah kâh chéu·a
any ใด ๆ dai dai
apartment ห้องคอนโด hôrng korn·doh
appendix (body) ไส้ติ่ง sâi ɖìng
apple แอปเปิ้ล àap·beun
appointment การนัด gahn nát
April เดือนเมษายน deu·an mair·săh·yon
archaeological ทางโบราณคดี tahng
    boh·rahn·ná·ká·dee
architect สถาปนิก sà·tăh·bà·ník
architecture สถาปัตยกรรม sà·tăh·bàt·
    ɖà·yá·gam
argue ทะเลาะ tá·ló
arm แขน kăan
aromatherapy การบำบัดโรคด้วยกลิ่นหอม
    gahn bam·bàt rôhk dôo·ay glìn hŏrm
arrest ⓥ จับกุม jàp gum
arrivals ขาเข้า kăh kòw

arrive มาถึง mah tĕung
art ศิลปะ sĭn·lá·bà
art gallery ห้องแสดงภาพ hôrng sà·daang
    pâhp
artist ศิลปิน sĭn·lá·bin
ashtray ที่เขี่ยบุหรี่ têe kèe·a bù·rèe
Asia ทวีปเอเชีย tá·wêep air·see·a
ask (a question) ถาม tăhm
ask (for something) ขอ kŏr
asparagus หน่อไม้ฝรั่ง nòr mái fà·ràng
aspirin ยาแอสไพริน yah àat·sà·pai·rin
asthma โรคหืด rôhk hèut
at ที่ têe
athletics การกรีฑา gahn gree·tah
atmosphere บรรยากาศ ban·yah·gàht
aubergine มะเขือ má·kĕu·a
August เดือนสิงหาคม deu·an sĭng·hăh·
    kom
aunt (father's younger sister) อา ah
aunt (older sister of either parent)
    ป้า bâh
Australia ประเทศออสเตรเลีย brà·têt
    or·sà·drair·lee·a
Australian Rules Football ฟุตบอล
    ออสเตรเลีย fút·born
    or·sà·drair·lee·a
automated teller machine (ATM)
    ตู้เอทีเอ็ม ɖôo air tee em
autumn หน้าใบไม้ร่วง nâh bai mái
    rôo·ang
avenue ถนน tà·nŏn
awful แย่ yâa

B

B&W (film) (ฟิล์ม) ขาวดำ (fim) kŏw dam
baby ทารก tah·rók
baby food อาหารทารก ah·hăhn tah·rók
baby powder แป้งทารก bâang tah·rók
babysitter พี่เลี้ยงเด็ก pêe lée·ang dèk
back (body) หลัง lăng
back (position) หลัง lăng
back street ซอย soy

backpack เป้ bâir

bacon หมูเบคอน mŏo bair-korn

bad เลว le-ou

bag ถุง tŭng

baggage กระเป๋า grà-bŏw

baggage allowance พิกัดน้ำหนักกระเป๋า pí-gàt nám nàk grà-bŏw

baggage claim ที่รับกระเป๋า têe ráp grà-bŏw

bakery ที่ขายขนมปัง têe kăi kà-nŏm bang

balance (account) รายยอด ขบัญชี rai yôrt (ban-chee)

balcony ระเบียง rá-bee-ang

ball ลูกบอล lôok born

ballet การเต้นบัลเล่ต์ gahn dên ban-lâir

bamboo ไม้ไผ่ mái pài

bamboo shoot(s) หน่อไม้ nòr mái

banana กล้วย glôo-ay

band (music) วงดนตรี wong don-dree

bandage ผ้าพันแผล păh pan plăa

Band-Aid ปลาสเตอร์ blah-sà-đeu

bandit โจร john

Bangkok กรุงเทพ grung têp

bank ธนาคาร tá-nah-kahn

bank account บัญชีธนาคาร ban-chee tá-nah-kahn

banknote ธนบัตร tá-ná-bàt

bar บาร์ bah

bar work งานในบาร์ ngahn nai bah

barber ช่างตัดผม châhng đàt pŏm

baseball เบสบอล bèt-born

basket ตะกร้า đà-grâh

basketball บาสเกตบอล bah-sà-gèt-born

bath อ่างน้ำ àhng nám

bathing suit ชุดว่ายน้ำ chút wâi nám

bathroom ห้องน้ำ hông nám

batik ปาเต๊ะ bah-đé

battery (flashlight) ถ่านไฟฉาย tàhn fai chăi

battery (car) หม้อแบตเตอรี่ môr bàat-đeu-rêe

bay อ่าว òw

be เป็น ben

beach ชายหาด chai hàht

beach volleyball วอลเลย์บอลชายหาด worn-lair-born chai hàht

bean ถั่ว tòo-a

beansprout ถั่วงอก tòo-a ngôrk

beautiful สวย sŏo-ay

beauty salon ร้านเสริมสวย ráhn sĕum sŏo-ay

because เพราะว่า pró-wâh

bed เตียง đee-ang

bed linen ผ้าปูที่นอน păh boo têe norn

bedding เครื่องนอน krêu-ang norn

bedroom ห้องนอน hông norn

bee ผึ้ง pêung

beef เนื้อวัว néu-a woo-a

beer เบียร์ bee-a

before ก่อน gòrn

beggar คนขอทาน kon kŏr tahn

behind ข้างหลัง kâhng lăng

Belgium ประเทศเบเยี่ยม prà-têt ben-yee-am

bell ระฆัง rá-kang

bell tower หอระฆัง hŏr rá-kang

below ข้างล่าง kâhng lâhng

beneath ใต้ đâi

beside ข้างๆ kâhng kâhng

best ดีที่สุด dee têe sùt

bet การพนัน gahn pá-nan

better ดีกว่า dee gwàh

between ระหว่าง rá-wàhng

bible คัมภีร์ไบเบิ้ล kam-pee bai-bêun

bicycle รถจักรยาน rót jàk-gà-yahn

big ใหญ่ yài

bigger ใหญ่กว่า yài gwàh

biggest ใหญ่ที่สุด yài têe sùt

bike chain โซ่จักรยาน sôh jàk-gà-yahn

bike lock กุญแจจักรยาน gun-jaa jàk-gà-yahn

bike path ทางจักรยาน tahng jàk-gà-yahn

bike repair shop ร้านซ่อมจักรยาน ráhn sôrm jàk-gà-yahn

bill (restaurant etc) บิลค์ bin

binoculars กล้องสองตา glông sŏrng đah

bird นก nók

birth certificate ใบเกิด bai gèut

birthday วันเกิด wan gèut

biscuit ขนม kà-nŏm

bite (dog) กัด gàt

bite (insect) ต่อย đòy

bitter ขม kŏm

black สีดำ sĕe dam

bladder ถุงปัสสาวะ tŭng bàt-săh-wá

blanket ผ้าห่ม pâh hòm

blind ตาบอด đah bòrt

blister รอยพอง roy porng

blocked ตัน đan

blood เลือด lêu·at

blood group กลุ่มเลือด glum lêu·at

blood pressure ความดันโลหิต kwahm dan loh-hìt

blood test การเจาะเลือด gahn jò lêu·at

blue (light) สีฟ้า sĕe fáh

blue (dark) สีน้ำเงิน sĕe nám ngeun

board (a plane, ship etc) ขึ้น kêun

boarding house บ้านพัก bâhn pák

boarding pass บัตรขึ้นเครื่องบิน bàt kêun krêu·ang bin

boat เรือ reu·a

body (living) ร่างกาย râhng gai

body (dead) ศพ sòp

boiled ต้ม đôm

boiled rice ข้าวต้ม kôw đôm

bone กระดูก grà-dòok

book หนังสือ năng-sĕu

book (make a booking) จอง jorng

book shop ร้านขายหนังสือ ráhn kăi năng-sĕu

booked out จองเต็มแล้ว jorng đem láa-ou

boot(s) รองเท้าบู๊ท rorng tów bút

border ชายแดน chai daan

bored เบื่อ bèu·a

boring น่าเบื่อ nâh bèu·a

borrow ยืม yeum

botanic garden สวนพฤกษาชาติ sŏo·an préuk-săh-châht

both ทั้งสอง táng sŏrng

bottle ขวด kòo·at

bottle opener เครื่องเปิดขวด krêu·ang bèut kòo·at

bottle shop ร้านขายเหล้า ráhn kăi lôw

bottom (body) ก้น gôn

bottom (position) ข้างล่าง kâhng lâhng

bowl ชาม chahm

box กล่อง glòrng

boxer นักมวย nák moo·ay

boxer shorts กางเกงขาขั้น gahng-geng kăh săn

boxing การต่อยมวย gahn đòy moo·ay

boy เด็กชาย dèk chai

boyfriend แฟนผู้ชาย faan pôo chai

bra ยกทรง yók song

bracelet กำไลมือ gam-lai meu

brakes เบรก brèk

brandy บรั่นดี bà-ràn-dee

brave กล้าหาญ glâh-hăhn

bread ขนมปัง kà-nŏm bang

bread rolls ขนมปังก้อน kà-nŏm bang górn

break หัก hàk

break down เสีย sĕe·a

breakfast อาหารเช้า ah-hăhn chów

breast (body) เต้านม đôw nom

breast (poultry) อก òk

breathe หายใจ hăi jai

bribe ⓝ สินบน sĭn bon

bridge สะพาน sà-pahn

briefcase กระเป๋าเอกสาร grà-bŏw èk-gà-săhn

brilliant ยอด yôrt

bring เอามา ow mah

brochure แผ่นพับโฆษณา pàan páp koh-sà-nah

broken หักแล้ว hàk láa-ou

broken down เสียแล้ว sĕe·a láa-ou

bronchitis โรคหลอดลมอักเสบ rôhk lòrt lom àk-sèp

brooch เข็มกลัด kěm glàt
brother (older) พี่ชาย pêe chai
brother (younger) น้องชาย nórng chai
brown สีน้ำตาล sěe nám dahn
bruise ① รอยช้ำ roy chám
brush แปรง braang
bucket ถัง tǎng
Buddha พระพุทธเจ้า prá-put-tá-jôw
Buddhism ศาสนาพุทธ sàht-sà-nǎh pút
Buddhist ชาวพุทธ chow pút
budget งบประมาณ ngóp brà-mahn
buffet อาหารบุฟเฟ่ต์ ah-hǎhn dang dòr
bug (insect) แมลง má-laang
build สร้าง sâhng
builder ช่างก่อสร้าง châhng gòr sâhng
building ตึก dèuk
bumbag กระเป๋าคาดเอว grà-bǒw kâht e-ou
bungalow บ้านในบังกะโหล bâhn nai bang-gà-lòh
Burma ประเทศพม่า brà-tèt pá-mâh
burn (injury) แผลไฟไหม้ plǎa fai mâi
burn ไฟไหม้ fai mâi ① เผา pǒw
burnt ไหม้แล้ว mâi láa-ou
bus (city) รถเมล์ rót mair
bus (intercity) รถโดยสาร rót bai bàt
bus station สถานีรถเมล์ sà-tǎhn-nee kon sòng
bus stop ป้ายรถเมล์ bâi rót mair
business ธุรกิจ tú-rá-gìt
business class ชั้นธุรกิจ chán tú-rá-gìt
business person นักธุรกิจ nák tú-rá-gìt tú-rá-gìt
busy ยุ่ง yûng
but แต่ว่า dàa wâh
butcher ผู้ขายเนื้อ kon kái néu-a
butcher's shop ร้านขายเนื้อ ráhn kái néu-a
butter เนย neu-i
butterfly ผีเสื้อ pěe séu-a
button กระดุม grà-dum
buy ซื้อ séu

c

cabbage ผักกะหล่ำปลี pàk gà-làm-blee
café ร้านกาแฟ ráhn gah-faa
cake เค้ก ka-nôm
cake shop ร้านขายเค้ก ráhn kái ka-nôm
calculator เครื่องคิดเลข krêu-ang kít lék
calendar ปฏิทิน bà-di-tin rée-ak
call โทร. rée-ak
Cambodia ประเทศกัมพูชา brà-tèt ka-mên
camera กล้องถ่ายรูป glôrng tái rôop
camera shop ร้านขายกล้องถ่ายรูป ráhn kái glòeng tái rôop
camp แคมป์ pàk raam
camp site พื้นที่ตั้งเต็นท์ têe bàk dén raam
camping ground พื้นที่ตั้งแคมป์ kái pák raam
camping store ร้านขายอุปกรณ์ ráhn kái kong kaam-bing
can (tin) กระป๋อง grà-bǒrng
can (have permission) ได้ dâi
can (be able) ทำได้ tam dâi
can opener ที่เปิดกระป๋อง têe krěu-ang beut grà-bǒrng
Canada ประเทศแคนาดา brà-tèt kaa-nah-dah
cancel ยกเลิก yók lêuk
cancer โรคมะเร็ง rôhk ma-reng
candle เทียนไข tee-an kǎi
candy ลูกอม lôok om
cantaloupe แคนตาลูป daang kaan-dàp-lòop
capital (provincial) เมืองหลวง am-peu meu-ang
capsicum พริกหวาน prík wǎhn
car รถยนต์ rót yon
car hire การเช่ารถ gahn chôw rót
car owner's title ใบกรรมสิทธิ์รถยนต์ bai gam-ma-sìt rót yon
car park ที่จอดรถ têe jòrt rót
car registration ทะเบียนรถ tá-bee-an rót
caravan รถคาราวาน rót kah-rah-wahn

cardiac arrest โรคหัวใจวาย rôhk hŏo-a jai wai

cards (playing) ไพ่ pâi

care (look after) ดูแล doo laa

Careful! ระวัง rá-wang

carpenter ช่างไม้ châhng mái

carrot แครอท kaa-rôrt

carry (in arms) อุ้ม ûm

carry (on back) แบก bàak

carry (in hands) หิ้ว hêw

carry (in pocket) พก pók

carry (over shoulder) สะพาย sà-nài

carton กล่อง glòrng

cash เงินสด ngeun sòt

cash (a cheque) แลก lâak

cash register เครื่องเก็บเงิน krêu-ang gèp ngeun

cashew มะม่วงหิมพานต์ má-môo-ang hĭm-má-pahn

cashier แคเชียร์ kaa-chee-a

casino กาสิโน gah-sì-noh

cassette ม้วนเทป móo-an tép

castle ปราสาท bràh-sàht

casual work งานชั่วคราว ngahn chôo-a krow

cat แมว maa-ou

cathedral โบสถ์ bòht

Catholic คริสตัง krít-sà-đang

cauliflower ดอกกะหล่ำ dòrk gà-làm

cave ถ้ำ tâm

CD ซีดี see-dee

celebration การฉลอง gahn chà-lŏrng

cemetery สุสาน sù-săhn

cent เซ็นต์ sen

centimetre เซนติเมตร sen-đi-mét

centre ศูนย์กลาง sŏon glahng

ceramics กระเบื้อง grà-bêu-ang

cereal ซีเรียล see-ree-an

certificate ใบประกาศ bai bprà-gàht

chain โซ่ sôh

chair เก้าอี้ gôw-êe

championships การแข่งขัน gahn kàang kăn

chance (opportunity) โอกาส oh-gàht

change ⓝ การเปลี่ยนแปลง gahn plèe-an plaang

change (coins) เงินปลีก ngeun bplèek

change ⓥ เปลี่ยนแปลง bplèe-an blaang

change (money) แลก lâak

changing room (in shop) ห้องเปลี่ยนเสื้อ hôrng bplèe-an sêu-a

charming มีเสน่ห์ mee sà-nàir

chat up เกี้ยว gêe-o

cheap ถูก tòok

cheat คนขี้โกง kon kêe gohng

check (banking) เช็ค chék

check (bill) บิลล์ bin

check ⓥ ตรวจ đròo-at

check-in (desk) เช็คอิน chék in

checkpoint ด่านตรวจ dàhn đròo-at

cheese เนยแข็ง neu-i kăang

chef พ่อครัว pôr kroo-a

chemist ร้านขายยา ráhn kăi yah

chemist (pharmacist) เภสัชกร pair-sàt-chá-gorn

cheque (banking) เช็ค chék

cheque (bill) บิลล์ bin

cherry ลูกเชอรี่ lôok cheu-rêe

chess หมากรุก màhk rúk

chess board กระดานหมากรุก grà-dahn màhk rúk

chest (body) หน้าอก nâh òk

chestnut ลูกเกาลัด lôok gow-lát

chewing gum หมากฝรั่ง màhk fà-ràng

chicken ไก่ gài

chicken pox อีสุกอีใส ee-sùk-ee-săi

chickpea ถั่วเขียว tòo-a kĕe-o

child เด็ก dèk

child seat ที่นั่งเฉพาะเด็ก têe nâng chà-pó dèk

childminding การดูแลเด็ก gahn doo laa dèk

children เด็กๆ dèk dèk
chilli พริก prík
chilli sauce น้ำพริก nám prík
China ประเทศจีน brà-têt jeen
Chinese จีน jeen
chiropractor หมอดัดสันหลัง mŏr dàt
   săn lăng
chocolate ช็อกโกแลต chórk-goh-lét
choose เลือก lêu-ak
chopping board เขียง kĕe-ang
chopsticks ไม้ตะเกียบ mái dà-gèe-ap
Christian ชาวคริสต์ chow krit
Christian name ชื่อ chêu
Christmas คริสต์มาส krít-màht
Christmas Day วันคริสต์มาส
   wan krít-màht
church โบสถ์ bòht
cigar ซิการ์ bù-rèe sí-gáh
cigarette บุหรี่ bù-rèe
cigarette lighter ไฟแช็ก fai cháak
cinema โรงหนัง rohng năng
circus ละครสัตว์ lá-korn sàt
citizenship สัญชาติ săn-châht
city เมือง meu-ang
city centre ใจกลางเมือง jai glahng
   meu-ang
civil rights สิทธิประชาชน sìt-tí prà-chah-
   chon
human rights สิทธิมนุษยชน sìt-tí má-nút-
   sà-yá-chon
class (category) ประเภท brà-pêt
class system ระบบแบ่งชั้น rá-bòp bàang
   chán
clean ⓐ สะอาด sà-àht
clean ⓥ ทำสะอาด tam sà-àht
cleaning การทำสะอาด gahn tam sà-àht
client ลูกค้า lôok káh
cliff หน้าผา nâh păh
climb ปีน been
cloakroom ห้องเก็บเสื้อ hôrng gèp sêu-a
clock นาฬิกา nah-lí-gah
close ⓥ ปิด bìt

close ⓐ ใกล้ glâi
closed ปิดแล้ว bìt láa-ou
clothesline ราวตากผ้า row đàhk pâh
clothing เสื้อผ้า sêu-a pâh
clothing store ร้านขายเสื้อผ้า ráhn kăi
   sêu-a pâh
cloud เมฆ mêk
cloudy ฟ้าคลุ้ม fáh klúm
clutch (car) คลัตช์ klát
coach (bus) รถทัวร์ rót too-a
coast ฝั่งทะเล fâng tá-lair
coat เสื้อคลุม sêu-a klum
cocaine โคเคน koh-ken
cockroach แมลงสาบ má-laang sàhp
cocktail ค็อกเทล kórk-ten
cocoa โกโก้ goh-gôh
coconut มะพร้าว má-prów
coconut juice น้ำมะพร้าว nám má-prów
coconut milk กะทิ gà-tí
coffee กาแฟ gah-faa
coins เหรียญ rĕe-an
cold (virus) หวัด wàt
cold เย็น yen
cold (feeling) หนาว nŏw
colleague เพื่อนงาน pêu-an ngahn
collect call โทรเก็บปลายทาง toh gèp
   blai tahng
college วิทยาลัย wít-tá-yah-lai
colour สี sĕe
comb หวี wĕe
come มา mah
comedy ละครตลก lá-korn đà-lòk
comfortable สบาย sà-bai
commission ค่าธรรมเนียม kâh tam-nee-am
communications (profession) การสื่อสาร
   gahn sèu săhn
communion (Christian ceremony) ศีล
   มหาสนิท sĕen-má-hăh-sà-nit
communist คอมมิวนิสต์ korm-mew-nít
companion เพื่อน pêu-an
company บริษัท bor-rí-sàt
compass เข็มทิศ kĕm tit

complain ร้องทุกข์ rórng túk

complaint คำร้องทุกข์ kam rórng túk

complementary (free) แถม tǎam

computer คอมพิวเตอร์ korm-pew-đeu

computer game เกมส์คอมพิวเตอร์ gem korm-pew-đeu

concert การแสดง gahn sà-daang

concussion มันสมองกระทบกระเทือน man sà-mǒrng grà-tóp grà-teu-an

conditioner (hair) ยานวดผม yah nôo-at pǒm

condom ถุงยางอนามัย tǔng yahng à-nah-mai

conference การประชุม gahn bràa-chum

confession การสารภาพผิด gahn sǎh-rá-páhp pìt

confirm (a booking) ยืนยัน yeun yan

congratulations ขอแสดงความยินดี kǒr sà-daang kwahm yin dee

conjunctivitis โรคตาแดง rohk đah daang

connection ข้อต่อ kôr đòr

connection (transport) การต่อ gahn đòr

conservative หัวเก่า hǒo-a gòw

constipation ท้องผูก tórng pòok

consulate กงสุล gong-sǔn

contact lens solution น้ำยาล้างเลนส์สัมผัส nám yah láhng len sǎm-pàt

contact lenses เลนส์สัมผัส len sǎm-pàt

contraceptives (pills) ยาคุมกำเนิด yah kum gam-nèut

contraceptives (condoms) ถุงยางอนามัย tǔng yahng à-nah-mai

contract ใบสัญญา bai sǎn-yah

convenience store ร้านขายของชำ ráhn kǎi kǒrng cham

convent คอนแวนต์ korn-waan

cook ① คนครัว kon kroo-a

cook ② ทำอาหาร tam ah-hǎhn

cookie ขนมกุ๊กกี้ kà-nǒm gúk-gêe

cooking การทำอาหาร gahn tam ah-hǎhn

cool เย็น yen

corkscrew เหล็กไขจุกขวด lèk kǎi jùk kòo-at

corn ข้าวโพด kôw pôht

corner มุม mum

cornflakes คอร์นเฟล็กซ์ korn-flèk

corrupt ทุจริต tú-jà-rìt

cost มีราคา mee rah-kah

cotton ฝ้าย fâi

cotton balls สำลี sǎm-lee

cotton buds ไม้สำลี mái sǎm-lee

cough ไอ ai

cough medicine ยาแก้ไอ yah gâa ai

count นับ náp

counter (at bar) โต๊ะกั้น đó gân

country ประเทศ bràa-têt

countryside ชนบท chon-ná-bot

coupon คูปอง koo-borng

court (legal) ศาล sǎhn

court (tennis) สนาม sà-nǎhm

cousin ลูกพี่ลูกน้อง lôok pêe lôok nórng

cover charge ค่าผ่านประตู kâh pàhn bràa-đoo

cow วัว woo-a

crab ปู boo

cracker ขนมปังกรอบ kà-nǒm bang gròrp

crafts หัตถกรรม hàt-tà-gam

crash ① ชน chon

crazy บ้า bâh

crèche ที่ฝากเลี้ยงเด็ก têe fàhk lée-ang dèk

credit เครดิต crair-dìt

credit card บัตรเครดิต bàt crair-dìt

crocodile จระเข้ jà-rá-kâir

crop พืชผล pêut pǒn

cross (religious) ไม้กางเขน mái gahng kěn

crowded แออัด aa àt

cucumber แตงกวา đaang gwah

cup ถ้วย tôo-ay

cupboard ตู้ đôo

currency exchange การแลกเงิน gahn lâak ngeun

current (electricity) กระแสไฟฟ้า grà-sǎa fai fáh

current affairs เหตุการณ์ปัจจุบัน kàw bàhn
tan-wah-kom

curry แกง gaang
mee-ang

custard apple น้อยหน่า nóy nàh

custom ประเพณี brà-pair-nee

customs ศุลกากร sùn-lá-gah-gorn

cut ⊙ ตัด dàt

cutlery ช้อนส้อม chórn sôm

CV ประวัติย่อ brà-wàt yôr
ngahn

cycle ⊙ ปั่นจักรยาน bàn jàk-gà-yahn
jàk-gà-yahn

cycling การปั่นจักรยาน gahn bàn jàk-gà-yahn
jàk-gà-yahn

cyclist คนปั่นรถจักรยานบนถนน kon ban rót

cystitis กระเพาะปัสสาวะอักเสบ
grà-pór bàt-sah-wá àk-sèp

D

dad พ่อ pôr

daily รายวัน rai wan

dance ⊙ เต้นรำ dên ram

dancing การเต้นรำ gahn dên ram

dangerous อันตราย an-dà-rai

dark มืด mûet

dark (of colour) สีเข้ม sée kêm

date (a person) นัดพบ nát póp

date (appointment) การนัดหมาย gahn nát mái

date (day) วันที่ wan têe

date (fruit) อินทผลัม in-tá-pá-lam

date of birth วันที่เกิด wan têe gèut

daughter ลูกสาว lôok sŏw

dawn รุ่งอรุณ a-run

day วัน wan

day after tomorrow (the) วันมะรืน
má-reun

day before yesterday (the) วันก่อนเมื่อวาน
meu-a wahn seun

dead ตายแล้ว dai láa-ou

deaf หูหนวก hŏo nòo-ak

deal (cards) แจก jàak

December เดือนธันวาคม deu-an
tan-wah-kom

decide ตัดสินใจ dàt sin jai

deep ลึก léuk

deforestation การตัดป่า gahn tam
lai

degrees (temperature) องศา ong-săh
wair-rah-lai

delay การล่าช้า gahn sée-a wair-rah-lai

deliver ส่ง sòng

democracy ประชาธิปไตย brà-chah-tí-
bà-dai

demonstration การสาธิต gahn săh-tí
ka-boo-an

Denmark ประเทศเดนมาร์ก brà-têt
den-mâhk

dental floss ไหมขัดฟัน chéu-ak sée fan

dentist หมอฟัน mŏr fan

deodorant ยาดับกลิ่น yah dàp glìn
doo-a

depart (leave) ออกเดินทาง òrk deun
tahng

department store ร้านสรรพสินค้า sàp-pá-
sin-káh

departure ขาออก kăh òrk

departure gate ประตูขึ้นเครื่อง brà-doo
kâh òrk

deposit เงินมัดจำ ngeun mát jam
gèe-a

derailleur ตีนผีรถจักรยาน tèe blèe-an

descendant ผู้สืบสายโลหิต sai

desert ทะเลทราย tá-lair sai

design ออกแบบ òrk bàap

dessert ของหวาน kŏrng wăhn

destination จุดหมายปลายทาง
blai tahng

details รายละเอียด rai la-èe-at
blai tahng

diabetes โรคเบาหวาน rôhk bow wăhn
toh-rá-sàp

dial tone สัญญาณหมุนโทรศัพท์ săn-yahn
toh-rá-sàp

diaper ผ้าอ้อม pâh ôm

diaphragm (body) กระบังลม ga-bang lom

diarrhoea ท้องร่วง tórng sée-a

diary สมุดบันทึก ban-téuk rai wan

dice ลูกเต๋า lôok dǒw

dictionary พจนานุกรม pót-jà-nah-nú-grom
die ตาย đai
diet อาหารพิเศษ ah-hǎhn pí-sèt
different ต่างกัน đàhng gan
different from ต่างจาก đàhng jàhk
difficult ยาก yâhk
dining car ตู้รับประทานอาหาร đôo ráp bà-tahn ah-hǎhn
dinner อาหารมื้อเย็น ah-hǎhn méu yen
direct ทางตรง tahng đrong
direct-dial โทรทางตรง toh tahng đrong
direction ทิศทาง tít tahng
director (film) ผู้กำกับ pôo gam-gàp
director (company) กรรมการผู้จัดการ gam-má-gahn pôo jàt gahn
dirty สกปรก sòk-gà-bròk
disabled พิการ pí-gahn
disco ดิสโก dit-sà-goh
discount ราคาส่วนลด rah-kah sòo-an lót
discrimination การแบ่งแยก gahn bàeng yâak
disease โรค rôhk
dish จาน jahn
disk (CD-ROM) แผ่นซีดี pàen see-dee
disk (floppy) แผ่นดิสก์ pàen dit
district เขต kèt
diving การดำน้ำ gahn dam nám
diving equipment อุปกรณ์ดำน้ำ ùp-bà-gorn dam nám
divorced หย่าแล้ว yàh láa-ou
dizzy เวียนหัว wee-an hǒo-a
do ทำ tam
doctor หมอ mǒr
documentary สารคดี sǎ-rá-ká-dee
dog หมา mǎh
doll ตุ๊กตา đúk-gà-đah
dollar ดอลลาร์ dorn-lah
door ประตู brà-đoo
dope (drugs) เนื้อ néu-a
double คู่ kôo
double bed เตียงคู่ đee-ang kôo
double room ห้องคู่ hôrng kôo

down ลง long
downhill ทางลง tahng long
dozen โหล lǒh
drama ละคร lá-korn
dream ฝัน fǎn
dress (n) กระโปรง grà-brohng
dried ตากแห้ง đàhk hâhng
dried fruit ผลไม้ตากแห้ง pǒn-lá-mái đàhk hâhng
drink (n) เครื่องดื่ม krêu-ang dèum
drink (v) ดื่ม dèum
drinking food กับแกล้ม gàp glâam
drinking water น้ำดื่ม nám dèum
drive ขับ kàp
drivers licence ใบขับขี่ bai kàp kèe
drug ยา yah
drug addiction การติดยา gahn đìt yah
drug dealer ผู้ค้ายาเสพติด pôo káh yah sèp đìt
drug trafficking การค้ายาเสพติด gahn káh yah sèp đìt
drug user ผู้ใช้ยาเสพติด pôo chái yah sèp đìt
drugs (illicit) ยาเสพติด yah sèp đìt
drum กลอง glorng
drunk เมา mow
dry (a) แห้ง hâhng
dry (hang out) ตากให้แห้ง đàhk hâi hâhng
duck เป็ด bèt
dummy (pacifier) หัวนมเทียม hǒo-a nom tee-am
durian ทุเรียน tú-ree-an
DVD ดีวีดี dee-wee-dee

E

each แต่ละ đàa-lá
ear หู hǒo
early เช้า chów
earn ทำรายได้ tam rai dâi
earplugs ที่อุดหู têe ùt hǒo
earrings ตุ้มหู đûm hǒo
Earth โลก lôhk

english-thai

E

enter เข้าไป kôw bai
entertainment guide คู่มือบันเทิง kôo meu ban-teung
entry การเข้า gahn kôw
envelope ซองจดหมาย sorng jòt-mǎi
environment สิ่งแวดล้อม sìng wâet lórm
epilepsy โรคลมชัก rôhk lom mhoo
equal opportunity โอกาสเท่าเทียมกัน oh-gàht tôw-am gan
equality ความเท่าเทียมกัน kwahm tôw-am gan pâhk
equipment อุปกรณ์ up-bpa-gorn
escalator บันไดเลื่อน ban-dai lêu-an
estate agency ตัวแทนซื้อขายบ้าน bor-ri-sàt à-sǎng-hǎh-ri-ma-sáp
euro ยูโร yu-roh
Europe ทวีปยุโรป tá-wêep yú-rohp
evening ตอนเย็น dorn yen
every ทุก túk
everyone ทุกคน túk kon
everything ทุกสิ่งทุกอย่าง túk sìng
exactly ถูกต้อง drong bé
example ตัวอย่าง dtoo-a yàhng
excellent ยอดเยี่ยม yôrt yée-am
excess (baggage) (น้ำหนัก) เกิน (nám nàk) geun
exchange (v) แลกเปลี่ยน lâek bìee-an
exchange (n) การแลกเปลี่ยน gahn lâek bìee-an
exchange rate อัตราแลกเปลี่ยน àt-drah lâek bìee-an
excluded ไม่รวม mâi yók wén
exhaust (car) ท่อไอเสีย tôr ai sěe-a
exhibition นิทรรศการ ní-tát-sà-gahn
exit ทางออก tahng òrk
expensive แพง paang
experience ประสบการณ์ brà-sòp gahn ow
exploitation การเอารัดเอาเปรียบ gahn ow rát ow bprée-ap
express ด่วน dòo-an
express mail (by) ไปรษณีย์ด่วน brai-sà-nee dòo-an

enough wo por
enjoy (oneself) เพลิดเพลิน pleut pleun
English อังกฤษ ang-grìt
England ประเทศอังกฤษ brà-têt ang-grìt
engineering วิศวกรรม wít-sà-wà-gam
engineer วิศวกร wít-sà-wà-gorn
engine เครื่องยนต์ krêu-ang
engagement การหมั้น gaan mân
engaged หมั้นแล้ว mân láe-ou
endangered species สัตว์ใกล้สูญพันธุ์ sàt glâi sòon pan
end จบ/สิ้นสุด jòp sîn sùt
empty ว่างเปล่า wâang
employer นายจ้าง nai jâang
employee ลูกจ้าง lôok jâang
emotional เจ้าอารมณ์ jâo aa-rom wai
emergency เหตุฉุกเฉิน hèt chùk-chěrn
embassy สถานทูต sà-tǎan tôot
embarrassed อับอาย àp ai
email อีเมล ee-men
elevator ลิฟต์ líp
elephant ช้าง cháang
electricity ไฟฟ้า fai fáh
electrical store ร้านขายอุปกรณ์ไฟฟ้า ráhn
kǎi up-ba-gorn fai fáh
election การเลือกตั้ง gaan lêu-ak dâng
eggplant มะเขือ ma-kěu-a
egg noodles บะหมี่ bà-mèe
egg ไข่ kài
education การศึกษา gaan sèuk-sǎh
editor บรรณาธิการ ban-nah-ti-gahn
eczema แผลเรื้อนกวาง plàa beuay
ecstasy (drug) ยาอี yah yah ee
economy class ชั้นประหยัด chán brà-yàt
eat (very formal) รับประทาน ráp brà-tahn
eat (polite) ทาน tahn
eat (informal) กิน gin
easy ง่าย ngâi
Easter เทศกาลอีสเตอร์ têt-sà-gahn èet
sa-děu
east ทิศตะวันออก tít dà-wan òrk
earthquake แผ่นดินไหว paan din wǎi

extension (visa) ต่ออายุ đòr ah-yú
eye ตา đah
eye drops ยาหยอดตา yah yòrt đah
eyes ตา đah

F

fabric เนื้อผ้า néu·a pâh
face ใบหน้า bai nâh
face cloth ผ้าเช็ดหน้า pâh chét nâh
factory โรงงาน rohng ngahn
factory worker คนทำงานในโรงงาน kon tam ngahn nai rohng ngahn
fall (autumn) หน้าใบไม้ร่วง nâh bai mái róo·ang
fall (down) ล้ม lóm
family ครอบครัว krôrp kroo·a
family name นามสกุล nahm sà·kun
famous มีชื่อเสียง mee chêu sěe·ang
fan (machine) พัดลม pát lom
fan (sport, etc) แฟน faan
fanbelt สายพาน săi pahn
far ไกล glai
fare ค่าโดยสาร kâh doy sǎhn
farm ไร่นา rǎi nah
farmer ชาวไร่ชาวนา chow rǎi chow nah
fashion แฟชั่น faa-chân
fast เร็ว re·ou
fat อ้วน ôo·an
father inf พ่อ pôr
father pol บิดา bi-dah
father-in-law พ่อตา pôr đah
faucet ก๊อกน้ำ górk nám
fault (someone's) ความผิด kwahm pìt
faulty บกพร่อง bok prôrng
fax machine เครื่องแฟกซ์ krêu·ang fàak
February เดือนกุมภาพันธ์ deu·an gum-pah-pan
feed เลี้ยงอาหาร lée·ang ah-hǎhn
feel (touch) คลำ klam
feel (sense) รู้สึก róo-sèuk
feeling (physical) ความรู้สึก kwahm róo-sèuk

feelings อารมณ์ ah-rom
female หญิง yǐng
female (of animals) เพศเมีย pêt mee·a
fence รั้ว róo·a
fencing (sport) การฟันดาบ gahn fan dàhp
ferry เรือข้ามฟาก reu·a kàhm fâhk
festival งาน ngahn
fever ไข้ kâi
few น้อย nóy
fiancé(e) คู่หมั้น kôo mân
fiction เรื่องแต่ง rêu·ang đàang
fight สู้ sôo
fill เติม đeum
fillet เนื้อไม่มีก้าน néu·a mái mee gâhn
film (cinema) ภาพยนตร์ pâhp-pá-yon
film (for camera) ฟิล์ม fim
film speed ความไวของฟิล์ม kawhm wai kǒrng fim
filtered กรอง grorng
find หาเจอ hǎh jeu
fine ดี dee
fine (penalty) ค่าปรับ kâh ɓràp
finger นิ้ว néw
finish ⓝ จุดจบ jùt jòp
finish ⓥ จบ jòp
Finland ประเทศฟินแลนด์ prà-têt fin-laan
fire ไฟ fai
fire extinguisher เครื่องดับเพลิง krêu·ang dàp pleung
firewood ฟืน feun
first ที่หนึ่ง têe nèung
first name ชื่อ chêu
first class ชั้นหนึ่ง chán nèung
first-aid kit ชุดปฐมพยาบาล chút ɓà-tǒm pá-yah-bahn
fish ปลา ɓlah
fish monger คนขายปลา kon kǎi plah
fish shop ร้านขายปลา ráhn kǎi plah
fisherman ชาวประมง chow ɓrà-mong
fishing การหาปลา gahn hǎh plah
fishing boat เรือประมง reu·a ɓrà-mong
flag ธง tong

flannel ผ้าสำลี pâh kŏn nôo
flash (camera) แฟลช fláet
flashlight ไฟฉาย fai chǎi
flat บ้าน bâan
flat (apartment) ห้องชุด hôrng chút
flat mái nîm
flea màt
fleamarket ตลาดขายของเก่า dà-làht
flight (aeroplane) เที่ยวบิน têe-o bin
floating market ตลาดน้ำ dà-làht nám
flood น้ำท่วม nám tôo-am
floor พื้น péun
floor (storey) ชั้น chán
florist คนขายดอกไม้ kon kǎi dòrk mái
flour แป้ง bâang
flower ดอกไม้ dòrk mái
flu ไข้หวัด kâi wàt
fly บิน bin
foggy มีหมอก mee mòrk
follow ตาม dahm
food อาหาร ah-hǎhn
food poisoning อาหารเป็นพิษ ah-hǎhn-ben-pít
food supplies เสบียง sà-bee-ang
foot เท้า tów
football (soccer) ฟุตบอล fút-born
footpath ทางเดิน tahng deun
foreign ต่างชาติ dàhng châht
foreigner คนต่างชาติ kon dàhng châht
foreigner (Westerner) ฝรั่ง fa-ràng
forest ป่า bàh
forever ตลอดไป dà-lòrt pai
forget ลืม leum
forgive ให้อภัย hâi a-pai
fork ส้อม sôrm
fortnight สองอาทิตย์ bâak
fortune teller หมอดู mŏr doo
foul (in football) ฟาวล์ fow
foyer ห้องโถง hôrng tŏhng
fragile บอบบาง bòrp bahng
rohng raam
France ประเทศฝรั่งเศส bra-tét fa-ràng-sèt

free (available) ว่าง wâhng
free (gratis) ฟรี free
free (not bound) อิสระ it-sà-rà
freezer ตู้แช่แข็ง dôo châe kǎang
fresh สด sòt
Friday วันศุกร์ wan sùk
fridge ตู้เย็น dôo yen
fried (deep) ทอด tôrt
fried rice ข้าวผัด kôw pàt
friend เพื่อน pêu-an
friendly เป็นมิตร ben mìt
frog กบ gòp
from จาก jàhk
frost น้ำค้างแข็ง nám káhng kǎang
frozen แช่แข็ง châe kǎang
fruit ผลไม้ pŏn-lá-mái
fruit juice น้ำผลไม้ nám pŏn-lá-mái
fruit picking การเก็บผลไม้ gahn gèp pŏn-lá-mái
fry (deep fry) ทอด tôrt
frying pan กระทะ grà-tá
full เต็ม dem
full-time เต็มเวลา dem wair-lah
fun สนุก sà-nùk
funeral งานศพ ngahn sòp
funny ตลก dà-lòk
furniture เฟอร์นิเจอร์ feu-ní-jeu
future อนาคต à-nah-kót

G

game (football) เกม gem
game (sport) เกม gem
garage (sport) อู่ซ่อมรถ òo sôrm rót
garbage ขยะ kà-yà
garbage can ถังขยะ tǎng kà-yà
garden สวน sŏo-an
gardener คนสวน chow sŏo-an
gardening การทำสวน gahn tam sŏo-an
garlic กระเทียม grà-tee-am

gas (for cooking) ก๊าซ gáht

gas (petrol) น้ำมันเบนซิน nám-man ben-sin

gas cartridge ถังแก๊ส tǎng gáat

gas station ปั๊มน้ำมัน ฿ám nám-man

gastroenteritis โรคกระเพาะอักเสบ rôhk grà-pó àk-sèp

gate (airport, etc) ประตู ฿rà-đoo

gauze ผ้าพันแผล pâh pan plăa

gay เกย์ gair

Germany ประเทศเยอรมัน ฿rà-têt yeu-rá-man

get เอา ow

get off (a train, etc) ลง long

ghost ผี pěe

gift ของขวัญ kŏrng kwăn

gig การแสดง gahn sà-daang

gin เหล้าจิน lôw jin

girl สาว sŏw

girlfriend แฟนสาว faan sŏw

give ให้ hâi

glandular fever โรคเริม rôhk reum

glass (drinking) แก้ว gâa-ou

glasses (spectacles) แว่นตา wâan đah

glove(s) ถุงมือ tŭng meu

glue กาว gow

go ไป ฿ai

go out ไปข้างนอก ฿ai kâhng nôrk

go out with ไปเที่ยวกับ ฿ai têe-o gàp

go shopping ไปซื้อของ ฿ai séu kŏrng

goal เป้าหมาย ฿ôw măi

goal (football) ประตู ฿rà-đoo

goalkeeper ผู้รักษาประตู pôo rák-sǎh ฿rà-đoo

goat แพะ paa

god (general) เทวดา tair-wá-dah

God พระเจ้า prá jôw

goggles (swimming) แว่นกันน้ำ wâan gan nám

gold ทองคำ torng kam

Golden Triangle สามเหลี่ยมทองคำ sǎhm lèe-am torng kam

goldsmith ช่างทอง châhng torng

golf ball ลูกกอล์ฟ lôok górp

golf course สนามกอล์ฟ sà-nǎhm górp

good ดี dee

goodbye ลาก่อน lah gòrn

government รัฐบาล rát-tà-bahn

gram กรัม gram

grandchild หลาน lǎhn

grandfather (maternal) ตา đah

grandfather (paternal) ปู่ ฿òo

grandmother (maternal) ยาย yai

grandmother (paternal) ย่า yâh

grapes องุ่น à-ngùn

grass หญ้า yâh

grass (marijuana) กัญชา gan-chah

grateful ปลื้มใจ ฿lêum jai

grave ที่ฝังศพ têe fǎng sòp

gray สีเทา sěe tow

great (fantastic) ยอด yôrt

green สีเขียว sěe kěe-o

green pepper พริกเขียว prík kěe-o

greengrocer คนขายผัก kon kǎi pàk

grey สีเทา sěe tow

grocery ร้านขายของชำ ráhn kǎi kŏrng cham

grow (a plant) ปลูก ฿lòok

grow (bigger) งอก ngôrk

grow (develop) เจริญ jà-reun

g-string จีสตริง jee sà-đring

guaranteed รับประกัน ráp ฿rà-gan

guess เดา dow

guesthouse บ้านพัก bâhn pák

guide (person) ไกด์ gai

guide dog สุนัขนำทางคนตาบอด sù-nák nam tahng kon đah bòrt

guidebook คู่มือนำเที่ยว kôo meu nam têe-o

guided tour ทัวร์ too-a

guilty มีความผิด mee kwahm pìt

guitar กีตาร์ gee-đah

gulf อ่าว òw

gum (chewing) หมากฝรั่ง màhk fà-ràng

gun ปืน ƀeun
gym (place) ห้อง ออกกำลังกาย hôrng òrk gam-lang gai
gymnastics ยิมนาสติก yim-nah-sà-đik
gynaecologist นรีแพทย์ ná-ree-pâat

H

hair ผม pǒm
hairbrush แปรง ƀraang
haircut การตัดผม gahn đàt pǒm
hairdresser ช่างตัดผม châhng đàt pǒm
halal อาหาร ที่จัดทำตามหลักศาสนาอิสลาม ah-hǎhn têe jàt tam đahm làk sàht-sà-nǎh it-sà-lahm
half ครึ่ง krêung
hallucination ภาพหลอน pâhp lǒrn
ham เนื้อแฮม néu-a haam
hammer ค้อน kórn
hammock เปลญวน plair yoo-an
hand มือ meu
handbag กระเป๋าพาย grà-ƀǒw pai
handicrafts เครื่อง หัตถกรรม krêu-ang hàt-tà-gam
handkerchief ผ้าเช็ดหน้า pâh chét nâh
handlebars มือจับ meu jàp
handmade ทำด้วยมือ tam dôo-ay meu
handsome รูปหล่อ rôop lòr
happy สุข sùk
harassment การเบียดเบียน gahn bèe-at bee-an
harbour อ่าว òw
hard (not soft) แข็ง kǎang
hard (difficult) ยาก yâhk
hard-boiled ต้มแข็ง đôm kǎang
hardware store ร้านขายอุปกรณ์ก่อสร้าง ráhn kǎi ùp-ƀà-gorn gòr sâhng
hat หมวก mòo-ak
have มี mee
have a cold เป็นหวัด ƀen wàt
have fun สนุก sà-nùk
hay fever โรคภูมิแพ้ rôhk poom páa
he เขา kǒw

head หัว hǒo-a
headache ปวดหัว ƀòo-at hǒo-a
headlights ไฟหน้ารถ fai nâh rót
health สุขภาพ sù-kà-pâhp
hear ได้ยิน dâi yin
hearing aid หูเทียม hǒo tee-am
heart หัวใจ hǒo-a jai
heart attack หัวใจวาย hǒo-a jai wai
heart condition โรคหัวใจ rôhk hǒo-a jai
heat ความร้อน kwahm rórn
heated เขาร้อน rôw rórn
heavy หนัก nàk
Hello. สวัสดีครับ/สวัสดีค่ะ sà-wàt-dee kráp/sà-wàt-dee kâ m/f
Hello. (answering telephone) ฮัลโหล han-lǒh
helmet หมวกกันน็อก mòo-ak gan nórk
help ① ความช่วยเหลือ kwahm chôo-ay lěu-a
help ⓥ ช่วย chôo-ay
Help! ช่วยด้วย chôo-ay dôo-ay
hepatitis โรคตับอักเสบ rôhk đàp àk-sèp
her ของ เขา kǒrng kǒw
herb สมุนไพร sà-mǔn-prai
herbalist คนขายสมุนไพร kon kǎi sà-mǔn-prai
here ที่นี่ têe née
hermit cave ถ้ำฤๅษี tâm reu-sěe
heroin เฮโรอีน hair-roh-een
high สูง sǒong
high school โรงเรียนมัธยม rohng ree-an mát-tá-yom
highchair เก้าอี้สูง gôw-êe sǒong
highway ทางหลวง tahng lǒo-ang
hike เดินป่า deun ƀàh
hiking การเดินป่า gahn deun ƀàh
hiking boots รองเท้าเดินป่า rorng tów deun ƀàh
hiking route ทางเดินป่า tahng deun ƀàh
hill เขา kǒw
Hindu ศาสนาฮินดู sàht-sà-nǎh hin-doo
hire เช่า chôw

his เขา kŏw

historical ทางประวัติศาสตร์ tahng brà-wàt-dì-sàht

history ประวัติศาสตร์ brà-wàt-dì-sàht

hitchhike โบกรถ bòhk rót

HIV ไวรัสเอชไอวี wai-rát èt ai wee

hockey ฮอกกี้ hók-kêe

holiday (public) วันหยุด wan yùt

holidays การพักร้อน gahn pák rón

home บ้าน bâhn

homeless ไม่มีบ้าน mâi mee bâhn

homemaker แม่บ้าน mâe bâhn

homosexual คนรักร่วมเพศ kon rák rôo-am pét

honey ผึ้ง pêung

honeymoon เดินทางฮันนีมูน dern taang hanee-moon

horoscope ดวงพระจันทร์ doo-ang prá jan

horse ม้า máh

horse riding การขี่ม้า gahn kèe máh

hospital โรงพยาบาล rohng pá-yaa-bahn

hospitality การรับแขก gahn ráp kàak

hostess (bar) โฮสเตส hôht-dèt

hot (spicy) เผ็ด pét

hot ร้อน rón

hot springs บ่อน้ำร้อน bòr nám rón

hot water น้ำร้อน nám rón

hotel โรงแรม rohng raem

hour ชั่วโมง chôo-a mohng

house บ้าน bâhn

housework งานบ้าน gahn bâhn

how อย่างไร yàhng rai

how much เท่าไหร่ tôw rai

hug กอด gòt

huge ใหญ่มหึมา yài má-hĕu-mah

human resources สรรพยากรมนุษย์ sàp-pá-yah-gorn má-nút

human rights สิทธิมนุษย์ sìt-tì má-nút-sà-yá-chon

humanities มนุษยศาสตร์ má-nút-sà-yá-sàht

hundred ร้อย róy

hungry (to be) หิว hĕw

hunting การล่าสัตว์ gahn lâh sàt

hurry (in a) รีบรีบ rêep rêep

hurt ทำให้เจ็บ hâi jèp

hurt (to be hurt) เจ็บ jèp

husband ผัว pŏo-a

I ผม/ดิฉัน pŏm/di-chǎn m/f

ice น้ำแข็ง nám kăang

ice cream ไอติม ai-dim

ice hockey ฮอกกี้น้ำแข็ง hók-gêe nám

ice-cream parlour ร้านขายไอศครีม ráhn kăang

identification หลักฐาน lák tăhn

identification card (ID) บัตรประจำตัว bàt

idiot ปัญญาอ่อน ban-yah ôm

if ถ้า tâh

ill ป่วย bòo-ay

immigration การตรวจคนเข้าเมือง dròo-at kon

important สำคัญ săm-kan

impossible เป็นไปไม่ได้ ben bai mâi dâi

in ใน nai

in front of ต่อหน้า dòr nâh

included รวมด้วย roo-am dôo-ay

income tax ภาษี pah-sĕe

India อินเดีย in-dee-a

indicator ไฟเลี้ยว fai lée-o

indigestion อาหารไม่ย่อย ah-hăhn

indoor ข้างใน kâhng nai

industry อุตสาหกรรม ùt-săh-gam

infection ติดเชื้อ dìt chéu-a

inflammation ที่อักเสบ tèe ak-sèp

influenza ไข้หวัด kâi wàt

information ข้อมูล kòr moon

ingredient ส่วนประกอบ sòo-an brà-gòrp

inject ฉีด chèet

injection การฉีด gahn chèet

injured บาดเจ็บ bàht jèp
injury บาดแผล tée bàht jèp
inner tube ยางใน yahng nai
innocent ไร้เดียงสา bor-rí-sùt
insect repellent ยากันแมลง yah gan má-laang
inside ข้างใน kâhng nai
instructor ผู้สอน pôo sŏrn
insurance การประกัน gahn bpra-gan
interesting น่าสนใจ nâh sŏn-jai
international ระหว่างประเทศ rá-wàhng bpra-tét
Internet อินเตอร์เน็ต in-deu-nèt
Internet café ร้านอินเตอร์เน็ต ráhn in-deu-nèt
interpreter ล่าม lâhm
interview การสัมภาษณ์ gahn săm-pâht
invite เชิญ choo-an
iron (for clothes) เตารีด dow rêet
island เกาะ gò
Israel ประเทศอิสราเอล bpra-tét-ì-sa-rah-airm
IT เทคโนโลยีสารสนเทศ ték-noh-loh-yee sāhn sŏn-tét
it มัน man
Italy ประเทศอิตาลี bpra-tét-i-dah-lee
itch คัน kan
itinerary รายการเดินทาง rai gahn

J

jacket เสื้อกันหนาว sêu-a gan nŏw
jail คุก kúk
jam แยม yaam
January เดือนมกราคม deu-an má-gà-rah-kom
Japan ประเทศญี่ปุ่น bpra-tét yêe-bùn
jar กระปุก grà-bùk
jaw ขากรรไกร kâh gan-grai
jealous อิจฉา ìt-chăh
jeans กางเกงยีน gahng geng yeen
jeep รถจี๊ป rót jéep
jellyfish แมงกะพรุน maang gà-prun

jet lag อาการเหนื่อยล้าจากการเดินทาง gahn bpùat ráhng gài gàp wair-lah tée
jewellery เครื่องประดับ dàak dahng
pet ploy
Jewish ชาวยิว chow yew
job งาน ngahn
jogging การวิ่งออกกำลังกาย gahn wîng òrk gam-lang
joke เรื่องตลก kam dà-lòk
journalist ผู้สื่อข่าว นักข่าว nák kèe-an
journey การเดินทาง gahn deun tahng náng-sěu pim
judge ผู้พิพากษา pôo pí-pâhk-săh
juice น้ำผลไม้ nám pŏn-lá-mái
July เดือนกรกฎาคม deu-an gà-rá-gà-dah-kom
jump กระโดด grà-dòht
jumper (sweater) เสื้อ sêu-a tàk
jumper leads สายพ่วงแบตเตอรี่ săi pòo-ang
June เดือนมิถุนายน deu-an mí-tù-nah-yon
jungle ป่า bpàh ròk
junk (boat) เรือสำเภา reu-a săm-pow

K

ketchup ซอสมะเขือเทศ sórt ma-kěu-a tét
key กุญแจ lòok gun-jae
keyboard คีย์บอร์ด kee-bòrt
kick เตะ dté
kidney ไต dai
kilo กิโล gì-loh
kilogram กิโลกรัม gì-loh-gram
kilometre กิโลเมตร gì-loh-mét
kind (nice) ใจดี jai dee
kindergarten อนุบาล à-nu-bahn
The King ในหลวง nai lŏo-ang
kiosk ร้านเล็ก ráhn lék
kiss จูบ ✓☺✓ jòop
kitchen ครัว kroo-a
knee หัวเข่า hŏo-a kòw
knife มีด mêet

know รู้ róo
kosher อาหารที่จัดทำตามลักษณะ ah-hăhn têe jàt tam dahm lák
sàht-sà-năh yew

L

labourer กรรมกร gam-ma-gorn
lace ลูกไม้ lôok mái
lake ทะเลสาบ tá-lair sàhp
land ประเทศ brà-tèt
landlord/landlady เจ้าของที่ jôw kŏrng têe
lane ซอย soy
language ภาษา paa-săh
Laos ประเทศลาว brà-têt low
laptop คอมพิวเตอร์โน๊ตบุ๊ค korm-pew-děu
large ใหญ่ yài
last (previous) ที่แล้ว tee láew
last (week) ที่แล้ว tee láew
late ช้า cháh
later ทีหลัง tee lăng
laugh หัวเราะ hŏo-a ró
launderette โรงซักรีด rohng sák réet
laundry (clothes) ผ้าซัก pâh sák
laundry (place) ที่ซักผ้า tèe sák pâh
laundry (room) ห้องซักผ้า hôrng sák pâh
law กฎหมาย gòt-mǎi
law (study, profession) การกฎหมาย gahn gòt-mǎi
lawyer ทนายความ gahn gòt-mǎi
laxative ยาระบาย yah rá-bai
lazy ขี้เกียจ kêe gèe-at
leader ผู้นำ pôo nam
leaf ใบไม้ bai mái
learn เรียน ree-an
leather หนัง núa năng
lecturer อาจารย์ ah-jahn
ledge ริมเชิงผา rá hìm cheung pàh
left (direction) ข้างซ้าย kâang sái
left luggage บริการกระเป๋าฝาก left luggage grà-bow fàhk
left luggage (office) left luggage bor jâi
horng ráp fáhk grà-bów

left-wing ฝ่ายซ้าย fài sái
leg ขา kǎh
legal ทางกฎหมาย tahng gòt-mǎi
legislation นิติบัญญัติ nì-dì-ban-yàt
legume ผักถั่ว pàk tòo-a
lemonade น้ำมะนาว nám-ma-now
lens เลนส์ layn
lentil ถั่วเขียว tòo-a kèe-o
lesbian เลสเบี้ยน lét-bee-an
less น้อยกว่า nóy gwàh
letter (mail) จดหมาย jòt-mǎi
lettuce ผักกาดหอม pàk gàht hŏrm
liar คนโกหก kon gôh-hòk
library ห้องสมุด hôrng sà-mùt
lice เหา hăw
licence plate number ป้ายเลขทะเบียน mái lêk ta-bee-an
licence ใบอนุญาต bai à-nu-yâht
lie (recline) นอน norm
lie (tell a lie) โกหก goh-hòk
life ชีวิต chee-wìt
life jacket เสื้อชูชีพ sêu-a choo chêep
lift (elevator) ลิฟท์ lip
light (electric) ไฟ fai
light (not heavy) เบา bow
light (of colour) อ่อน ôrn
light bulb หลอดไฟ lòrt fai
lighter (cigarette) ไฟแช็ค fai cháak
like ชอบ chôrp
lime มะนาว má-now
linen (material) ผ้าลินิน pâh li-nin
linen (sheets etc) ผ้าปู pâh boo
lip balm ขี้ผึ้งทาที่นอน kêe pêung tah tée norm
lips ริมฝีปาก rim fěe bàhk
lipstick ลิปสติก lip-sà-dìk
liquor store ร้านเหล้า ráhn lôw
listen (to) ฟัง fang
little (small) น้อย nóy
little (not much) นิดหน่อย nít-nòy
live (somewhere) อยู่ yòo

machine เครื่อง krêu-ang

mackerel ปลาทู blah too

M

luxury หรูหรา rŏo rǎh

lung ปอด bòt

lunch อาหารกลางวัน ah-hăhn glahng wan

lump ก้อน gôm

luggage tag ป้ายติดกระเป๋า bâi dtìt gra-bow

luggage lockers ตู้เก็บกระเป๋า dôo fàhk gra-bow

luggage กระเป๋า gra-bow

lucky โชคดี chôhk dee

luck โชค chôhk

lubricant น้ำมันหล่อลื่น nám man lòr leun

low ต่ำ dam

lover คู่รัก kôo rák

love รัก rák

love ความรัก kwahm rák

loud ดัง dang

(a) lot มากมาย mâhk

lost property office ที่รับแจ้งของหาย jâeng kŏng hăi

lost หาย hăi

lose ทำหาย tam hăi

loose change เงินปลีก ngern blèek

loose หลวม lŏo-am

lookout จุดชมวิว tée chom tew-tàt

look for หา hăh

look after ดูแล gùa doo laa

look ดู doo

long ยาว yow

lollies ลูกอม lôok om

locked ล็อกไว้แล้ว sài gun-jaa láo-ou

lock ล็อก sài gun-jaa

local ท้องถิ่น tórng tìn

lobster กุ้งทะเลตัวใหญ่ gûng tá-lair dtua yài

lizard (monitor) ตัวเงินตัวทอง dta-gòo-at

lizard (house) จิ้งจก jîng-jòk

lizard (gecko) ตุ๊กแก dúk-gaa

liver ตับ dàp

---

magazine นิตยสาร หนังสือ náng sĕu wah-rá-săhn

magic mushrooms เห็ดขี้ควาย hèt kêe kwai

mail (letters) จดหมาย jòt-măi

mail (postal system) ไปรษณีย์ brai-sà-nee

mailbox ตู้ไปรษณีย์ dôo brai-sà-nee

main หลัก lòhk

main road ถนนสายหลัก tà-nŏn săi lòhk tahng lŏo-ang

make ทำ tam

make-up เครื่องสำอาง krêu-ang săm-ahng

mammogram เอ็กซ์เรย์เต้านม ék-sà-rai dòw nom

man ผู้ชาย pôo jai

manager ผู้จัดการ pôo jàt gahn

mandarin ส้มเขียวหวาน sôm kĕe-o wăhn

mango มะม่วง má-môo-ang

manual worker กรรมกร gam-ma-gorn

many เยอะ yúh

map แผนที่ păan têe

March มีนาคม mee-nah-kom

margarine เนยเทียม nui i-tee-am

marijuana กัญชา gan-chah

marital status สถานะการสมรส sà-tăh-na-gahn sŏm-rót

market ตลาด dta-làht

married แต่งงานแล้ว dàang ngahn láa-ou

marry แต่งงาน dàang ngahn

martial arts ศิลปะการต่อสู้ sin-la-bà gahn dòr sôo

Mass (Catholic) พิธีมิสซา pí-tee mít-sah

massage นวด nôo-at

masseur/masseuse หมอนวด mŏr nôo-at

mat เสื่อ sèu-a

matches (for lighting) ไม้ขีดไฟ mái kèet fai

material (cloth) ผ้า pâh kèet tai

mattress ฟูก fôok

May เดือนพฤษภาคม deu-an préut-sà-pah-kom

maybe บางที bahng tee
mayonnaise น้ำสลัด nám ráht
mayor นายกเทศมนตรี nah-yók têt-sà-mon-dree
me ผม/ฉัน pǒm/di-chán m/f
meal อาหารมื้อ meu ah-hǎhn
measles โรคหัด rôhk hàt
meat เนื้อ néu-a
mechanic ช่างเครื่อง châhng krêu-ang
media สื่อมวลชน séu moo-an chon
medicine (medication) ยา yah
medicine (study, profession) การแพทย์ gahn pâet
meditation การนั่งสมาธิ gahn tam sà-mah-tí
meditation centre ศูนย์สมาธิ sŏon pah-wá-nah
meet พบ póp
Mekong catfish ปลาบึก blah bèuk
melon แตง 1 daang
member สมาชิก sà-mah-chík
menstruation ระดู rá-doo
menu รายการอาหาร rai gahn ah-hǎhn
message ข้อความ kôr kwahm fàhk
metal โลหะ mét lék
metro (sky train) รถไฟฟ้า rót fai fáh
metro station สถานีรถไฟฟ้า sà-tǎh-nee
microwave (oven) เตาไมโครเวฟ doh
midday เที่ยงวัน têe-ang wan
midnight เที่ยงคืน têe-ang keun
migraine ไมเกรน mai-gren
military ทหาร tá-hǎhn
military service การรับราชการทหาร gahn ben
milk นมสด milk nám nom
millilitre มิลลิลิตร min-li-mét
million ล้าน láhn

mince มีน sáp
mineral water น้ำแร่ nám ráa
minivan รถตู้ rót dôo
minute นาที nah-tee
mirror กระจก grà-jòk
miscarriage การแท้ง gahn táang
miss (feel absence of) คิดถึง kít teung
mistake ความผิด ⊙ kwǎhm pìt plâht
mix ผสม pà-sòm
mobile phone โทรศัพท์มือถือ toh-rá-sàp meu teu
modern ทันสมัย tahn moh-dem
moisturiser ครีมบำรุงผิว bam-rung kwǎhm chéun
monastery วัด wát
Monday วันจันทร์ wan jan
money เงิน ngern
monk พระ prá
monk's living quarters กุฏิ gù-dì
monsoon มรสุม mor-rá-sum
month เดือน deu-an
monument อนุสาวรีย์ à-nu-săh-wá-ree
noon เที่ยง prá jan
moped รถมอเตอร์ไซค์ rót mor-dern-sai
more (than before) มากขึ้น mâhk kêun
more (than something else) อีก èek
morning เช้า dorn chów
morning sickness แพ้ท้อง páa tórng
mosque มัสยิด mát-sà-yìt
mosquito ยุง yung
mosquito coil ยากันยุง yah jùt gan
mosquito net มุ้ง múng
mother แม่ mâa
mother-in-law (mother of husband) พ่อผัว pol pǒo-a mahn-dah
mother-in-law (mother of wife) แม่ยาย mâa yai

N

nail clippers กรรไกรตัดเล็บ gan-grai dtàt lép
name ชื่อ chêu
napkin ผ้าเช็ดปาก pâh chét bpàak
nappy ผ้าอ้อม pâh ôm

di-chán
my (for a woman) ของฉัน kŏng chán
my (for a man) ของผม kŏng pŏm
mute ใบ้ bâi
mussel หอยแมลงภู่ hŏy ma-laeng pôo
Muslim ชาวอิสลาม chow it-sà-lahm
musician นักดนตรี nák don-dree
music shop ร้านขายดนตรี rahn don-dree
music ดนตรี don-dree
mushroom เห็ด hèt
museum พิพิธภัณฑ์ pí-pít-tá-pan
muscle กล้ามเนื้อ glâhm néu-a
murder (v) ฆ่า kâh
murder (n) การฆาตกรรม kâht-dà-gam
mumps โรคคางทูม rôhk kahng toom
mum แม่ mâe
mud โคลน kohn klohn
Miss/Ms นางสาว nahng sŏw
Mrs นาง nahng
Mr นาย nai
movie หนังภาพยนตร์ năng pâhp-pá-yon
mouth ปาก bpàak
mouse หนู nŏo
mountaineering การปีนเขา gahn been kŏw
mountain range เทือกเขา têuk-kŏw
mountain path ทางขึ้นเขา tahng khêun kŏw
mountain goat เลียงผา lee-ang pǎh
mountain bike จักรยานภูเขา jàk-grà-yahn poo kŏw
mountain ภูเขา poo kŏw
dòo-an
motorway (tollway) ทางด่วน tahng dòo-an
motorcycle รถจักรยานยนต์ rot mor-deu-sai yon
motorboat เรือยนต์ reu-a yon
motorbike รถจักรยานยนต์ rot mor-deu-sai

nappy rash ผื่นผ้าอ้อม phèun pàa ut-tá-yahn
national park อุทยานแห่งชาติ ut-ta-yahn hàang châht
nationality สัญชาติ săn-châht
nature ธรรมชาติ tam-ma-châht
naturopathy การรักษาโรคด้วยวิธีธรรมชาติ wi-tee tam-ma-châht
nausea คลื่นไส้ khleun sâi
near ใกล้ glâi
nearby ที่อยู่ใกล้ๆ tée yòo glâi-ang
nearest ใกล้ที่สุด glâi têe-sùt
necessary จำเป็น jam-ben
necklace สร้อยคอ sôy kor
need ต้องการ dtông gahn
needle (sewing) เข็ม kěm
needle (syringe) เข็มฉีดยา kěm chèet
negative ฟิล์มเนกาทีฟ dtah-kài
net ตาข่าย dtah-kài
Netherlands ประเทศเนเธอร์แลนด์ pra-têt nair-teu-laan
network เครือข่าย krea-a kài
never ไม่เคย mâi keu-I
new ใหม่ mài
New Year's Day วันปีใหม่ wan bpee mài
New Year's Eve คืนวันปีใหม่ keun wan sin bee
New Zealand ประเทศนิวซีแลนด์ pra-têt new see-laan
news ข่าว kòw
news stand แผงหนังสือพิมพ์ têe kâi nǎng-sěu pim
newsagency ร้านขายหนังสือพิมพ์ rahn kǎi nǎng-sěu pim
newspaper หนังสือพิมพ์ nǎng-sěu pim
next (month) หน้า nâh
next to ถัดไป tàt bpai kâhng kâng
nice (food etc) อร่อย a-ròy
nickname ชื่อเล่น chêu lên
niece หลานสาว lǎhn sŏw
night คืน keun

night out เที่ยวกลางคืน têe-o glahng keun
nightclub ไนท์คลับ nai klap
no ไม่ mâi
no vacancy ไม่มีห้องว่าง mâi mee hông wâhng
noisy เสียงดัง sĕe-ang dang
none ไม่มีเลย mâi mee loie
non-smoking ห้ามสูบบุหรี่ mâi sòop bu-rèe
noodle shop ร้านก๋วยเตี๋ยว ráhn gŏoay-dĕe-o
noodles เส้น sen
noon เที่ยง têe-ang
north ทิศเหนือ tít nĕu-a
Norway ประเทศนอร์เวย์ brà-têt nor-wair
nose จมูก jà-mòok
not ไม่ mâi
notebook สมุดบันทึก sà-mùt ban-téuk
nothing ไม่มีอะไร mâi mee à-rai
November พฤศจิกายน préut-sà-ji-gah-yon
nuclear energy พลังงานนิวเคลียร์ pá-lang ngahn new-klee-a
nuclear testing การทดลองนิวเคลียร์ gahn tót long new-klee-a
nuclear waste กากนิวเคลียร์ gàhk new-klee-a
number (figure) ตัวเลข măi lêk
number (quantity) จำนวน jam-noo-an
numberplate แผ่นป้ายทะเบียน pàen bâi tá-bee-an
nurse (man) บุรุษพยาบาล bù-rút pá-yah-bahn
nurse (woman) นางพยาบาล nahng pá-yah-bahn
nut ถั่ว tòo-a

O

oats ข้าวโอ๊ต kôw óht
ocean มหาสมุทร ma-hăh sà-mut
October เดือนตุลาคม deu-an dù-lah-kom

off (spoiled) เสีย sĕe-a
office (place) สำนักงาน săm-nák ngahn
office worker พนักงานสำนักงาน pá-nák ngahn săm-nák ngahn
often บ่อยๆ bòi bòi
oil น้ำมัน náhm man
oil (motor) น้ำมันเครื่อง náhm man krêu-ang
old (person) แก่ gàe
old (thing) เก่า gòw
olive มะกอก ma-gòrk
olive oil น้ำมันมะกอก náhm man ma-gòrk
Olympic Games กีฬาโอลิมปิก gee-lah oh-lim-bìk
omelette ไข่เจียว kài jee-o
on บน bon
on (not off) เปิด bèut
on time ตรงเวลา drong way-lah
once ครั้งเดียว kráng dee-o
one หนึ่ง nèung
one-way (ticket) เที่ยวเดียว têe-o dee-o
onion หอมหัวใหญ่ hŏrm hŏo-a yài
only เท่านั้น tôw nán
open (v) เปิด bèut
opening hours เวลาเปิด-ปิด way-lah bèut-bìt
opera house โรงอุปรากร rohng ùp-bà-rah-gorn
opera อุปรากร ùp-bà-rah-gorn
operation (medical) การผ่าตัด gahn pàh dàt
operator (telephone) พนักงานโทรศัพท์ pá-nák ngahn toh-rá-sàp
opinion ความคิดเห็น kwahm kít hĕn
opposite ตรงกันข้าม drong gan kâhm
optometrist หมอตรวจสายตา mŏr dròo-at săi dah
or หรือ rĕu
orange (colour) สีส้ม sĕe sôm
orange (fruit) ส้ม sôm
orange juice น้ำส้ม náhm sôm
orchestra วงดุริยางค์ wong du-ri-yahng
order (v) สั่ง sàng
order (n) ใบสั่ง bai sàng

ordinary ธรรมดา tam-ma-dah

orgasm จุดสุดยอด jùt sùt yôrt

original ดั้งเดิม dâng deum

our ของเรา kŏrng rao

out of order เสีย sĕe-a

outside ข้างนอก kâhng nôrk

ovarian cyst ถุงน้ำในรังไข่ tŭng nám nai rang kài

ovary รังไข่ rang kài

oven เตาอบ dao òp

overcoat เสื้อคลุม sêu-a klum

overdose ใช้ยาเกินขนาด chái yah geun yah geun
kà-nàht

overnight ค้างคืน káhng keun

overseas ต่างประเทศ dàhng bprà-têt

owner เจ้าของ jôw kŏrng

oxygen ออกซิเจน órk-sí-jen

oyster หอยนางรม hŏy nahng rom

ozone layer ชั้นโอโซนในชั้นบรรยากาศ chán
ozone layer

p

pacifier (dummy) หัวนมหลอกของเด็ก hŏo-a nom
tee-am

packet (general) ห่อ hòr

package ห่อ hòr

paddy field นา nah

padlock แม่กุญแจ mâe gun-jaa

page หน้า nâh

pain ความเจ็บปวด kwahm bòo-at

painful เจ็บ jèp

painter ช่างทาสี châhng tah sĕe

painting (a work) ภาพเขียน pâhp kĕe-an

painting (the art) การวาดภาพ gahn

pair (couple) คู่ kôo

Pakistan ประเทศปากีสถาน bprà-têt
bah-gee-sà-tăhn

palace วัง wang

---

pan กระทะ grà-tá

pandanus leaf ใบเตย bai deu-i

pants (trousers) กางเกง gahng-geng

pantyhose ถุงน่อง tŭng nông

panty liners ผ้าอนามัยแบบบาง pâh a-na-mai

paper กระดาษ grà-dàht

pap smear การตรวจภายในของผู้หญิง gahn dròo-at pai nai

paperwork เอกสาร èk-gà-săhn

paraplegic คนอัมพาต kon am-ma-pâht

parcel ห่อ hòr

parents พ่อแม่ pôr mâe

park (a car) จอดรถ jòrt rót

park สวนสาธารณะ sŏo-an săh-tah-rá-ná

parliament รัฐสภา rát-tà-sà-pah

part (component) ส่วนประกอบ sòo-an

part-time ไม่เต็มเวลา mâi dem wair-lah

party (night out) งานเลี้ยง ngahn lée-ang

party (politics) พรรค pák

pass ผ่าน pàhn

passenger ผู้โดยสาร pôo doy săhn

passport หนังสือเดินทาง năng-sĕu deun
tahng

passport number หมายเลขหนังสือเดินทาง
mái lêk năng-sĕu deun tahng

past อดีต à-dèet

pasta เส้น sên

pastry ขนมอบ ka-nŏm

path ทาง tahng

pay จ่าย jài

payment การจ่ายเงิน gahn jài ngern

pea ถั่วลันเตา tòo-a lan-dow

peace สันติภาพ săn-dì-pâhp

peak (mountain) ยอดเขา yôrt kŏw

peanut ถั่วลิสง tòo-a lí-song

pear ลูกแพร lôok paa

pedal บันไดรถ ban-dai rót

pedestrian คนเดินถนน kon deun tŏn
jàk-gà-yahn

pedicab สามล้อรับจ้าง săhm lór

pedicab (motorised) รถตุ๊กตุ๊ก rót dúk dúk

pen (ballpoint) ปากกา (ลูกลื่น) pàhk-gah
(lôok lêun)

P

penis อวัยวะเพศชาย ong-ká-châht

penknife มีดพับ mêet páp

pensioner ผู้รับเงินบำนาญ kon gin ngeun bam-nahn

people คน kon

pepper (bell) พริกหยวก prík tai

pepper พริกไทย prík

per (day) ต่อ dòr

per cent เปอร์เซ็นต์ beu-sen

perfect สมบูรณ์แบบ sŏm-boon

performance การแสดง sà-daang

perfume น้ำหอม nám hŏrm

period pain ปวดประจำเดือน bòo-at ra-doo-

permission การอนุญาต à-nu-yâht

permit ใบอนุญาต bai à-nu-yâht

person คน kon

petition ยื่นคำร้อง nâng-sĕu rórng

petrol น้ำมัน ben-sin

petrol station ปั๊มน้ำมัน bâm nám-man

pharmacist เภสัชกร pair-sàt-chá-gorn

pharmacy ร้านขายยา ráhn kăi yah

phone book สมุดโทรศัพท์ sà-mut toh-

phone box ตู้โทรศัพท์ dôo toh-ra-sàp

phone card บัตรโทรศัพท์ bàt toh-ra-sàp

photo รูปถ่าย rôop tài

photographer ช่างภาพ châhng tài páp

photography การถ่ายรูป páp

phrasebook หนังสือรวมคำ kôo meu

pickaxe อีเต้อ plôo-a

pickles ผักดอง kŏrng dorng

pickpocket (v) นักล้วงกระเป๋า ka-moy

picnic ปิกนิก bìk-nìk

pie พายไส้ต่างๆ ka-nŏm pai

piece ชิ้น chín

pier ท่าเรือ tâh reu-a

pig หมู mŏo

big ใหญ่ yài

pill (the) ยาเม็ด yah kum gam-neut

pillow หมอน mŏm

pillowcase ปลอกหมอน block mŏm

pineapple สับปะรด sàp-bà-rót

pink สีชมพู sĕe chom-poo

pipe (smoking) กล้องยาสูบ glôrng sòop yah

pistachio ถั่วพิสตาชิโอ tòo pí-sà-dah-chi-oh

place สถานที่ sà-tăhn-têe

place of birth สถานที่เกิด sà-tăhn-têe gèut

plane (aeroplane) เครื่องบิน krêu-ang bin

planet ดาวเคราะห์ dow krŏ

plant พืช pêut

plastic พลาสติก plah-sà-dìk

plate จาน jahn

plateau ที่ราบสูง têe râhp sŏong

platform ชานชาลา chahn chah-lah

play (cards) เล่นไพ่ lên

play (guitar) เล่นกีตาร์ lên

play (theatre) ละคร lá-korn

plug (bath) จุก jùk

plug (electricity) ปลั๊กไฟ plák

poached ต้มน้ำ nám tôm

pocket (shirt, jacket) กระเป๋าเสื้อ gra-bŏw sêu-a

pocket (pants) กระเป๋ากางเกง gra-bŏw gahng geng

pocket knife มีดพับ mêet páp

poetry บทกวี kam glorm

point (n) จุด jùt

point (v) ชี้ chée

poisonous มีพิษ mee pit

police ตำรวจ dam-ròo-at

police officer เจ้าหน้าที่ตำรวจ dam-ròo-at

police station สถานีตำรวจ sà-tăh-nee dam-ròo-at

policy นโยบาย ná-yoh-bai

politician นักการเมือง nák gahn meu-ang

politics การเมือง gahn meu-ang

pollen ละอองเกสร gair-sŏrn dòrk mái

pollution มลภาวะ mon-lá-pah-wá

pool (game) สนุกเกอร์ sà-núk-geu

pool (swimming) สระว่ายน้ำ sà wâi nám

poor จน jon

poppy ดอกฝิ่น dòrk fin

popular เป็นที่นิยม ben têe ní-yom

pork เนื้อหมู néu-a mŏo

pork sausage ไส้กรอกหมู sâi-gròrk mŏo

port (sea) ท่าเรือ tâh reu-a

porter คนขนของ kon kŏn kŏrng

positive (optimistic) มองในแง่ดี morng nai ngâa dee

positive (certain) แน่นอน nâa norn

possible เป็นไปได้ ben bai dâi

post code รหัสไปรษณีย์ rá-hàt brai-sà-nee

post office ที่ทำการไปรษณีย์ têe tam gahn brai-sà-nee

postage ค่าส่ง kâh sòng

postcard ไปรษณียบัตร brai-sà-nee-yá-bàt

poster ภาพโปสเตอร์ pâhp boh-sà-đeu

pot (ceramics) หม้อดิน môr din

pot (dope) กัญชา gan-chah

potato มันฝรั่ง man fà-ràng

pottery การปั้นหม้อ gahn bân môr

pound (money, weight) ปอนด์ born

poverty ความยากจน kwahm yâhk jon

powder ผง pŏng

power อำนาจ am-nâht

prawn กุ้ง gûng

prayer บทสวดมนต์ bòt sòo-at mon

prayer book หนังสือสวดมนต์ năng-sĕu sòo-at mon

prefer นิยม ní-yom

pregnancy test kit ชุดตรวจการตั้งท้อง chút đròo-at gahn đâng tórng

pregnant ตั้งครรภ์ đâng kan

premenstrual tension ความเครียดก่อนเป็นระดู kwahm krêe-at gòrn ben rá-doo

prepare เตรียม đree-am

prescription ใบสั่งยา bai sàng yah

present (gift) ของขวัญ kŏrng kwăn

present (time) ปัจจุบัน bàt-jù-ban

present ⓥ มอบ môrp

president ประธานาธิบดี bra-tah-nah-tí-bà-dee

pressure ความดัน kwahm dan

pretty สวย sŏo-ay

price ราคา rah-kah

priest บาทหลวง bàht lŏo-ang

prime minister นายกรัฐมนตรี nah-yók rát-tà-mon-đree

printer (computer) เครื่องพิมพ์ krêu-ang pim

prison คุก kúk

prisoner นักโทษ nák tôht

private ส่วนตัว sòo-an đoo-a

produce ⓥ ผลิต pà-lìt

profit กำไร gam-rai

program โครงการ krohng gahn

program (computer) โปรแกรม broh-graam

projector เครื่องฉายภาพ krêu-ang chăi pâhp

promise สัญญา săn-yah

prostitute โสเภณี sŏh-pair-nee

protect ป้องกัน bôrng gan

protected (species) (สัตว์) สงวน (sàt) sà-ngŏo-an

protest ⓝ การประท้วง gahn bra-tóo-ang

protest ⓥ ประท้วง bra-tóo-ang

province จังหวัด jang-wàt

provincial capital อำเภอเมือง am-peu meu-ang

provisions เสบียง sà-bee-ang

pub (bar) ผับ bàp

public gardens สวนสาธารณะ sŏo-an săh-tah-rá-ná

public relations การประชาสัมพันธ์ gahn bra-chah săm-pan

public telephone โทรศัพท์สาธารณะ toh-rá-sàp săh-tah-rá-ná

public toilet สุขาสาธารณะ sù-kăh săh-tah-rá-ná

publishing การพิมพ์ gahn pim
pull ดึง deung
pump สูบ sòop
pumpkin ฟักทอง fák torng
puncture ยางแตก yahng đàak
pure บริสุทธิ์ bor-rí-sùt
purple สีม่วง sĕe môo-ang
purse กระเป๋าเงิน grà-bŏw ngeun
push ผลัก plùk
put on ใส่ sài

Q

quadriplegic คนอัมพาต kon am-má-pâht
qualifications คุณวุฒิ kun-ná-wút
quality คุณภาพ kun-ná-pâhp
quarantine ด่านกักโรค đàhn gàk rôhk
quarter หนึ่งส่วนสี่ nèung sòo-an sèe
queen พระราชินี prá rah-chí-nee
question คำถาม kam tăhm
queue คิว kew
quick เร็ว re-ou
quiet เงียบ ngêe-ap
quit (a job) ลาออก lah òrk
quit (a habit) เลิก lêuk

R

rabbit กระต่าย grà-đài
race (sport) การแข่ง gahn kàang
racetrack สนามแข่ง sà-năhm kàang
racing bike จักรยานแข่ง jàk-gà-yahn kàang
racism ลัทธิแบ่งผิว lát-tí bàang pĕw
racquet ไม้ตี mái đee
radiator (car) หม้อน้ำ môr nám
radio วิทยุ wít-tá-yú
radish หัวผักกาด hŏo-a pàk gàht
railway station สถานีรถไฟ sà-tăh-nee rót fai
rain ฝน fŏn
raincoat เสื้อกันฝน sêu-a gan fŏn
rainy season หน้าฝน nâh fŏn

raisin ลูกเกด lôok gèt
rally การชุมนุม gahn chum-num
rape ⓝ การข่มขืน gahn kòm kĕun
rape ⓥ ข่มขืน kòm kĕun
rare (food) ไม่สุกมาก mâi sùk mâhk
rare (uncommon) หายาก hăh yâhk
rash ผื่น pèun
rat หนู nŏo
rave งานเต้นรำ ngahn đên ram
raw ดิบ dìp
razor มีดโกน mêet gohn
razor blade ใบมีดโกน bai mêet gohn
read อ่าน àhn
reading การอ่าน gahn àhn
ready พร้อม prórm
real estate agent คนขายอสังหาริมทรัพย์
   kon kăi à-săng-hăh-rim-má-sáp
realistic สมจริง sŏm jing
rear (seat etc) หลัง lăng
reason เหตุ hèt
receipt ใบเสร็จ bai sèt
recently เร็วๆนี้ re-ou re-ou née
recommend แนะนำ náa nam
record (sound) อัดเสียง àt sĕe-ang
recording การบันทึก gahn ban-téuk
recyclable รีไซเคิลได้ ree-sai-kêun dâi
recycle รีไซเคิล ree-sai-kêun
red สีแดง sĕe daang
red pepper พริกแดง prík daang
referee กรรมการผู้ตัดสิน gam-má-gahn
   pôo đàt sĭn
reference ที่อ้างอิง têe âhng ing
reflexology การนวดเส้น gahn nôo-at sên
refrigerator ตู้เย็น đôo yen
refugee คนอพยพ kon òp-pá-yop
refund เงินคืน ngeun keun
refuse ปฏิเสธ pà-đì-sèt
regional พื้นเมือง péun meu-ang
registered mail (post by)
   ไปรษณีย์ลงทะเบียน bprai-sà-nee long
   tá-bee-an
rehydration salts เกลือแร่ gleu-a râa

relationship ความสัมพันธ์ kwahm săm-pan

relax ผ่อนคลาย pòrn klai

relic วัตถุโบราณ wát-tù boh-rahn

religion ศาสนา sàht-sà-năh

religious ทางศาสนา tahng sàht-sà-năh

remote ห่างไกล hàhng glai

remote control รีโมท ree-môht

rent เช่า chôw

repair ซ่อม sôrm

republic สาธารณรัฐ săh-tah-rá-ná-rát

reservation (booking) การจอง gahn jorng

rest พัก pák

restaurant ร้านอาหาร ráhn ah-hăhn

resume (CV) ประวัติการทำงาน brà-wàt gahn tam ngahn

retired ปลดเกษียณ blòt gà-sĕe-an

return (ticket) ไปกลับ bai glàp

return (come back) กลับ glàp

review คำวิจารณ์ kam wí-jahn

rhythm จังหวะ jang-wà

rib ซี่โครง sêe krohng

rice ข้าว kôw

rice field นา nah

rich (wealthy) รวย roo-ay

ride ⓝ เที่ยว têe-o

ride ⓥ ขี่ kèe

right (correct) ถูก tòok

right (direction) ขวา kwăh

right-wing ฝ่ายขวา fài kwăh

ring (on finger) แหวน wăen

ring (phone) โทร toh

rip-off การโกง gahn gohng

risk ⓝ ความเสี่ยง kwahm sèe-ang

risk ⓥ เสี่ยง sèe-ang

river แม่น้ำ mâa nám

road ถนน tà-nŏn

road map แผนที่ถนน păan tèe tà-nŏn

rob ขโมย kà-moy

rock หิน hĭn

rock (music) ดนตรีร็อค don-đree rórk

rock climbing การปีนหน้าผา gahn been nâh păh

rock group วงดนตรีร็อค wong don-đree rórk

rockmelon แตงหวาน đaang wăhn

roll (bread) ขนมปังก้อน kà-nŏm bang gôrn

rollerblading การเล่นโรลเลอร์เบลด gahn lên rohn-leu-blèt

romantic โรแมนติก roh-maan-đik

roof หลังคา lăng-kah

room ห้อง hôrng

room number หมายเลขห้อง măi lêk hôrng

rope เชือก chêu-ak

round กลม glom

roundabout วงเวียน wong wee-an

route สาย săi

rowing การพายเรือ gahn pai reu-a

rubbish ขยะ kà-yà

rubella โรคหัดเยอรมัน rôhk hàt yeu-rá-man

rug เสื่อ sèu-a

rugby รักบี้ rák-bêe

ruins ซากโบราณสถาน sâhk boh-rahn-ná sà-tăhn

rule กฎ gòt

rum เหล้ารัม lôw ram

run ⓥ วิ่ง wîng

running การวิ่ง gahn wîng

runny nose น้ำมูกไหล nám môok lăi

S

sad เศร้า sôw

saddle อานม้า ahn máh

safe ⓝ ตู้เซฟ đôo sép

safe ⓐ ปลอดภัย blòrt pai

safe sex เพศสัมพันธ์แบบปลอดภัย pêt săm-pan bàap blòrt pai

saint (Christian) นักบุญ nák bun

saint (Buddhist) พระอรหันต์ prá à-rá-hăn

salad ผักสดรวม pàk sòt roo-am

salami ไส้กรอก sâi gròrk

salary เงินเดือน ngeun deu-an

sale ลดราคา lót rah-kah

sales tax ภาษีมูลค่าเพิ่ม pah-sĕe moon kâh pêum

salmon ปลาแซลมอน blah saan-morn

salt เกลือ gleu·a

same เหมือน mĕu·an

sampan เรือสำปั้น reu·a săm-bân

sand ทราย sai

sandal รองเท้าแตะ rorng tów đaa

sanitary napkin ผ้าอนามัย pâh à-nah-mai

sardine ปลาซาร์ดีน blah sah-deen

Saturday วันเสาร์ wan sŏw

sauce น้ำซอส nám sórt

saucepan หม้อ môr

sauna ซาวน่า sow-nâh

sausage ไส้กรอก sâi gròrk

say ว่า wâh

scalp หนังศีรษะ năng sĕe-sà

scarf ผ้าพันคอ pâh pan kor

school โรงเรียน rohng ree·an

science วิทยาศาสตร์ wít-tá-yah-sàht

scientist นักวิทยาศาสตร์ nák wít-tá-yah-sàht

scissors กรรไกร gan-grai

score ⓥ คะแนน ká-naan

scoreboard กระดานบอกคะแนน grà-dahn bòrk ká-naan

Scotland ประเทศสก๊อตแลนด์ brà-têt sà-górt-laan

scrambled กวน goo·an

sculpture (moulded) รูปปั้น rôop bân

sculpture (cut) รูปสลัก rôop sà-làk

sea ทะเล tá-lair

sea gypsies ชาวน้ำ chow nám

seafood อาหารทะเล ah-hăhn tá-lair

seasick เมาคลื่น mow klêun

seaside ริมทะเล rim tá-lair

season หน้า nâh

seat (place) ที่นั่ง têe nâng

seatbelt เข็มขัดนิรภัย kĕm kàt ni-rá-pai

second (of time) วินาที wí-nah-tee

second (place) ที่สอง têe sŏrng

second class ชั้นสอง chán sŏrng

second-hand มือสอง meu sŏrng

second-hand shop ร้านขายของ มือสอง ráhn kăi kŏrng meu sŏrng

secretary เลขา lair-kăh

see เห็น hĕn

self-employed ทำธุรกิจส่วนตัว tam tú-rá-git sòo·an đoo·a

selfish เห็นแก่ตัว hĕn gàa đoo·a

sell ขาย kăi

send ส่ง sòng

sensible มีเหตุผล mee hèt pŏn

sensual น่าใคร่ nâh krâi

separate ต่างหาก đàhng hàhk

September เดือนกันยายน deu·an gan-yah-yon

serious (earnest) เอาจริง เอาจัง ow jing ow jang

serious (important) สำคัญ săm-kan

service การบริการ gahn bor-rí-gahn

service charge ค่าบริการ kâh bor-rí-gahn

service station ปั๊มน้ำมัน bám nám-man

serviette ผ้าเช็ดปาก pâh chét bàhk

several หลาย lăi

sew เย็บ yép

sex (gender) เพศ pêt

sex (the act) การร่วมเพศ gahn rôo·am pêt

sexism เพศนิยม pêt ní-yom

sexy เซ็กซี่ sek-sêe

shade ร่ม rôm

shadow เงา ngow

shampoo น้ำยาสระผม nám yah sà pŏm

shape รูปทรง rôop song

share (a dorm etc) รวมกันใช้ rôo·am gan chái

share (with) แบ่ง bàang

shave โกน gohn

shaving cream ครีมโกนหนวด kreem gohn nòo·at

she เขา kŏw

sheep แกะ gàa

sheet (bed) ผ้าปูนอน pâh boo norn

shelf ชั้น chán

shingles (illness) โรคงูสวัด rôhk ngoo
sa-wàt
ship เรือ reu-a
shirt เสื้อเชิ้ต séu-a chéut
shoe รองเท้า rong tów
shoes รองเท้า rong tów
shoot ⊙ ยิง ying
shop ⊙ ร้าน ráhn
shopping การซื้อของ gahn séu kŏrng
shophouses ห้องแถว hông tâa-ou
shopping centre ศูนย์สรรพสินค้า sŏon sàp-pa-sin-káh
short (height) เตี้ย dêe-a
short (length) สั้น sân
shortage ความขาดแคลน kwahm kàht klaan
shorts กางเกงขาสั้น gahng-geng kǎh sân
shoulder ไหล่ lài
show ⊙ การแสดง gahn sa-daang
show ⊙ แสดง sa-daang
shower ฝักบัว fàk boo-a
shrimp กุ้ง gôong
shrine (Buddhist) แท่นพระ tâan prá
shut ปิด bìt
shy อาย ai
sick ป่วย bòo-ay
side ข้าง kâhng
side street ซอย soy
sign ป้าย bâi
signature ลายเซ็น lai sen
silk ผ้าไหม pâh mǎi
silver เงิน ngeun
similar คล้ายคลาย klái klái
simple ง่าย ngâi
since (May) ตั้งแต่ dâng dàa
sing ร้องเพลง rórng pleng
Singapore ประเทศสิงคโปร์ bra-tèt
sing-ka-boh
singer นักร้อง nák rórng
single (person) โสด Tàra sòht

single room ห้องเดี่ยว hông dèe-o
singlet เสื้อกล้าม séu-a glâhm
sister (older) พี่สาว pêe sǒw
sister (younger) น้องสาว nórng sǒw
sit นั่ง nâng
size (general) ขนาด ka-nàht
skate สเก็ต lên sa-gèt
skateboarding การเล่นกระดานสเก็ต gahn
lêh gra-dahn sa-gèt
ski สกี lên sa-gee
skimmed milk นมพร่องมันเนย
prôhng nom néu-i
skin ผิวหนัง pěw nǎng
skirt กระโปรง gra-brohng
skull กะโหลกศีรษะ ga-lòhk sée-sà
sky ท้องฟ้า tórng fáh
sleep ⊙ นอน non
sleeping bag ถุงนอน tǒong non
sleeping berth ที่นอน têe non
nai dôo non
sleeping car ตู้นอน dôo non
sleeping pills ยานอนหลับ yah non làp
sleepy ง่วงนอน ngôo-ang non
slice ฝาน fǎn chín
slide (film) ฟิล์มสไลด์ fim sa-lái
slow ช้า cháh
slowly อย่างช้าๆ yàhng cháh
small เล็ก lék
smaller เล็กกว่า lék gwàh
smallest เล็กที่สุด lék têe sùt
smell ⊙ กลิ่น glìn
smile ⊙ ยิ้ม yím
smoke ⊙ ควัน kwan
snack ⊙ ของว่าง ah-hǎhn wâhng
snail หอย hǒy
snake งู ngoo
snorkelling การดำน้ำดูปะการังโดยใช้ท่อ gahn
dam nám chái tòr hǎi jai
snow ⊙ หิมะ hì-má
snow pea ถั่วลันเตา tòo-a lan-dow
soap สบู่ sa-bòo

soap opera ละครโทรทัศน์ lá-korn toh-rá-tát

soccer ฟุตบอล fút-born

social welfare การประชาสงเคราะห์ gahn brà-chah sŏng-kró

socialist คนถือลัทธิสังคมนิยม kon tĕu lát-tí săng-kom ní-yom

sock(s) ถุงเท้า tŭng tów

soft drink น้ำอัดลม nám àt lom

soft-boiled ลวก lôo-ak

soldier ทหาร tá-hăhn

someone คนใดคนหนึ่ง kon dai kon nèung

something สิ่งใดสิ่งหนึ่ง sìng dai sìng nèung

sometimes บางครั้ง bahng kráng

son ลูกชาย lôok chai

song เพลง pleng

soon เร็วๆ นี้ re·ou re·ou née

sore เจ็บ jèp

soup น้ำซุป nám súp

south ทิศใต้ tít đâi

souvenir ของที่ระลึก kŏrng têe rá-léuk

souvenir shop ร้านขายของที่ระลึก ráhn kăi kŏrng têe rá-léuk

soy milk นมถั่วเหลือง nom tòo·a lĕu·ang

soy sauce ซอสซีอิ๊ว sôrt see-éw

space ที่ว่าง têe wâhng

Spain ประเทศสเปน brà-tèt sà-ben

sparkling wine เหล้าองุ่นสปาร์คลิ้ง lôw à-ngùn sà-bah-kling

speak พูด pôot

special พิเศษ pí-sèt

specialist ผู้เชี่ยวชาญเฉพาะทาง pôo chêe·o chahn chá-pó tahng

speed ความเร็ว kwahm re·ou

speed limit กำหนดความเร็ว gam-nòt kwahm re·ou

speedometer เครื่องวัดความเร็ว krêu·ang wát kwahm re·ou

spider แมงมุม má-laang mum

spinach ผักโขม pàk kŏhm

spirit shrine ศาลเจ้า săhn jôw

spoiled เสีย sĕe·a

spoke ซี่ล้อรถ sêe lór rót

spoon ช้อน chórn

sport กีฬา gee-lah

sports store ร้านขายอุปกรณ์กีฬา ráhn kăi ùp-bà-gorn gee-lah

sportsperson นักกีฬา nák gee-lah

sprain ความเคล็ด kwahm klét

spring (coil) ขดลวดสปริง kòt lôo·at sà-bring

spring (season) หน้าใบไม้ผลิ nâh bai mái plì

squid ปลาหมึก blah mèuk

stadium สนามกีฬา sà-năhm gee-lah

stairway บันได ban-dai

stale ไม่สด mâi sòt

stamp แสตมป์ sà-đàam

star ดาว dow

(four-) star (สี่) ดาว (sèe) dow

start (beginning) จุดเริ่ม jùt rêum

start เริ่ม rêum

start (a car) สตาร์ท sà-đáht

station สถานี sà-tăh-nee

stationer's (shop) ร้านขายอุปกรณ์เขียน ráhn kăi ùp-bà-gorn kĕe·an

statue รูปหล่อ rôop lòr

stay (at a hotel) พัก pák

stay (in one place) หยุด yùt

steak (beef) เนื้อสะเต๊ะ néu·a sà-đé

steal ขโมย kà-moy

steep ชัน chan

step ขั้น kân

stereo สเตริโอ sà-đair-ree-o

sticky rice ข้าวเหนียว kôw nĕe·o

still water น้ำเปล่า nám blòw

stock (food) ซุปก้อน súp gôrn

stockings ถุงน่อง tŭng nôrng

stolen ขโมยแล้ว kà-moy láa·ou

stomach ท้อง tórng

stomachache (to have a) เจ็บท้อง jèp tórng

stone หิน hĭn

stoned (drugged) เมา mow

stop (bus, tram, etc) ป้าย bâi

stop (cease) หยุด yùt

stop (prevent) ห้าม hâhm

stop หยุด yùt

storm พายุ pah-yú

story นิทาน ní-tahn

stove เตาอบ dao òp

straight ตรง drong

strange แปลก bplàek

stranger คนแปลกหน้า kon bplàek nâh

strawberry สตรอเบอรี่ sa-dror-beu-rêe

stream ลำธาร lam tahn

street ถนน ta-nǒn

street market ตลาดนัด da-làht nát

strike (เลิกงาน) การนัดหยุดงาน gahn nát yùt ngahn sa-drai

string เชือก chêu·ak

stroke (health) เส้นเลือดในสมองแตก sên lêu·at nai sa-mŏrng dàek

stroller รถเข็นเด็ก rót ken dèk

strong แข็งแรง kǎeng raang

stubborn ดื้อ dêu

student นักศึกษา nák sèuk-sǎh

studio (for recording) ห้องอัดเสียง hông àt sĕe·ang

stupa พระสถูป prá sa-tòop

stupid โง่ ngôh

style สไตล์ sa-dai

subtitles คำบรรยาย kam ban-yai

suburb ชานเมือง chahn meu·ang

subway (train) รถไฟใต้ดิน rót fai dtâi din

sugar น้ำตาล nám dahn

suitcase กระเป๋าเดินทาง gra-bŏw deun tahng

sultana องุ่นแห้ง a-ngùn hâeng

sun cream ครีมทากันแดด kreem tah gan dàat pew ah-tít

sun พระอาทิตย์ prá-aa-tít

sunburn ผิวที่ถูกแดดเผา pĕw têe tòok dàat pǎo

sunblock ครีมกันแดด kreem gan dàat

Sunday วันอาทิตย์ wan aa-tít

sunglasses แว่นกันแดด wâen gan dàat

sunny มีแดด mee dàat

sunrise พระอาทิตย์ขึ้น prá-aa-tít dà-wan kêun

sunset พระอาทิตย์ตกดิน prá-aa-tít dà-wan dòk

sunstroke โรคแพ้แดด rôhk páa dàat

superstition ความเชื่อเรื่องโชคลาง kwahm chêu·a pêe·ang rêu·ang mah-gèt

supermarket ซุปเปอร์มาร์เก็ต soo-beu-mah-gèt

supporter (politics) ผู้สนับสนุน pôo sa-nàp sa-nún

supporter (sport) แฟนบอล faan bon

surf โต้คลื่น dôh klêun

surface mail ไปรษณีย์ธรรมดา brai-sa-nee tahng tam-ma-dah

surfboard กระดานโต้คลื่น gra-dahn dôh kleun

surfing การโต้คลื่น gahn dôh klêun

surname นามสกุล nahm sa-gun

surprise ความประหลาดใจ kwahm bra-làht jai

swamp หนองน้ำ nŏng nám

sweater เสื้อไหมพรม sêu·a mǎi prom

Sweden ประเทศสวีเดน bra-tèt sa-wee-den

sweet หวาน wǎhn

sweet & sour เปรี้ยวหวาน brêe·o wǎhn

sweets ขนมหวาน ka-nŏm wǎhn

swelling ความบวมอักเสบ kwahm boo·am-

swim ว่ายน้ำ wâi nám

swimming (sport) การว่ายน้ำ gahn wâi nám

swimming pool สระว่ายน้ำ sà wâi nám

Switzerland ประเทศสวิตเซอร์แลนด์ bra-tèt sà-wít-seu-laan

synagogue โบสถ์ยิว bòht yew

synthetic ที่สังเคราะห์ têe sǎng-kró

syringe กระบอกฉีดยา kràbòk chèet yah

T

table โต๊ะ dó

table tennis ปิงปอง bing borng

tablecloth ผ้าปูโต๊ะ pâh boo dó

tail หาง hǎhng

tailor ช่างตัดเสื้อ châhng đàt sêu·a
take เอาไป ow bai
take a photo ถ่ายรูป tài rôop
talk พูด pôot
tall สูง sŏong
tampon แทมพอน taam-porn
tanning lotion ครีมอาบแดด kreem àhp dàat
tap ก๊อกน้ำ górk nám
tap water น้ำประปา nám bra-bah
tasty อร่อย à-ròy
tax ภาษี pah-sĕe
taxi รถแท็กซี่ rót táak-sêe
taxi stand ที่จอดรถแท็กซี่ têe jòrt rót táak-sêe
tea น้ำชา nám chah
tea (leaves) ใบชา bai chah
teacher อาจารย์ ah-jahn
team ทีม teem
teaspoon ช้อนชา chórn chah
technique เทคนิค ték-ník
teeth ฟัน fan
telegram โทรเลข toh-rá-lêk
telephone ⓝ โทรศัพท์ toh-rá-sàp
telephone ⓥ โทร toh
telephone box ตู้โทรศัพท์ đôo toh-rá-sàp
telephone centre ศูนย์โทรศัพท์ sŏon toh-rá-sàp
telescope กล้องส่องทางไกล glôrng sòrng tahng glai
television โทรทัศน์ toh-rá-tát
tell บอก bòrk
temperature (fever) ไข้ kâi
temperature (weather) อุณหภูมิ un-hà-poom
temple วัด wát
temple fair งานวัด ngahn wát
tennis เทนนิส ten-nít
tennis court สนามเทนนิส sà-năhm ten-nít
tent เต็นท์ đén
tent peg หลักปักเต็นท์ làk bàk đén
terrible แย่ yâa

test การสอบ gahn sòrp
Thai ไทย tai
Thailand ประเทศไทย bra-têt tai
thank ขอบใจ kòrp jai
Thank you. ขอบคุณ kòrp kun
that (one) (อัน) นั้น (an) nán
theatre โรงละคร rohng lá-korn
their ของเขา kŏrng kŏw
there ที่นั่น têe nán
therefore ฉะนั้น chà-nán
thermometer ปรอท bà-ròrt
they เขา kŏw
thick หนา năh
thief ขโมย kà-moy
thin (general) บาง bahng
thin (of a person) ผอม pŏrm
think คิด kít
third ที่สาม têe săhm
thirsty (to be) หิวน้ำ hĕw nám
this (month etc) (เดือน) นี้ (deu·an) née
thread เส้นด้าย sên dâi
throat คอหอย kor hŏy
thrush (health) เชื้อรา chéu·a rah
thunderstorm พายุฟ้าร้อง pah-yú fáh rórng
Thursday วันพฤหัสบดี wan pá-réu-hàt
ticket ตั๋ว đŏo·a
ticket collector คนเก็บตั๋ว kon gèp đŏo·a
ticket machine เครื่องบริการตั๋ว krêu·ang bor-rí-gahn đŏo·a
ticket office ช่องขายตั๋ว chôrng kăi đŏo·a
tide น้ำขึ้นน้ำลง nám kêun nám long
tight แน่น nâan
time เวลา wair-lah
time difference ความต่างของเวลา kwahm đàhng kŏrng wair-lah
timetable ตารางเวลา đah-rahng wair-lah
tin (can) กระป๋อง grà-bŏrng
tin opener เครื่องเปิดกระป๋อง krêu·ang bèut grà-bŏrng
tiny เล็กนิดเดียว lék nít dee·o
tip (gratuity) เงินทิป ngeun típ

english-thai

T

toy ของเล่น kǒrng lên
toy shop ร้านขายของเล่น ráhn kǎi kǒrng lên
track (path) ทาง tahng
track (sport) ลู่ lôo
trade การค้า gahn káh
tradesperson พ่อค้า pôr káh
traffic จราจร ja-rah-jorn
traffic light ไฟจราจร fai ja-rah-jorn
trail ทางเดิน tahng deun
train รถไฟ rót fai
train station สถานีรถไฟ sa-thǎh-nee rót fai
transsexual คนแปลงเพศ kon bplaang-pêt
transit lounge ห้องพักผู้โดยสาร hôrng pák sǎm-ráp kon deun
translate แปล bplaa
transport ⓝ การขนส่ง gahn kǒn sòng
transvestite กระเทย ga-teu-i
travel ⓥ เดินทาง deun tahng
travel agency บริษัทนำเที่ยว bor-rí-sàt
tôrng têe-o
travel sickness (car) เมารถ mow rót
travel sickness (boat) เมาเรือ mow reu-a
travel sickness (air) เมาเครื่องบิน mow krêu-ang
travellers cheque เช็คเดินทาง chék deun
tahng
tree ต้นไม้ dôn mái
trip (journey) เที่ยว têe-o
trolley รถเข็น rót kěn
trousers กางเกง gahng-geng
truck รถบรรทุก rót ban-túk
trust ไว้ใจ wái jai
try (try out) ลอง lorng
try (attempt) พยายาม pá-yah-yahm
T-shirt เสื้อยืด sêu-a yêut
Tuesday วันอังคาร wan ang-kahn
tumour เนื้องอก néu-a ngôrk
tuna ปลาทูน่า blah too-nah
tune ทำนองเพลง tam-norng pleng

tired เหนื่อย nèu-ay
tissues กระดาษทิชชู gra-dàht-tít-chôo
to ถึง têung
toast ขนมปังปิ้ง ka-nǒm bang bîng
toaster เครื่องปิ้งขนมปัง krêu-ang bîng ka-nǒm bang
tobacco ยาสูบ yah sèrp
tobacconist ร้านขายยาสูบ ráhn kǎi yah sòop
today วันนี้ wan née
toe นิ้วเท้า néw tów
tofu เต้าหู้ dôw-hôo
together ด้วยกัน dôo-ay gan
toilet ห้องน้ำ hôrng nám
toilet paper กระดาษชำระ gra-dàht
tomato มะเขือเทศ ma-kěu-a têt
tomato sauce ซอสมะเขือเทศ sórt ma-kěu-a tét
tomorrow พรุ่งนี้ prûng née
tomorrow afternoon พรุ่งนี้บ่าย prûng née bài
tomorrow evening พรุ่งนี้เย็น prûng née yen
tomorrow morning พรุ่งนี้เช้า prûng née chów
tonight คืนนี้ keun née
too (expensive etc) เกินไป geun bai
toothache ปวดฟัน bòo-at fan
toothbrush แปรงสีฟัน braang sěe fan
toothpaste ยาสีฟัน yah sěe fan
toothpick ไม้จิ้มฟัน mái jîm fan
torch (flashlight) ไฟฉาย fai chǎi
touch แตะ dàa
tour ทัวร์ too-a
tourist นักท่องเที่ยว nák tôrng têe-o
tourist office สำนักงานท่องเที่ยว sǎm-nák
ngahn tôrng têe-o
towards ไปทาง bai teung
towel ผ้าเช็ดตัว pâh chét doo-a
tower หอคอย hǒr koy
toxic waste ขยะมีพิษ ka-yà mee pít

turkey ไก่งวง gài ngoo-ang
turn เลี้ยว lée-o
TV ทีวี toh-rá-tát
tweezers แหนบ nàap
twin beds เตียงคู่ dtee-ang dée-ang
twins ฝาแฝด făh fàat
two สอง sŏng
type พิมพ์ tam-má-dah
typical ธรรมดา tam-má-dah
tyre ยางรถ yahng rót

U

ultrasound อัลตราซาวด์ un-drah-sow
umbrella ร่ม rôm
uncomfortable ไม่สบาย mâi sà-bai
underneath ใต้ dâi
understand เข้าใจ kôw jai
underwear กางเกงใน gahng-geng nai
unemployed ตกงาน dòk ngahn
unfair ไม่ยุติธรรม mâi yút-dì-tam
uniform เครื่องแบบ krêu-ang bàap
universe จักรวาล jàk-gà-wahn
university มหาวิทยาลัย ma-hăh-wít-tá-yah-lai
unleaded ไร้สารตะกั่ว rái săhn dà-gòo-a
unsafe ไม่ปลอดภัย mâi bplòt pai
until (Friday, etc) จนถึง jon teung
unusual แปลก bplàak
up ขึ้น kêun
uphill ทางขึ้น tahng kêun
urgent ด่วน dòo-an
urinary infection การติดเชื้อที่ท่อ tòr
bàt-săh-wá ak-sèp
USA สหรัฐอเมริกา sà-hà-rát a-mair-rí-gah
useful มีประโยชน์ mee bprà-yòht

V

vacancy ตำแหน่งว่าง hâwng wâhng
vacant ว่าง wâhng
vacation การพักผ่อน têe-o pák pòrn
vaccination การฉีดวัคซีน chèet wák-seen

vagina ช่องคลอด chôrng klôrt
validate ทำให้ถูกต้อง tam hâi tòok dtông
valley หุบเขา hòop kŏw
valuable มีค่า mee kâh
value (price) ราคา rah-kah
van รถตู้ rót dôo
veal เนื้อลูกวัว néu-a lôok woo-a
vegetable ผัก pàk
vegetarian มังสวิรัติ kon gin jair
vein เส้นเลือด sên lêu-at
venereal disease กามโรค gahm-ma-rôhk
venue สถานที่ sà-tăhn têe
very มาก mâhk
video recorder หัวอัดวีดีโอ glôrng tài
wee-dee-oh
video tape เทปวีดีโอ têp wee-dee-oh
view วิว wiw
village หมู่บ้าน mòo bâhn
villager ชาวบ้าน chow bâhn
vine (not grape) เถาวัลย์ tŏw-wan
vinegar น้ำส้ม nám sôm
vineyard ไร่องุ่น râi à-ngùn
virus ไวรัส wai-rát
visa วีซ่า wee-sâh
visit (v) ไปเยี่ยม bpai yêe-am
vitamins วิตามิน wí-dtah-min
vodka วอดก้า lôw wôrt-gáh
voice เสียง sĕe-ang
volleyball (sport) วอลเลย์บอล worm-
lair-born
volume (sound) ระดับเสียง kwahm dang
volume (capacity) ปริมาตร bpà-rí-mâht
vomit อาเจียน òo-ak
vote การลงคะแนนเสียง long ká-naan sĕe-ang

W

wage ค่าจ้าง kâh raang
wait (for) รอ ror
waiter พนักงานเสิร์ฟ kon deun ôh
waiting room ห้องพักรอ hôrng pák ror
wake someone up ปลุก bplùk
wake up ตื่น dèun

walk เดิน deun
wall (outer) กำแพง gam-paang
want อยาก yàhk
war สงคราม sŏng-krahm
wardrobe ตู้เสื้อผ้า đôo sêu·a pâh
warm อุ่น ùn
warn เตือน đeu·an
wash (oneself) ล้าง láhng
wash (something) ล้าง láhng
wash (clothes) ซัก sák
wash cloth (flannel) ผ้าขนหนู pâh kŏn nŏo
washing machine เครื่องซักผ้า krêu·ang sák pâh
watch ⓝ นาฬิกา nah-lí-gah
watch ⓥ ดู doo
water น้ำ nám
water bottle ขวดน้ำ kòo·at nám
waterfall น้ำตก nám đòk
watermelon แตงโม đaang moh
waterproof ชุดกันน้ำ chút gan nám
waterskiing สกีน้ำ sà·gee nám
wave ⓝ คลื่น klêun
way ทาง tahng
we เรา row
weak อ่อน òrn
wealthy รวย roo·ay
wear ใส่ sài
weather อากาศ ah-gàht
wedding งานแต่ง ngahn đàang
wedding cake ขนมฉลองงานแต่งงาน kà·nŏm chà·lŏng wan đàang ngahn
wedding present ของขวัญแต่งงาน kŏrng kwăn đàang ngahn
Wednesday วันพุธ wan pút
week อาทิตย์ ah-tít
(this) week อาทิตย์ (นี้) ah-tít (née)
weekend วันเสาร์อาทิตย์ wan sŏw ah-tít
weigh ชั่ง châng
weight น้ำหนัก nám-nàk
weights ขนาดน้ำหนัก jahn nám-nàk
welcome ต้อนรับ đôrn ráp

welfare (well-being) ความเผาสุข kwahm păh-sùk
well ดี dee
west ทิศตะวันตก tít đà-wan đòk
Western ฝรั่ง fà-ràng
Westerner ฝรั่ง fà-ràng
wet เปียก bèe·ak
what อะไร à-rai
wheel ล้อ lór
wheelchair รถเข็น rót kĕn
when เมื่อไร mêu·a rai
where ที่ไหน têe năi
which อันไหน an năi
whisky เหล้าวิสกี้ lôw wít-sà-gêe
white สีขาว sĕe kŏw
who ใคร krai
wholemeal bread ขนมปังทำด้วยแป้งข้าวสาลีที่ไม่ได้เอารำออก kà·nŏm bang tam dôo·ay bâang kôw săh-lee têe mâi dâi ow ram òrk
why ทำไม tam mai
wide กว้าง gwâhng
wife เมีย mee·a
win ชนะ chá-ná
wind ลม lom
window หน้าต่าง nâh đàhng
windscreen กระจกหน้ารถ grà-jòk nâh rót
windsurfing การเล่นกระดานโต้ลม gahn lên grà-dahn đôh lom
wine เหล้าไวน์ lôw wai
wings ปีก bèek
winner ผู้ชนะ pôo chá-ná
winter หน้าหนาว nâh nŏw
wire ลวด lôo·at
wish ⓥ ปรารถนา bràh-tà-năh
with กับ gàp
within (an hour) ภายใน pai nai
without ไม่มี mâi mee
wok กระทะ grà-tá
woman ผู้หญิง pôo yĭng
wonderful ดีเยี่ยม dee yêe·am
wood ไม้ mái

wool ขนแกะ kŏn gàa
word ศัพท์ sàp
work ⓝ งาน ngahn
work ⓥ ทำงาน tam ngahn
work experience ประสบการณ์ในการทำงาน
  Ъrà-sòp gahn nai gahn tam ngahn
work permit ใบแรงงาน bai raang ngahn
workout การออกกำลังกาย gahn òrk
  gam-lang gai
workshop ห้องทำงาน hôrng tam ngahn
world โลก lôhk
World Cup บอลโลก born lôhk
worms (intestinal) พยาธิ pá-yáht
worried กังวล gang-won
worship บูชา boo-chah
wraparound (for men) ผ้าขะม้า
  pâh kà-máh
wraparound (for women) ผ้าถุง pâh tŭng
wrist ข้อมือ kôr meu
write เขียน kĕe-an
writer นักเขียน nák kĕe-an
wrong ผิด pìt

Y

year ปี ƀee
(this) year ปี (นี้) ƀee (née)
yellow สีเหลือง sĕe lĕu-ang
yes ใช่ châi
(not) yet ยัง yang
yesterday เมื่อวาน mêu-a wahn
yoga โยคะ yoh-ká
yogurt โยเกิร์ต yoh-gèut
you inf เธอ teu
you pl พอ pol kun
young หนุ่ม nùm
your ของคุณ kŏrng kun
youth hostel บ้านเยาวชน báhn yow-
  wá-chon

Z

zip/zipper ซิป síp
zodiac สิบสองราศี sìp-sŏrng rah-sĕe
zoo สวนสัตว์ sŏo-an sàt

If you're having trouble understanding Thai, or if a Thai-speaking person wants to communicate with you in English, point to the text below. This gives directions on how to to look up words in Thai and show you the English translation.

ใช้พจนานุกรมไทย–อังกฤษนี้เพื่อช่วยชาวต่างชาติคนนั้นเข้าใจสิ่งที่คุณอยากจะพูด ค้นหาศัพท์จากรายการศัพท์ภาษาไทย แล้วชี้ให้เห็นศัพท์ภาษาอังกฤษที่ตรงกับศัพท์นั้น

ก

กงสุล gong-sŭn **consulate**
กรรไกร gan-grai **scissors**
กระจก grà-jòk **mirror**
กระดาษ grà-dàht **paper**
กระดาษทิชชู grà-dàht tít-chôo **tissues**
กระดาษห้องน้ำ grà-dàht hôrng nám **toilet paper**
กระดุม grà-dum **button**
กระป๋อง grà-bŏrng **can • tin**
กระเป๋า grà-bŏw **baggage • luggage**
กระเป๋าเงิน grà-bŏw ngeun **purse**
กระเป๋าเดินทาง grà-bŏw deun tahng **suitcase**
กระโปรง grà-brohng **dress • skirt**
กระแสไฟฟ้า grà-săa fai fáh **current (electricity)**
กรัม gram **gram**
กรุงเทพ grung têp **Bangkok**
กล้องถ่ายรูป glôrng tài rôop **camera**
กล้องถ่ายวิดีโอ glôrng tài wee-dee-oh **video recorder**
กลับ glàp **return (come back)**
กลิ่น glìn **smell**
กลุ่มเลือด glum lêu-at **blood group**
กษัตริย์ gà-sàt **king**
ก๊อกน้ำ górk nám **tap**
กับแกล้ม gàp glâam **drinking food**
กางเกง gahng-geng **pants • trousers**

กางเกงขาสั้น gahng-geng kăh săn **shorts**
กางเกงใน gahng geng nai **underwear**
กางเกงยีน gahng geng yeen **jeans**
ก๊าซ gáht **gas (for cooking)**
กาแฟ gah-faa **coffee**
การกฎหมาย gahn gòt-măi **law (study, professzion)**
การเขียนภาพ gahn kĕe-an pâhp **painting (the art)**
การจอง gahn jorng **reservation (booking)**
การจ่าย gahn jài **payment**
การช้าเวลา gahn cháh wair-lah **delay**
การเช่ารถ gahn chôw rót **car hire**
การดูแลเด็ก gahn doo laa dèk **childminding**
การต่อ gahn dòr **connection (transport)**
การตัดผม gahn dàt pŏm **haircut**
การเต้นรำ gahn dên ram **dancing**
การถ่ายภาพ gahn tài pâhp **photography**
การทำสะอาด gahn tam sà-àht **cleaning**
การนัด gahn nát **appointment**
การบริการ gahn bor-rí-gahn **service**
การประกัน gahn brà-gan **insurance**
การประชุม gahn brà-chum **conference**
การปรับร่างกายกับเวลาที่แตกต่าง gahn bràp râhng gai gàp wair-lah têe đàak đahng **jet lag**
การพักร้อน gahn pák rórn **holidays**
การแพ้ gahn páa **allergy**

241

การแพทย์ gahn pâat **medicine (study, profession)**
การร่วมเพศ gahn rôo·am pêt **sex (the act)**
การเล่นสกี gahn lên sà·gee **skiing**
การแลกเงิน gahn lâak ngeun **currency exchange**
การสัมภาษณ์ gahn sǎm·pâht **interview**
การแสดง gahn sà·daang **concert**
การต่อยมวย gahn dòy moo·ay **boxing**
กำหนดความเร็ว gam·nòt kwahm re·ou **speed limit**
กิน gin **eat** inf
กิโลกรัม gì·loh·gram **kilogram**
กิโลเมตร gì·loh·mêt **kilometre**
เกม gem **match (sports)**
เกย์ gair **gay**
เก่า gòw **old (thing)**
เก้าอี้ gôw·êe **chair**
เกาะ gò **island**
เงินไป geun bai **too (expensive etc)**
แก่ gàa **dark (of colour)**
แก่ gàa **old (person)**
แก้ว gâa·ou **glass (drinking)**
โกน gohn **shave**
ใกล้ glâi **close • near**
ใกล้เคียง glâi kee·ang **nearby**
ใกล้ที่สุด glâi têe·sùt **nearest**
ไก่ gài **chicken**
ไกด์ gai **guide (person)**

ขนแกะ kǒn gàa **wool**
ขนมปัง kà·nǒm bang **bread**
ขนมปังปิ้ง kà·nǒm bang bîng **toast**
ขนาด kà·nàht **size (general)**
ขม kǒm **bitter**
ขโมยแล้ว kà·moy láa·ou **stolen**
ขยะ kà·yà **garbage**
ขวด kòo·at **bottle**
ขวา kwǎh **right (direction)**
ข้อความฝาก kôr kwahm fàhk **message**

ของขวัญ kǒrng kwǎn **present (gift)**
ของเขา kǒrng kǒw **his • her**
ของดิฉัน kǒrng dì·chǎn **my (for a woman)**
ของท้องถิ่น kǒrng tórng tìn **local**
ของที่ระลึก kǒrng têe rá·léuk **souvenir**
ของผม kǒrng pǒm **my (for a man)**
ของเรา kǒrng row **our**
ของหวาน kǒrng wǎhn **dessert**
ข้อต่อ kôr dòr **connection**
ข้อเท้า kôr tów **ankle**
ขอบคุณ kòrp kun **thank you**
ข้อมูล kôr moon **information**
ขอแสดงความยินดี kôr sà·daang kwahm yin dee **congratulations**
ขับ kàp **drive**
ขา kǎh **leg**
ขากรรไกร kǎh gan·grai **jaw**
ขาเข้า kǎh kôw **arrivals**
ข้างนอก kâhng nôrk **outside**
ข้างใน kâhng nai **inside**
ข้างหลัง kâhng lǎng **behind**
ข้างๆ kâhng kâhng **beside**
ข่าว kòw **news**
ขาวดำ kǒw dam **B&W (film)**
ขาออก kǎh òrk **departures**
ขึ้น kêun **board (a plane, ship etc)**
ขึ้น kêun **up**
เข็ม kěm **needle (sewing)**
เข็มขัดนิรภัย kěm kàt ní·rá·pai **seatbelt**
เข็มฉีด kěm chèet **needle (syringe)**
เขา kǒw **he, she, they**
แข็ง kǎng **hard (not soft)**
แขน kǎan **arm**
ไข้ kâi **fever**
ไข้หวัด kâi wàt **influenza • flu**

คนกินเงินบำนาญ kon gin ngeun bam·nahn **pensioner**
คนกินเจ kon gin jair **vegetarian**
คนขายผัก kon kǎi pàk **greengrocer**
คนครัว kon kroo·a **cook**
คนเดินโต๊ะ kon deun dó **waiter**

คนต่างชาติ kon đàhng cháht **foreigner**
คนรักร่วมเพศ kon rák rôo·am pêt
 homosexual
ครอบครัว krôrp kroo·a **family**
คริสต์มาส krít-máht **Christmas**
ครีมกันแดด kreem gan dàat **sunblock**
ครีมโกนหนวด kreem gohn nòo·at
 shaving cream
ครีมทาหลังโกนหนวด kreem tah lăng gohn
 nòo·at **aftershave**
ครีมอาบแดด kreem àhp dàat **tanning
 lotion**
คลื่นไส้ klêun sâi **nausea**
ควัน kwan **smoke**
ความเคล็ด kwahm klét **sprain**
ความต่างเขตเวลา kwahm đàhng kèrt wair-
 -lah **time difference**
ความปวด kwahm bòo·at **pain**
ความร้อน kwahm rórn **heat**
ความรัก kwahm rák **love**
ความไวของฟิล์ม kawhm wai kŏng fim
 film speed
ค็อกเทล kórk-ten **cocktail**
คอมพิวเตอร์ korm-pew-đeu **computer**
คอมพิวเตอร์แล็ปท็อป korm-pew-đeu láap-
 -tórp **laptop**
คอหอย kor hŏy **throat**
คัน kan **itch**
ค่าเข้า kâh kôw **admission (price)**
ค่าธรรมเนียม kâh tam-nee·am
 commission
ค่าบริการ kâh bor-rí-gahn **service charge**
ค่าปรับ kâh bràp **fine (penalty)**
ค่าผ่านประตู kâh pàhn brà-đoo **cover
 charge**
ค่ายพักแรม kâi pák raam **camping ground**
คำตลก kam đà-lòk **joke**
คำบรรยาย kam ban-yai **subtitles**
คำร้องทุกข์ kam rórng túk **complaint**
คืน keun **night**
คืนนี้ keun née **tonight**
คืนวันสิ้นปี keun wan sîn bee **New Year's
 Eve**
คุก kúk **jail**

คุณ kun **you** pl pol
คู่มือนำเที่ยว kôo meu nam têe·o
 guidebook
คู่มือสนทนา kôo meu sŏn-tá-nah
 phrasebook
เครดิต crair-dit **credit**
เครือข่าย kreu·a kài **network**
เครื่องเก็บเงิน krêu·ang gèp ngeun **cash
 register**
เครื่องคิดเลข krêu·ang kit lêk **calculator**
เครื่องซักผ้า krêu·ang sák păh **washing
 machine**
เครื่องดื่ม krêu·ang dèum **drink**
เครื่องนอน krêu·ang norn **bedding**
เครื่องบริการตั๋ว
 krêu·ang bor-rí-gahn đŏo·a
 ticket machine
เครื่องบิน krêu·ang bin **aeroplane**
เครื่องปิ้งขนมปัง
 krêu·ang bîng kà-nŏm bang **toaster**
เครื่องเปิดกระป๋อง
 krêu·ang bèut grà-bŏrng
 can opener • tin opener
เครื่องเปิดขวด krêu·ang bèut kòo·at
 bottle opener
เครื่องพิมพ์ krêu·ang pim **printer
 (computer)**
เครื่องเพชรพลอย krêu·ang pét ploy
 jewellery
เครื่องสำอาง krêu·ang săm-ahng **make-up**
เครื่องหัตถกรรม krêu·ang hàt-tà-gam
 handicrafts
แคชเชียร์ kaa-chee·a **cashier**
ใคร krai **who**

ง

งบประมาณ ngóp brà-mahn **budget**
งาน ngahn **festival**
งาน ngahn **job**
งานเต้นรำ ngahn đên ram **rave • dance
 party**
งานเลี้ยง ngahn lée·ang **party
 (celebration)**

งานแสดง ง ngahn sà-daang **show**
เงิน ngeun **money**
เงิน ngeun **silver**
เงินคืน ngeun keun **refund**
เงินทิป ngeun tip **tip (gratuity)**
เงินปลีก ngeun blèek **change (coins)**
เงินมัดจำ ngeun mát jam **deposit**
เงินสด ngeun sòt **cash**
เงียบ ngêe-ap **quiet**

จ

จดหมาย jòt-mǎi **letter • mail**
จนถึง jon tĕung **until (Friday, etc)**
จมูก jà-mòok **nose**
จอง jorng **book (make a booking)**
จอด jòrt **park (a car)**
จาน jahn **dish**
จาน jahn **plate**
จีสตริง jee sà-đring **g-string**
จุ๊ก jùk **plug (bath)**
จุดหมายปลายทาง jùt mǎi blai tahng
   destination
จูบ jòop **kiss**
เจ็บ jèp **painful**
เจ็บท้อง jèp tórng **stomachache (to
   have a)**
ใจกลางเมือง jai glahng meu-ang **city centre**

ฉ

ฉะนั้น chà-nán **therefore**
ฉีดวัคซีน chèet wák-seen **vaccination**

ช

ชนบท chon-ná-bot **countryside**
ช่วยด้วย chôo-ay dòo-ay **Help!**
ช็อกโกแลต chórk-goh-lét **chocolate**
ช่อขายตั๋ว chôrng kǎi đǒo-a **ticket office**
ช้อน chórn **spoon**
ช้อนชา chórn chah **teaspoon**
ช้อนส้อม chórn sôrm **cutlery**

ชอบ chôrp **like**
ชั้นธุรกิจ chán tú-rá-git **business class**
ชั้นสอง chán sǒrng **second class**
ชั่วโมง chôo-a mohng **hour**
ช้า cháh **late**
ช่างตัดผม châhng đàt pǒm **hairdresser**
ช่างตัดเสื้อ châhng đàt sêu-a **tailor**
ช่างถ่ายภาพ châhng tài pâhp
   photographer
ช่างทาสี châhng tah sěe **painter**
ชานชาลา chahn chah-lah **platform**
ชาม chahm **bowl**
ชายแดน chai daan **border**
ชายหาด chai hàht **beach**
ชาวยิว chow yew **Jewish**
ชาวไร่ชาวนา chow rài chow nah **farmer**
ชิ้น chín **slice**
ชี้ chée **point**
ชื่อ chêu **name**
ชุดว่ายน้ำ chút wâi nám **swimsuit**
เช็ค chék **cheque • check**
เช็คเดินทาง chék deun tahng **travellers
   cheque**
เช็คอิน chék in **check-in (desk)**
เช่า chôw **hire • rent**
เชือกสีฟัน chêu-ak sěe fan **dental floss**
ใช่ châi **yes**

ซ

ซ่อม sôrm **repair**
ซัก sák **wash (clothes)**
ซากโบราณสถาน sâhk boh-rahn-ná
   sà-tǎhn **ruins**
ซ้าย sái **left (direction)**
ซิป síp **zip/zipper**
ซีดี see-dee **CD**
ซื้อ séu **buy**
ซื้อของ séu kǒrng **shop**
ซูเปอร์มาร์เก็ต soo-beu-mah-gèt
   supermarket
เซนติเมตร sen-đi-mét **centimetre**

ด

คนตรี don-dree **music**
คนตรีร็อก don-dree rórk **rock (music)**
ด่วน dòo-an **urgent**
ด้วยกัน dôo-ay gan **together**
ดอกไม้ dòrk mái **flower**
ดอลลาร์ dorn-lah **dollar**
ดัง dang **loud**
ดินสอ din-sŏr **pencil**
ดี dee **good**
ดีกว่า dee gwàh **better**
ดีที่สุด dee têe sùt **best**
ดื่ม dèum **drink**
ดื่มน้ำผึ้งพระจันทร์ dèum nám pêung prá jan
    honeymoon
เด็ก dèk **child**
เด็กชาย dèk chai **boy**
เด็กๆ dèk dèk **children**
เดิน deun **walk**
เดินทางธุรกิจ deun tahng tú-rá-git
    business trip
เดินป่า deun bàh **hike**
เดี่ยว dèe-o **alone**
เดี๋ยวนี้ dĕe-o née **now**
เดือน deu-an **month**
ได้ยิน dâi yin **hear**

ต

ตรงเวลา drong wair-lah **on time**
ตรวจคนเข้าเมือง dròo-at kon kôw meu-ang
    immigration
ตลาด đà-làht **market**
ตลาดนัด đà-làht nát **street market**
ตลาดน้ำ đà-làht nám **floating market**
ต่อ đòr **per (day)**
ตอนเช้า đorn chów **morning**
ตอนบ่าย đorn bài **afternoon**
ตะวันขึ้น đà-wan kêun **sunrise**
ตะวันตก đà-wan đòk **sunset**
ตั้งครรภ์ đâng kan **pregnant**
ตัด đàt **cut**
ตัน đan **blocked**

ตั๋ว đŏo-a **ticket**
ตา đah **grandfather (maternal)**
ต่างกัน đàhng gan **different**
ต่างจาก đàhng jàhk **different from**
ต่างชาติ đàhng châht **foreign**
ต่างประเทศ đàhng brà-têt **overseas**
ตารางเวลา đah-rahng wair-lah **timetable**
ตำรวจ đam-ròo-at **police**
ตึก đèuk **building**
ตื่น đèun **wake up**
ตู้เซฟ đôo sép **safe**
ตู้โทรศัพท์ đôo toh-rá-sàp **phone box**
ตู้โทรศัพท์ đôo toh-rá-sàp **telephone box**
ตู้นอน đôo norn **sleeping car**
ตู้ไปรษณีย์ đôo brai-sà-nee **mailbox**
ตู้ฝากกระเป๋า đôo fàhk grà-bŏw **luggage**
    lockers
ตู้ไมโครเวฟ đôo mai-kroh-wép
    microwave (oven)
ตู้เย็น đôo yen **refrigerator**
ตู้รับประทานอาหาร đôo ráp brà-tahn
    ah-hăhn **dining car**
ตู้เอทีเอ็ม đôo air tee em **automated teller**
    machine (ATM)
เต้นรำ đên ram **dance**
เต้าหู้ đôw-hôo **tofu**
เตี้ย đêe-a **short (height)**
เตียง đee-ang **bed**
เตียงคู่ đee-ang kôo **double bed**
แต่งงานแล้ว đàang ngahn láa-ou **married**
ใต้ đâi **beneath**

ถ

ถนน tà-nŏn **road**
ถนน tà-nŏn **street**
ถ้วย tôo-ay **cup**
ถังแก๊ส tăng gáat **gas cartridge**
ถังขยะ tăng kà-yà **garbage can**
ถ้า tâh **if**
ถ่านไฟฉาย tàhn fai chăi **battery**
    (flashlight)
ถ่ายรูป tài rôop **take a photo**
ถึง tĕung **to**

tee êe at

north tít nĕua north
direction tít tahng direction
south tít dtâi south
west tít dta-wan dòk west
view tew tát view
cook tam ah-hăhn cook
validate someone? tam hâi dtòok dtâwng validate
someone?
hurt (to hurt) tam hâi jèp hurt (to hurt)
clean tam sà-àht clean
why tam mai why
handmade tam dôo-ay meu handmade
baby tah-rók baby
eat (polite) tahn eat (polite)
highway tahng lŏo-ang highway
direct tahng drong direct
aisle (on plane) tahng deun aisle (on plane)
motorway (tollway) tahng doo-an motorway (tollway)
path tahng path
guided tour • tour too-a guided tour • tour
modern tan sà-măi modern
lake tá-lair sàhp lake
both táng sŏrng both
all táng mòt all
sea tá-lair sea
car registration bai ta-bee-an rót car registration
lawyer ta-nai kwahm lawyer
diarrhoea tórng sĕe-a diarrhoea
constipation tórng pòok constipation
stomach tórng stomach
gold tong kam gold

ŋ

complementary (free) taam complementary (free)
cheap tòok cheap
condom condom
sleeping bag tŏong yahng à-mai sleeping bag
stockings tŏong nông stockings
pantyhose tŏong nông pantyhose
bag tŏong bag

---

telegram toh-rá-lêk telegram
direct-dial toh-rá-sàp drong direct-dial
TV toh-rá-tát TV
television toh-rá-tát television
collect call toh gèp blai tahng collect
call
telephone toh telephone
tampon taam-porn tampon
vacation bpai pák vacation
flight (aeroplane) têe-o flight (aeroplane)
one-way (ticket) têe-o dee-o one-way (ticket)
night out têe-o glahng keun night out
midday têe-ang wan midday
midnight têe-ang keun midnight
foot táo foot
video tape têp wee-dee-oh video tape
tennis ten-nít tennis
IT săhn sòn-tét IT
address têe yòo address
where têe năi where
later tee lăng later
last (previous) tee láew last (previous)
claim
baggage gra-bŏw baggage
accommodation têe pák accommodation
crèche têe fàhk lée-ang dèk crèche
there têe nân there
here têe nêe here
child seat têe nâng child seat
seat (place) têe nâng seat (place)
sleeping berth
post office brai-sà-nee post office
laundry (place) têe sák laundry (place)
property office
lost têe jàang kŏng hăi lost
stand
taxi têe jòt rót táak-sêe taxi
ashtray têe kèe-a bu-rèe ashtray
bakery têe kăi ka-nŏm bang bakery

telephone โทรศัพท์ toh-rá-sàp telephone

mobile phone โทรศัพท์มือถือ toh-rá-sàp meu těu mobile

public telephone โทรศัพท์สาธารณะ toh-rá-sàp sǎh-tah-rá-ná public telephone

ธ

banknote ธนบัตร tá-na-bàt banknote

bank ธนาคาร tá-nah-kahn bank

business ธุรกิจ tú-rá-gìt business

you inf เธอ teu you inf

น

massage นวด nôo-at massage

brother (younger) น้องชาย nórng chaai brother (younger)

sleep นอนหลับ norn làp sleep

scientist นักวิทยาศาสตร์ nák wít-tá-yah-sàht scientist

student นักศึกษา nák sèuk-sǎh student

actor นักแสดง nák sà-daang actor

that (one) นั้น nán (an) that (one)

this (one) นี้ nêe (an) this (one)

water น้ำ nám water

ice น้ำแข็ง nám kǎang ice

Mrs นาง naang Mrs

nurse นางพยาบาล naang pá-yah-bahn nurse (woman)

Miss/Ms นางสาว naang sǒw Miss/Ms

minute นาที nah-tee minute

boring น่าเบื่อ nâh bèu-a boring

family name • surn นามสกุล naam sà-kun family name • surn

Mr นาย naai Mr

watch นาฬิกา nah-lí-gah watch

alarm clock นาฬิกาปลุก nah-lí-gah blùk alarm clock

soup น้ำแกง nám gɛɛng soup

milk น้ำนม nom milk

juice น้ำผลไม้ nám pòn-lá-mái juice

oil น้ำมัน nám man oil

oil (motor) น้ำมันเครื่อง nám man krêu-ang oil (motor)

gas (petrol) น้ำมันเบนซิน nám man ben-sin gas (petrol)

lubricant น้ำมันหล่อลื่น nám man lòr lêun lubricant

mineral water น้ำแร่ nám ráa mineral water

perfume น้ำหอม nám hǒrm perfume

toe นิ้วเท้า new tów toe

cheese เนยแข็ง neu-i kǎang cheese

meat เนื้อ néu-a meat

recommend แนะนำ náa-nam recommend

in ใน nai in

the King ในหลวง nai lǒo-ang the King

บ

on บน bon on

company บริษัท bor-rí-sàt company

travel agency บริษัทท่องเที่ยว bor-rí-sàt tôrng têe-o travel agency

fragile บอบบาง bòrp bahng fragile

bank account บัญชีธนาคาร ban-chee tá-nah-kahn bank account

account บัญชี ban-chee account

boarding pass บัตรขึ้นเครื่องบิน bàt kêun krêu-ang bin boarding pass

credit card บัตรเครดิต bàt crair-dìt credit card

phone card บัตรโทรศัพท์ bàt toh-rá-sàp phone card

stairway บันได ban-dai stairway

diary บันทึกรายวัน ban-téuk rai wan diary

home • house บ้าน bâan home • house

boarding house บ้านพัก bâan pák boarding house

youth hostel บ้านเยาวชน bâan yow-wá-chon youth hostel

bar บาร์ bah bar

bill (restaurant etc) บิล bin bill (restaurant etc)

check (bill) บิล bin check (bill)

nurse บุรุษพยาบาล bù-rùt pá-yah-bahn nurse (man)

cigarette บุหรี่ bù-rèe cigarette

cigar บุหรี่ซิการ์ bù-rèe sì-gâh cigar

petrol เบนซิน ben-sin petrol

brakes เบรก brèk brakes

beer เบียร์ bee-a beer

light (not heavy) เบา bow light (not heavy)

share (with) แบ่ง bàang share (with)

cathedral โบสถ์ boht cathedral

church โบสถ์ boht church

ใบกรรมสิทธิ์รถยนต์ bai gam-má-sìt rót
  yon **car owner's title**
ใบขับขี่ bai kàp kèe **drivers licence**
ใบมีดโกน bai mêet gohn **razor blade**
ใบสั่งยา bai sàng yah **prescription**
ใบเสร็จ bai sèt **receipt**
ใบหน้า bai nâh **face**

ป

ปรอท bà-ròrt **thermometer**
ประตู bprà-đoo **door**
ประตู bprà-đoo **gate (airport, etc)**
ประเทศแคนาดา bprà-têt kaa-nah-dah
  Canada
ประเทศนิวซีแลนด์ prà-têt new see-laan
  New Zealand
ประเทศเนเธอร์แลนด์ bprà-têt nair-teu-laan
  Netherlands
ประเทศฝรั่งเศส bprà-têt fà-ràng-sèt **France**
ประเทศสก็อตแลนด์ bprà-têt sà-gòrt-laan
  Scotland
ประเทศออสเตรเลีย
  bprà-têt or-sà-đrair-lee-a **Australia**
ประเพณี bprà-pair-nee **custom**
ปรับอากาศ bpràp ah-gàht **air-conditioned**
ปราสาท bprah-sàht **castle**
ปลอกหมอน bplòrk mŏrn **pillowcase**
ปลั๊ก bplák **plug (electricity)**
ปลุก bplùk **wake someone up**
ปวดฟัน bòo-at fan **toothache**
ปวดหัว bòo-at hŏo-a **headache**
ป่วย bòo-ay **sick • ill**
ปอนด์ bporn **pound (money, weight)**
ปัญญาอ่อน ban-yah òrn **idiot**
ปั๊มน้ำมัน bám nám-man **petrol station**
ปั๊มน้ำมัน bám nám-man **service station**
ปาก bàhk **mouth**
ปากกา (ลูกลื่น) pàhk-gah (lôok lêun) **pen
  (ballpoint)**
ผ้าเต๊ะ bah-đé **batik**
ป้ายรถเมล์ bâi rót mair **bus stop**
ป่ารก bàh rók **jungle**

ปิกนิก bìk-ník **picnic**
ปิด bìt **close • shut**
ปิดแล้ว bìt láa-ou **closed**
ปี bee **year**
ปู่ bòo **grandfather (paternal)**
เป้ bâir **backpack**
เป็นไปไม่ได้ ben bai mâi dâi **impossible**
เปลี่ยนแปลง blèe-an blaang **change
  (general)**
แปรง braang **brush**
แปรงสีฟัน braang sĕe fan **toothbrush**
แปล blaa **translate**
ไป bai **go**
ไปกลับ bai glàp **return (ticket)**
ไปข้างนอก bai kâhng nôrk **go out**
ไปซื้อของ bai séu kŏrng **go shopping**
ไปเที่ยวกับ bai têe-o gàp **go out with**
ไปรษณีย์ brai-sà-nee **mail (postal
  system)**
ไปรษณีย์ทางธรรมดา brai-sà-nee tahng
  tam-má-dah **surface mail**
ไปรษณียบัตร brai-sà-nee-yá-bàt **postcard**
ไปรษณีย์ลงทะเบียน brai-sà-nee long tá-
  -bee-an **registered mail (post by)**
ไปรษณีย์อากาศ prai-sà-nee ah-gàht
  airmail

ผ

ผม pŏm **hair**
ผม/ดิฉัน pŏm/đi-chăn m/f l • **me**
ผลไม้ pŏn-lá-mái **fruit**
ผัก pàk **vegetable**
ผับ pàp **pub (bar)**
ผ้าเช็ดตัว pâh chét đoo-a **towel**
ผ้าเช็ดปาก pâh chét bàhk **napkin**
ผ้าซัก pâh sák **laundry (clothes)**
ผ้าปูที่นอน pâh boo têe norn **bed linen**
ผ้าพันคอ pâh pan kor **scarf**
ผ้าพันแผล pâh pan plăa **bandage**
ผ้าลินิน pâh li-nin **linen (material)**
ผ้าห่ม pâh hòm **blanket**
ผ้าไหม pâh măi **silk**

ผ้าอนามัย pâh à-nah-mai **panty liners**
ผ้าอนามัย pâh à-nah-mai **sanitary napkin**
ผ้าอ้อม pâh ôrm **diaper**
ผ้าอ้อม pâh ôrm **nappy**
ผิวเกรียมแดด pĕw gree-am dàat **sunburn**
ผู้จัดการ pôo jàt gahn **manager**
ผู้ชาย pôo chai **man**
ผู้โดยสาร pôo doy săhn **passenger**
ผู้หญิง pôo yĭng **woman**
เผ็ด pèt **hot (spicy)**
เผา pŏw **burn**
แผ่นซีดี pàan see-dee **disk (CD-ROM)**
แผ่นดิสก์ pàan dìt **disk (floppy)**
แผนที่ păan têe **map**
แผ่นพับโฆษณา pàan páp koh-sà-nah
   brochure
แผลไฟไหม้ plăa fai măi **burn**

ฝ

ฝน fŏn **rain**
ฝรั่ง fà-ràng **foreigner (Westerner)**
ฝักบัว fàk boo-a **shower**
ฝ้าย fâi **cotton**

พ

พจนานุกรม pót-jà-nah-nú-grom
   dictionary
พระอาทิตย์ prá ah-tít **sun**
พริกเขียว prík kĕe-o **green pepper**
พรุ่งนี้ prûng née **tomorrow**
พรุ่งนี้เช้า prûng née chów
   tomorrow morning
พรุ่งนี้บ่าย prûng née bài
   tomorrow afternoon
พรุ่งนี้เย็น prûng née yen
   tomorrow evening
พ่อครัว pôr kroo-a **chef**
พ่อแม่ pôr mâe **parents**
พิกัดน้ำหนักกระเป๋า
   pí-gàt nám nàk grà-bŏw **baggage**
   allowance
พิการ pí-gahn **disabled**

พิพิธภัณฑ์ pí-pít-tá-pan **museum**
พี่ชาย pêe chai **brother (older)**
พี่เลี้ยงเด็ก pêe lée-ang dèk **babysitter**
พูด pôot **speak**
เพศ pêt **sex (gender)**
เพศสัมพันธ์แบบปลอดภัย pêt săm-pan bàap
   blòrt pai **safe sex**
เพื่อน pêu-an **companion**
เพื่อน pêu-an **friend**
เพื่อนงาน pêu-an ngahn **colleague**

ฟ

ฟรี free **free (gratis)**
ฟัง fang **listen (to)**
ฟิล์ม fim **film (for camera)**
ฟิล์มสไลด์ fim sà-lái **slide (film)**
ฟุตบอล fút-born **football (soccer)**
ฟูก fôok **mattress**
แฟนผู้ชาย faan pôo chai **boyfriend**
แฟนสาว faan sŏw **girlfriend**
แฟลช flâat **flash (camera)**
ไฟ fai **light (electric)**
ไฟฉาย fai chăi **torch (flashlight)**
ไฟแช็ก fai cháak **cigarette lighter**
ไฟหน้ารถ fai nâh rót **headlights**

ภ

ภาพเขียน pâhp kĕe-an **painting (a work)**
ภาพถ่าย pâhp tài **photo**
ภาพยนตร์ pâhp-pá-yon **film • movie**
ภาษา pah-săh **language**
ภาษีสนามบิน pah-sĕe sà-năhm bin
   airport tax
ภูเขา poo kŏw **mountain**
เภสัชกร pair-sàt-chá-gorn **pharmacist**

ม

ม้วนเทป móo-an tép **cassette**
มหาวิทยาลัย má-hăh-wít-tá-yah-lai
   university
มะม่วงหิมพานต์ má-môo-ang hĭm-má-pahn
   cashew

มันสมองกระทบกระเทือน man sà-mǒrng grà-
-tóp grà-teu-an **concussion**
มากกว่า mâhk gwàh **more (than**
something else)
มากขึ้น mâhk kêun **more (than before)**
มิลลิเมตร mín-lí-mét **millimetre**
มีค่า mee kâh **valuable**
มีด mêet **knife**
มีดโกน mêet gohn **razor**
มีดตัดเล็บ mêet dàt lép **nail clippers**
มีดพับ mêet páp **penknife**
มีราคา mee rah-kah **cost**
มืด mêut **dark**
มือ meu **hand**
มือจับ meu jàp **handlebars**
มื้ออาหาร méu ah-hǎhn **meal**
เม็ดยา mét yah **pill**
เมตร mét **metre**
เม็ดอามันด์ má-lét ah-man **almond**
เมา mow **drunk**
เมาคลื่น mow klêun **travel**
sickness (boat)
เมาเครื่อง mow krêu-ang **travel**
sickness (air)
เมารถ mow rót **travel sickness (car)**
เมีย mee-a **wife**
เมือง meu-ang **city**
เมื่อไร mêu-a rai **when**
เมื่อวาน mêu-a wahn **yesterday**
เมื่อวานซืน mêu-a wahn seun **day before**
yesterday
แม่กุญแจ mâh gun-jaa **padlock**
แม่น้ำ mâa nám **river**
แม่ผัว mâa pǒo-a **mother-in-law (mother**
of husband)
แม่ยาย mâa yai **mother-in-law (mother**
of wife)
โมเดม moh-dem **modem**
ไม่ mâi **no**
ไม้ขีดไฟ mái kèet fai **matches (for**
lighting)
ไม่มี mâi mee **without**
ไม่มีห้องว่าง mâi mee hôrng wâhng **no**

vacancy
ไม่มีอะไร mâi mee à-rai **nothing**
ไม่สบาย mâi sà-bai **uncomfortable**
ไม่สูบบุหรี่ mâi sòop bù-rèe **non-smoking**

ย

ยกทรง yók song **bra**
ยกเลิก yók lêuk **cancel**
ยอด yôrt **great (fantastic)**
ยา yah **drug**
ยา yah **medicine (medication)**
ย่า yâh **grandmother (paternal)**
ยาก yâhk **hard (difficult)**
ยากันแมลง yah gan má-laeng **insect**
repellent
ยาแก้ปวด yah gâa bòo-at **painkiller**
ยาแก้ไอ yah gâa ai **cough medicine**
ยาคุมกำเนิด yah kum gam-nèut
contraceptives (pills)
ยาฆ่าเชื้อ yah kâh chéu-a **antiseptic**
ยาดับกลิ่นตัว yah dàp glin đoo-a
deodorant
ยานวดผม yah nôo-at pǒm
conditioner (hair)
ยาปฏิชีวนะ yah pà-đi-chee-wá-ná
antibiotics
ยาย yai **grandmother (maternal)**
ยาระบาย yah rá-bai **laxative**
ยาว yow **long**
ยาสีฟัน yah sěe fan **toothpaste**
ยาเสพติด yah sèp đit **drugs (illicit)**
ยาแอสไพริน yah àat-sà-pai-rin **aspirin**
ยืนยัน yeun yan **confirm (a booking)**
ยุ่ง yûng **busy**
เย็น yen **cool • cold**
แย่ yâa **awful**

ร

รถเข็น rót kěn **trolley**
รถเข็น rót kěn **wheelchair**
รถเข็นเด็ก rót kěn dèk **stroller**
รถจักรยาน rót jàk-gà-yahn **bicycle**

รถแท็กซี่ rót táak-sêe **taxi**
รถบัส rót bàt **bus (intercity)**
รถพยาบาล rót pá-yah-bahn **ambulance**
รถไฟ rót fai **train**
รถมอเตอร์ไซค์ rót mor-đeu-sai **motorcycle**
รถเมล์ rót mair **bus (city)**
รถยนต์ rót yon **car**
ร่ม róm shade • **umbrella**
ร่วมกันใช้ rôo-am gan chái **share (a dorm etc)**
รหัสไปรษณีย์ rá-hàt brai-sà-nee **post code**
รอ ror **wait (for)**
รองเท้า rorng tów **shoe**
รองเท้าบู๊ท rorng tów bút **boot**
ร้อน rórn **hot**
รอยพอง roy porng **blister**
ระวัง rá-wang **Careful!**
รัก rák **love**
รัฐบาล rát-tà-bahn **government**
รับประกัน ráp brà-gan **guaranteed**
รับประทาน ráp brà-tahn **eat (very formal)**
ราคา rah-kah **price**
ราคาส่วนลด rah-kah sòo-an lót **discount**
ร้าน ráhn **shop**
ร้านกาแฟ ráhn gah-faa **cafe**
ร้านขายขนม ráhn kǎi kà-nǒm **cake shop**
ร้านขายของชำ ráhn kǎi kǒrng cham **convenience store**
ร้านขายของที่ระลึก ráhn kǎi kǒrng têe rá-léuk **souvenir shop**
ร้านขายเนื้อ ráhn kǎi néu-a **butcher's shop**
ร้านขายยา ráhn kǎi yah **chemist • pharmacy**
ร้านขายรองเท้า ráhn kǎi rórng tów **shoe shop**
ร้านขายเสื้อผ้า ráhn kǎi sêu-a pâh **clothing store**
ร้านขายหนังสือพิมพ์ ráhn kǎi nǎng-sěu pim **newsagency**
ร้านขายเหล้า ráhn kǎi lôw **liquor store**
ร้านขายอุปกรณ์กีฬา ráhn kǎi ùp-bà-gorn gee-lah **sports store**

ร้านขายอุปกรณ์เขียน ráhn kǎi ùp-bà-gorn kěe-an **stationer's (shop)**
ร้านดนตรี ráhn don-đree **music shop**
ร้านเสริมสวย ráhn sěum sǒo-ay **beauty salon**
ร้านอาหาร ráhn ah-hǎhn **restaurant**
ร้านอินเตอร์เนต ráhn in-đeu-nét **Internet cafe**
รายการ rai gahn **itinerary**
รายการอาหาร rai gahn ah-hǎhn **menu**
รายวัน rai wan **daily**
รีโมท ree-môht **remote control**
รูปหล่อ rôop lòr **handsome**
เรือ reu-a **boat**
เรือข้ามฟาก reu-a kâhm fâhk **ferry**
เรือสำเภา reu-a sǎm-pow **junk (boat)**
แรมคืน raam keun **overnight**
โรคกระเพาะอักเสบ rôhk grà-pó àk-sèp **gastroenteritis**
โรคตับอักเสบ rôhk đàp àk-sèp **hepatitis**
โรคเบาหวาน rôhk bow wǎhn **diabetes**
โรคหัวใจ rôhk hǒo-a jai **heart condition**
โรงซักรีด rohng sák rêet **launderette**
โรงพยาบาล rohng pá-yaa-bahn **hospital**
โรงแรม rohng raam **hotel**
โรงละคร rohng lá-korn **theatre**
โรงหนัง rohng nǎng **cinema**
โรแมนติก roh-maan-đik **romantic**
ไร่นา râi nah **farm**

ล
ลอง longo **try (try out)**
ละคร lá-korn **play (theatre)**
ลาก่อน lah gòrn **goodbye**
ล้าง láhng **wash (something)**
ล่าม lâhm **interpreter**
ลิปสติก líp-sà-đik **lipstick**
ลิฟต์ líp **lift (elevator)**
ลูกค้า lôok káh **client**
ลูกชาย lôok chai **son**
ลูกสาว lôok sǒw **daughter**
เล็ก lék **small**
เล็กกว่า lék gwàh **smaller**

เล็กที่สุด lék têe sùt **smallest**
เลนส์ len **lens**
เลนส์สัมผัส len săm-pàt **contact lenses**
เลว le-ou **bad**
เล็สเบียน lét-bee-an **lesbian**
เลือด lêu-at **blood**
แลก lâak **cash (a cheque)** • **change (money)**
แลก lâak
และ láe **and**

ว

วีดนตรี wong don-dree **band (music)**
วัง wang **palace**
วัตถุโบราณ wát-tù boh-rahn **antique**
วัน wan **day**
วันเกิด wan gèut **birthday**
วันปีใหม่ wan kêun bee mài **New Year's Day**
วันที่ wan têe **date (day)**
วันที่เกิด wan têe gèut **date of birth**
วันนี้ wan née **today**
วันมะรืน wan má-reun **day after tomorrow**
วันเสาร์อาทิตย์ wan sŏw ah-tít **weekend**
ว่าง wâhng **free (available)**
ว่าง wâhng **vacant**
ว่ายน้ำ wâi nám **swim**
วิทยาศาสตร์ wít-tá-yah-sàht **science**
วิทยุ wít-tá-yú **radio**
วีซ่า wee-sâh **visa**
เวลาเปิด wair-lah bèut **opening hours**
แว่นกันแดด wâen gan dàat **sunglasses**
แว่นตา wâen đah **glasses (spectacles)**
ไวรัสเอชไอวี wai-rát èt ai wee **HIV**

ศ

ศาสนาฮินดู sàht-sà-năh hin-doo **Hindu**
ศิลปะ sĭn-lá-bà **art**
ศิลปิน sĭn-lá-bin **artist**
ศุลกากร sŭn-lá-gah-gorn **customs**
ศูนย์กลาง sŏon glahng **centre**

ส

สกปรก sòk-gà-bròk **dirty**
ส่ง sòng **deliver**
สไตรค์ sà-drái **strike**
สถานี sà-tăh-nee **station**
สถานีขนส่ง sà-tăh-nee kŏn sòng **bus station**
สถานีตำรวจ sà-tăh-nee đam-ròo-at **police station**
สถานีรถไฟ sà-tăh-nee rót fai **railway station**
สถานีรถไฟ sà-tăh-nee rót fai **train station**
สถานีรถไฟฟ้า sà-tăh-nee rót fai fáh **metro station**
สนามเทนนิส sà-năhm ten-nít **tennis court**
สนามบิน sà-năhm bin **airport**
สบาย sà-bai **comfortable**
สบู่ sà-bòo **soap**
สมุดโทรศัพท์ sà-mùt toh-rá-sàp **phone book**
สมุดบันทึก sà-mùt ban-téuk **notebook**
สรรพสินค้า sàp-pá-sĭn-káh **department store**
สรรพสินค้า sàp-pá-sĭn-káh **shopping centre**
สร้อยคอ sôy kor **necklace**
สระว่ายน้ำ sà wâi nám **swimming pool**
สวน sŏo-an **garden**
สวนสัตว์ sŏo-an sàt **zoo**
สวนสาธารณะ sŏo-an săh-tah-rá-ná **park**
ส้วม sôo-am **toilet**
สวย sŏo-ay **beautiful**
สวัสดีครับ/สวัสดีค่ะ sà-wàt-dee kráp/ sà-wàt-dee kà m/f **Hello.**
สหรัฐอเมริกา sà-hà-rát à-mair-rí-gah **USA**
สอง sŏrng **two**
สองเตียง sŏrng đee-ang **twin beds**
สะพาน sà-pahn **bridge**
สะอาด sà-àht **clean**
สัญญาณโทรศัพท์ săn-yahn toh-rá-sàp **dial tone**
สามเหลี่ยมทองคำ săhm lèe-am torng kam **Golden Triangle**
สายการบิน săi gahn bin **airline**

สายฟ้า sǎi póo-ang jumper leads
สำคัญ sǎm-kan important
สำนักงานท่องเที่ยว sǎm-nák ngahn tòrng
  têe-o tourist office
สำลี sǎm-lee cotton balls
สี sěe colour
สีขาว sěe kǒw white
สีเขียว sěe kěe-o green
สีชมพู sěe chom-poo pink
สีดำ sěe dam black
สีแดง sěe daang red
สีน้ำเงิน sěe nám ngeun blue (dark)
สีน้ำตาล sěe nám đahn brown
สีฟ้า sěe fáh blue (light)
สีส้ม sěe sôm orange (colour)
สีเหลือง sěe lěu-ang yellow
สุข sùk happy
สุขภาพ sù-kà-pâhp health
สุขสาธารณะ sù-kǎh sǎh-tah-rá-ná
  public toilet
สุสาน sù-sǎhn cemetery
เสีย sěe-a off (spoiled)
เสีย sěe-a out of order
เสียงดัง sěe-ang dang noisy
เสียแล้ว sěe-a láa-ou broken down
เสื้อกันฝน sêu-a gan fǒn raincoat
เสื้อกันหนาว sêu-a gan nǒw jacket
เสื้อคลุม sêu-a klum coat
เสื้อชูชีพ sêu-a choo chêep life jacket
เสื้อเชิ้ต sêu-a chéut shirt
เสื้อถัก sêu-a tàk jumper • sweater
เสื้อผ้า sêu-a pâh clothing
เสื้อยืด sêu-a yêut T-shirt
แสตมป์ sà-đãam stamp
โสด sòht single (person)
โสเภณี sõh-pair-nee prostitute
ใส่กุญแจ sài gun-jaa lock
ใส่กุญแจแล้ว sài gun-jaa láa-ou locked

ห

หนัก nàk heavy
หนัง nǎng leather
หนังสือ nǎng-sěu book

หนังสือเดินทาง nǎng-sěu deun tahng
  passport
หนังสือพิมพ์ nǎng-sěu pim newspaper
หน้า nâh next (month)
หน้า nâh season
หน้าต่าง nâh đàhng window
หน้าใบไม้ผลิ nâh bai mái pli spring (season)
หน้าฝน nâh fǒn rainy season
หน้าร้อน nâh rórn summer
หนาว nǒw cold (sensation)
หน้าหนาว nâh nǒw winter
หน้าอก nâh òk chest (body)
หนึ่ง nèung one
หมอ mǒr doctor
หมอน mǒrn pillow
หมอนวด mǒr nôo-at masseur/masseuse
หม้อแบตเตอรี่ mǒr bàat-đeu-rêe
  battery (car)
หม้อแปลง mór blaang adaptor
หมอฟัน mǒr fan dentist
หมา mǎh dog
หมายเลขหนังสือเดินทาง mǎi lêk nǎng-sěu
  deun tahng passport number
หมายเลขห้อง mǎi lêk hôrng room number
หย่าแล้ว yàh láa-ou divorced
หยุด yùt Stop!
หรูหรา rõo ráh luxury
หลัง lǎng after
หลัง lǎng back (body)
หลัง lǎng rear (seat etc)
หลาน lǎhn grandchild
หวาน wǎhn sweet
หวี wěe comb
ห่อ hòr package
ห้อง hôrng room
ห้องเก็บเสื้อ hôrng gèp sêu-a cloakroom
ห้องคอนโด hôrng korn-doh apartment
ห้องคู่ hôrng kôo double room
ห้องเดี่ยว hôrng dèe-o single room
ห้องนอน hôrng norn bedroom
ห้องน้ำ hôrng nám bathroom/toilet
ห้องเปลี่ยนเสื้อ hôrng blèe-an sêu-a
  changing room (in shop)

ห้องพักรอ hôrng pák ror **waiting room**
ห้องพักสำหรับคนเดินทางผ่าน hôrng pák
    sǎm-ràp kon deun tahng pàhn **transit
    lounge**
ห้องรับฝากกระเป๋า hôrng ráp fàhk grá-bǒw
    left luggage (office)
ห้องว่าง hôrng wâhng **vacancy**
ห้องสมุด hôrng sà-mút **library**
ห้องแสดงภาพ hôrng sà-daang pâhp
    art gallery
หักแล้ว hàk láa-ou **broken**
หัตถกรรม hàt-tà-gam **crafts**
หัว hǒo-a **head**
หัวใจ hǒo-a jai **heart**
หัวใจวาย hǒo-a jai wai **heart attack**
หัวนมเทียม hǒo-a nom tee-am
    dummy • pacifier
หาย hǎi **lost**
หายาก hǎh yâhk **rare (uncommon)**
หิวน้ำ hěw nám **thirsty (to be)**
หูเทียม hǒo tee-am **hearing aid**
เหนื่อย nèu-ay **tired**
เหรียญ rěe-an **coins**
เหล็กไขจุกขวด lèk kǎi jùk kòo-at **corkscrew**
เหล้า lôw **alcohol**
เหล้าไวน์ lôw wai **wine**
แห้ง hâang **dry**
แหนบ nàap **tweezers**
แหวน wǎan **ring (on finger)**
ใหญ่ yài **big**
ใหญ่กว่า yài gwàh **bigger**
ใหม่ mài **new**
ไหล่ lài **shoulder**

อ

อึ๊กชาติ ong-ká-châht **penis**
อย่างช้า yàhng cháh **slowly**
อร่อย à-ròy **tasty**

อรุณ à-run **dawn**
อ้วน ôo-an **fat**
ออกเดินทาง òrk deun tahng **depart (leave)**
อ่อน òrn **light (of colour)**
อันตราย an-đà-rai **dangerous**
อาบน้ำ àhng nám **bath**
อาจารย์ ah-jahn **teacher**
อาทิตย์ ah-tít **week**
อารมณ์ ah-rom **feelings**
อาหาร ah-hǎhn **food**
อาหารกลางวัน ah-hǎhn glahng wan
    lunch
อาหารเช้า ah-hǎhn chów **breakfast**
อาหารตี้โต๊ะ ah-hǎhn đàng đó **buffet**
อาหารทารก ah-hǎhn tah-rók **baby food**
อาหารที่จัดทำตามหลักศาสนายิว ah-hǎhn
    têe jàt tam đahm làk sàht-sà-nǎh yew
    kosher
อาหารที่จัดทำตามหลักศาสนาอิสลาม ah-hǎhn
    têe jàt tam đahm làk sàht-sà-nǎh it-sà-
    -lahm **halal**
อาหารมื้อเย็น ah-hǎhn méu yen **dinner**
อาหารไม่ย่อย ah-hǎhn mâi yôy
    indigestion
อาหารว่าง ah-hǎhn wâhng **snack**
อินเตอร์เน็ต in-đeu-nét **Internet**
อีก ZvyoX soÃ′ èek (an) nèung
    another
อุณหภูมิ un-hà-poom **temperature
    (weather)**
อุ่น ùn **warm**
อุบัติเหตุ ù-bàt-đi-hèt **accident**
เอกสาร èk-gà-sǎhn **paperwork**
ไอ ai **cough**
ไอติม ai-đim **ice cream**